Sadlier

# We Are God's People

**Grade Six**

**Sadlier**

A Division of William H. Sadlier, Inc.

*Nihil Obstat*
Reverend John G. Stillmank, S.T.L.
*Censor Librorum*

*Imprimatur*
✠ Most Reverend William H. Bullock
Bishop of Madison
March 6, 2003

The *Nihil Obstat* and *Imprimatur* are official declarations that a book or pamphlet is free of doctrinal or moral error. No implication is contained therein that those who have granted the *Nihil Obstat* and *Imprimatur* agree with the contents, opinions, or statements expressed.

## Acknowledgments

Excerpts from the English translation of the *Catechism of the Catholic Church* for the United States of America, copyright © 1994, United States Catholic Conference, Inc.—Libreria Editrice Vaticana. English translation of the *Catechism of the Catholic Church: Modifications from the Editio Typica* copyright © 1997, United States Catholic Conference, Inc.—Libreria Editrice Vaticana. Used with permission.

Scripture excerpts are taken from the *New American Bible with Revised New Testament and Psalms* Copyright © 1991, 1986, 1970 Confraternity of Christian Doctrine, Inc., Washington, DC. Used with permission. All rights reserved. No part of the *New American Bible* may be reproduced by any means without permission in writing from the copyright owner.

Excerpts from the English translation of *Lectionary for Mass* © 1969, 1981, International Committee on English in the Liturgy, Inc. (ICEL); excerpts from the English translation of *Rite of Holy Week* © 1972, ICEL; excerpts from the English translation of *The Roman Missal* © 1973, ICEL; excerpts from the English translation of *Rite of Penance* © 1974, ICEL; excerpts from the English translation of *The Liturgy of the Hours* © 1974, ICEL; excerpts from the English translation of *A Book of Prayers* © 1982, ICEL; excerpts from the English translation of *Order of Christian Funerals* © 1985, ICEL; excerpts from the English translation of *Book of Blessings* © 1988, International Committee on English in the Liturgy, Inc. All rights reserved.

Excerpts from *Catholic Household Blessings and Prayers* © 1988 United States Catholic Conference, Inc. Washington, DC. Used with permission. All rights reserved.

Excerpts from *Prayers, Blessings, and Hymns* © 1954, KTAV Publishing House, Hoboken, NJ. Used with permission. All rights reserved.

"Family History Poll," Reprinted with the permission of FamilyEducation.com.

Chinese proverb 2238 from *The Columbia World of Quotations*, edited by Robert Andrews, Mary Biggs, and Michael Seidel, et al. © 1996 Columbia University Press. Reprinted with the permission of the publisher.

English translation of the Glory to the Father, Lord's Prayer, Apostles' Creed, Nicene Creed, *Te Deum Laudamus*, and the *Sanctus* by the International Consultation on English Texts (ICET).

"We Believe, We Believe in God," © 1979, North American Liturgy Resources (NALR), 5536 NE Hassalo, Portland, OR 97213. All rights reserved. Used with permission. "God, Creator, God Most High," © 1998, Janet Vogt. Published by OCP Publications, 5536 NE Hassalo, Portland OR 97213. All rights reserved. Used with permission. "I Know You Are God," © 1995, Janet Vogt. Published by OCP Publications, 5536 NE Hassalo, Portland OR 97213. All rights reserved. Used with permission. "And It Was Good," © 1990, North American Liturgy Resources (NALR), 5536 NE Hassalo, Portland, OR 97213. All rights reserved. Used with permission. "Water of Life (Aqua de Vida)," © 1994, Jaime Cortez. Published by OCP Publications, 5536 NE Hassalo, Portland OR 97213. All rights reserved. Used with permission. "Be Not Afraid," © 1975, 1978, Robert J. Dufford, SJ and New Dawn Music, 5536 NE Hassalo, Portland, OR 97213. All rights

reserved. "City of God," © 1981, Daniel L. Schutte and New Dawn Music, 5536 NE Hassalo, Portland, OR 97213. All rights reserved. Used with permission. "Wherever You Go," Weston Priory, Gregory Norbet, OSB. Copyright © 1972, from the recording "Wherever You Go," The Benedictine Foundation of the State of Vermont Inc., Weston Priory, Weston, Vermont, USA. Used with permission. "Psalm 122: Qué Alegría/I Rejoiced," Music and verse text © 1997, Jaime Cortez. Published by OCP Publications, 5536 NE Hassalo, Portland, OR 97213. All rights reserved. Used with permission. English refrain © 1969, 1981, ICEL. Spanish refrain © 1982, Sobicain. All rights reserved. Used with permission. The English translation of Psalm 122 response from *Lectionary for Mass* © 1969, 1981, 1997, International Committee on English in the Liturgy, Inc. All rights reserved. "Prepare the Way," © 1997, Paul Inwood. Published by OCP Publications, 5536 NE Hassalo, Portland, OR 97213. All rights reserved. Used with permission. "Psalm 98: All the Ends of the Earth," Music © 1999, 2000, Barbara Bridge. Published by OCP Publications, 5536 NE Hassalo, Portland, OR 97213. All rights reserved. Used with permission. Refrain © 1969, ICEL. Verse © 1970, CCD. All rights reserved. The English translation of Psalm 98 response from *Lectionary for Mass* © 1969, 1981, 1997, International Committee on English in the Liturgy, Inc. All rights reserved. "Though the Mountains May Fall," © 1975, Daniel L. Schutte and New Dawn Music, 5536 NE Hassalo, Portland, OR 97213. All rights reserved. Used with permission. "Christ, Be Our Light," © 1993, Bernadette Farrell. Published by OCP Publications, 5536 NE Hassalo, Portland, OR 97213. All rights reserved. Used with permission. "Luke 1: Magnificat/Benedictus," © 1992, 2000, Paule Freeburg, DC and Christopher Walker. Published by OCP Publications, 5536 NE Hassalo, Portland, OR 97213. All rights reserved. Used with permission. "My God, My God," © 1988, 1989, 1990, Christopher Walker. Published by OCP Publications, 5536 NE Hassalo, Portland, OR 97213. All rights reserved. Used with permission. "Resucitó/He Is Risen," Music © 1973, Ediciones Musical Pax. Sole U.S. Agent: OCP Publications. English text © 1988, OCP Publications, 5536 NE Hassalo, Portland, OR 97213. All rights reserved. Used with permission. "Pescador de Hombres/Lord, You Have Come," Spanish text and music © 1979, Cesáreo Gabaráin. English translation by Robert C. Trupia, © 1987 by OCP Publications, 5536 NE Hassalo, Portland, OR 97213. All rights reserved. Used with permission. "Jesus Is Risen," Music © 1992, Barbara Bridge. Text © 1992, Barbara Bridge and Owen Alstott. Published by OCP Publications, 5536 NE Hassalo, Portland, OR 97213. All rights reserved. Used with permission. "Spirit of God, Come to Us," © 1989, Sr. Veronica McGrath and Carey Landry. Administered by OCP Publications, 5536 NE Hassalo, Portland, OR 97213. All rights reserved. Used with permission. "God Has Chosen Me," © 1990, Bernadette Farrell. Published by OCP Publications, 5536 NE Hassalo, Portland, OR 97213. All rights reserved. Used with permission. "Who Am I?" Music and text © 1999, Christopher Walker and Paule Freeburg, DC. Published by OCP Publications, 5536 NE Hassalo, Portland, OR 97213. All rights reserved. Used with permission. "Envía Tu Espíritu," © 1988, Bob Hurd. Published by OCP Publications, 5536 NE Hassalo, Portland, OR 97213. All rights reserved. Used with permission.

William H. Sadlier, Inc.
9 Pine Street
New York, NY 10005-1002

ISBN: 0-8215-5406-9
123456789/07 06 05 04 03

The Ad Hoc Committee to Oversee the Use of the Catechism,
United States Conference of Catholic Bishops,
has found this catechetical text, copyright 2004,
to be in conformity with the *Catechism of the Catholic Church*.

The Sadlier *We Believe* Program was developed by nationally recognized experts in catechesis, curriculum, and child development. These teachers of the faith and practitioners helped us to frame every lesson to be age-appropriate and appealing. In addition, a team including respected catechetical, liturgical, pastoral, and theological experts shared their insights and inspired the development of the program.

The Program is truly based on the wisdom of the community, including:

Gerard F. Baumbach, Ed.D.
Executive Vice President and Publisher

Carole M. Eipers, D.Min.
Director of Catechetics

## Catechetical and Liturgical Consultants

Reverend Monsignor John F. Barry
Pastor, American Martyrs Parish
Manhattan Beach, CA

Sister Linda Gaupin, CDP, Ph.D.
Director of Religious Education
Diocese of Orlando

Mary Jo Tully
Chancellor, Archdiocese of Portland

Reverend Monsignor John M. Unger
Assoc. Superintendent for Religious Education
Archdiocese of St. Louis

## Curriculum and Child Development Consultants

Brother Robert R. Bimonte, FSC
Former Superintendent of Catholic Education
Diocese of Buffalo

Gini Shimabukuro, Ed.D.
Associate Director/Associate Professor
Institute for Catholic Educational Leadership
School of Education, University of
San Francisco

## Catholic Social Teaching Consultants

John Carr
Secretary, Department of Social Development
and World Peace, USCCB

Joan Rosenhauer
Coordinator, Special Projects
Department of Social Development and
World Peace, USCCB

## Inculturation Consultants

Reverend Allan Figueroa Deck, SJ, Ph.D.
Executive Director, Loyola Institute for
Spirituality, Orange, CA

Kirk Gaddy
Principal, St. Katharine School
Baltimore, MD

Reverend Nguyễn Việt Hưng
Vietnamese Catechetical Committee

Dulce M. Jiménez-Abreu
Director of Spanish Programs
William H. Sadlier, Inc.

# Contents

# WE BELIEVE

The *We Believe* program will help us to

**learn**

**celebrate**

**share**

and

**live our Catholic faith.**

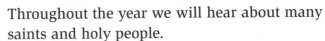

Throughout the year we will hear about many saints and holy people.

| | |
|---|---|
| Saint Agnes | Saint Jerome |
| Saint Alphonsus Liguori | Saint Lawrence |
| Saint Angela de Merici | Saint Martin of Tours |
| Saint Bonaventure | Mary, Mother of God |
| Saint Catherine of Siena | Saint Mary Magdalene |
| Saint Catherine Laboure | Saint Maximilian Kolbe |
| Saint Cecilia | Saint Paul |
| Saint Elizabeth of Portugal | Blessed Pierre Toussaint |
| Saint Genevieve of Paris | Saint Stephen |
| Saint Ignatius of Loyola | Saint Thomas Aquinas |
| Saint John | |

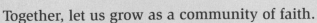

Together, let us grow as a community of faith.

# Welcome!

## ✝ We Gather in Prayer

**Leader:** Welcome, everyone, to Grade 6 *We Believe*. As we begin each chapter, we gather in prayer. We pray to God together. Sometimes, we will read from Scripture, other times we will say the prayers of the Church or sing a song of thanks and praise to God.

Today, let us sing the *We Believe* song!

## ♫ We Believe, We Believe in God

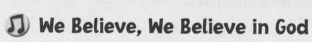

Refrain:

We believe in God;
We believe, we believe in Jesus;
We believe in the Spirit who gives us life.
We believe, we believe in God.

We believe in the Holy Spirit,
Who renews the face of the earth.
We believe we are part of a living Church,
And forever we will live with God.

(Refrain)

# Each day we learn more about God.

In each chapter, we find four main faith statements. They start the day's lesson. They focus us on what we will be learning about in the lesson.

## WE GATHER

✝ *Thank you, God, for all our classmates.*

Then we

think about
talk about
act out
draw about
write about

**Life**

at school
at home
in our parish
in our world
in our neighborhood

Talk about your life right now. What groups, teams, or clubs do you belong to?

Why do you like being a part of these groups?

What does belonging to these groups tell other people about you?

When we see **We Gather**, we begin by taking a moment to pray.

## WE BELIEVE

We learn about:

- the Blessed Trinity—God the Father, God the Son, and God the Holy Spirit

- Jesus, the Son of God, who became one of us

- the Church and its history and teachings

- the Mass and the sacraments

- our call to be a disciple of Jesus.

When we see **We Believe** we learn more about our Catholic faith.

## UNIT 1 — Forming the Covenant

"I praise you, so wonderfully you made me;
wonderful are your works!"          (Psalm 139:14)

## UNIT 2 — Building the Covenant Nation

"Sing to the LORD, for he is gloriously
triumphant."                              (Exodus 15:21)

## UNIT 3 — Redefining the Covenant People

"Rise up in splendor! Your light has come,
the glory of the Lord shines upon you." (Isaiah 60:1)

## UNIT 4 — The Covenant Fulfilled in Jesus

"And a voice came from the heavens, saying, 'This is my
beloved Son, with whom I am well pleased.'"(Matthew 3:17)

> A major theme in your **We Believe** textbook this year is learning more about God's love for his people, and his action in their lives throughout history. Your book is divided into four units.

## Watch for these special signs:

Whenever we see ✝ we make the sign of the cross. We pray and begin our day's lesson.

📖 is an open Bible. When we see it, or a reference like this (John 13:34), we hear the word of God. We hear about God and his people. We hear about Jesus and the Holy Spirit.

When we see 🧍 we do an activity. We might:

- talk together
- write a story
- draw a picture
- act out a story or situation
- imagine ourselves doing something
- sing a song together, or make up one
- work together on a special project.

There are all kinds of activities! We might see 🧍 in any part of our day's lesson. Be on the lookout!

Can you guess what 🎵 means? That's right, it means it is time to sing, or listen to music. We sing songs we know, make up our own, and sing along with those in our *We Believe* music program.

When we see **Key Words** we review the meanings of important words we have learned in the day's lesson.

## As Catholics...

Here we discover something special about our faith. We reflect on what we have discovered and try to make it a part of our life. Don't forget to read it!

## WE RESPOND

We can respond by:

- thinking about ways our faith affects the things we say and do

- sharing our thoughts and feelings

- praying to God.

Then in our home, neighborhood, school, parish, and world, we say and do the things that show love for God and others.

When we see **We Respond** we reflect and act on what we have learned about God and our Catholic faith.

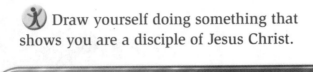 Draw yourself doing something that shows you are a disciple of Jesus Christ.

We are so happy you are with us!

## Review

Here we check to see what we have learned in this chapter.

## Reflect & Pray

We take a few moments to think about our faith and to pray.

## Key Words

We review the meanings of important words from the chapter.

---

Grade 6
Chapter 1

### Review

**Write the letter that best defines each term.**

1. _____ Divine Revelation
2. _____ Bible
3. _____ Tradition
4. _____ divine inspiration

a. written record of God's Revelation and his relationship with his people

b. a type of writing used to get a message across

c. the special guidance that the Holy Spirit gave to the human authors of the Bible

d. God's making himself known to us

e. the Revelation of the good news of Jesus Christ as lived out in the Church, past and present

**Write True or False next to the following sentences. Then change the false sentences to make them true.**

5. _____ The Magisterium is the living, teaching office of the Church.

6. _____ The Bible is the word of God.

7. _____ We learn about God's relationship with the people of Israel in the New Testament.

8. _____ Tradition is the written record of God's Revelation and relationship with his people.

**Write a paragraph to answer this question.**

9–10. How has God revealed himself to us?

**ASSESSMENT** Design a computer screensaver that sends this message: God makes himself known to us.

28

### We Respond in Faith

#### Reflect & Pray

When I read the Bible I _____

God, thank you for revealing yourself to me through _____

**Key Words**
Divine Revelation (p. 23)
Blessed Trinity (p. 23)
Bible (p. 25)
divine inspiration (p. 25)
Tradition (p. 25)

#### Remember

- We can know God through his creation.
- God makes himself known through Divine Revelation.
- God's Revelation is handed down through the Bible and Tradition.
- The Bible is a collection of books.

#### OUR CATHOLIC LIFE

**Saint Jerome**

Saint Jerome was born during the fourth century. He studied in Rome and learned Greek and Latin. He became a monk, but he worried that his love for the lifestyle and writings of non-Christians would take away from his love for God. After several years he went to live in the desert to fast, pray, and focus on God. Jerome studied the writings of the Old Testament and the Hebrew language with another monk. With skill in Hebrew and Greek, Jerome later translated the Bible into Latin. Because of his translation of the Bible, many people were able to read and study Scripture.

In his later years Jerome lived in Bethlehem where he studied the Bible, prayed, and wrote letters and books about the Bible. Saint Jerome is one of the Church's great biblical scholars, and we celebrate his feast day on September 30.

---

## ASSESSMENT

We do a chapter activity in which we show that we have discovered more about our Catholic faith.

## OUR CATHOLIC LIFE

Here we read an interesting story about the ways people make the world better by living out their Catholic faith.

## Remember

We recall the four main faith statements of the chapter.

# SHARING FAITH
## with My Family

At the end of each chapter, you will bring a page like this home to your family. It will offer fun activities that the whole family can enjoy!

## Sharing What I Learned

Discuss the following with your family.

**WE GATHER**

**WE BELIEVE**

**WE RESPOND**

## A Family Prayer

Lead your family in prayer.

People who love us make love grow. Thank you, God, for our family.

People who love us make love grow. Thank you, God, for all the friends of our family.

Most of all, thank you, God, for loving us!

## We✚Believe

### Family Contract

As a **We Believe** family, this year we promise to

_____

_____

Names

_____

_____

_____

Look here for connections to the Web and to the Catechism.

Visit Sadlier's

**www.WeBelieveweb.com**

**Connect to the Catechism of the Catholic Church**
For adult background and reflection, Catechism paragraph references are given here.

# Forming the Covenant

# SHARING FAITH as a Family

## Bring the Bible Home

This year your sixth grader will learn more about God's great love for his people, as shown through God's actions in the lives of all our ancestors in faith. The stories, poems, songs, and events that they discuss are all recorded in the Bible. So this is an ideal time to incorporate the reading of the Bible into your family life.

The only way to get comfortable with the Bible is to use it regularly. Incorporating the reading of the Bible in the home is a great place to start.

A simple way to use the Bible on a weekly basis is to use the readings that will be read at Sunday Mass. These are published in your parish bulletin. That way you will be hearing the word of God as recorded in both the Old and New Testaments of the Bible.

Using a personal study edition of a Bible is helpful because it contains notes and annotations. These provide a background of information on scriptural passages and explain terms that might not be familiar. You may want to look for companion resources that can help explain the context of a particular passage and stimulate reflection on how Scripture connects with daily life. The Internet provides many such resources.

## What Your Child Will Learn in Unit 1

Grade 6 of the *We Believe* program focuses on the story of God's people as recorded in the Old Testament, and the fulfillment of God's covenant in and through Jesus Christ. As Unit 1 begins, the children are presented with an overview of the books of the Old Testament and the New Testament. The Book of Genesis is the focus of Unit 1. The children are introduced to the first story of creation.

The second story of creation is then presented. The children discover that all human beings are equal in dignity and see what our responsibilities are as stewards of creation. The children will next hear of God's promise of a Savior and recognize that Jesus is the Promised One. The children learn about God's covenant with Abraham and his descendants. They also will appreciate that God loves his people and calls on each one of us to trust in him completely.

## Plan & Preview

▶ Have scissors, markers, pencils, or pens available for the activities on the family pages.

▶ Pieces of cardboard or stiff paper can be used for the *We Believe* Trading Cards. The front and back of the cards can be glued to the cardboard, to form a sturdy trading card.

## Note the Quote

"The family that perseveres in good works will surely have an abundance of blessings."

Chinese proverb

## From the Catechism

"The relationships within the family bring an affinity of feelings, affections, and interests, arising above all from the members' respect for one another."

*(Catechism of the Catholic Church, 2206)*

## Did You Know?

In a recent Internet poll, the following question was asked. How much do your kids know about their ancestors? Here are the results:

**9%** know their family tree down to the roots

**34%** know the general idea of their family tree

**46%** know about their living relatives

**8%** know almost nothing about their ancestors

(Reprinted with the permission of Family Education.com)

## Our Old Testament Roots

### The Old City of Jerusalem

Many people consider the ancient city of Jerusalem the most holy city in the world. Judaism, Christianity, and Islam each have a long, rich history in this city. Events central to the traditions of each of these faiths are believed to have taken place in Jerusalem. To the Jewish people it is the site of Abraham's sacrifice. To the Christians it is where the crucifixion and the Resurrection of Jesus took place. To the Muslims it is where the prophet Muhammad ascended to heaven.

The word *bible* means

The Old Testament contains
_____ books about the

The New Testament contains
_____ books about the

THE BIBLE

# God's Revelation

## ✝ We Gather in Prayer

**Leader:** O living God,
Our journey of faith leads us on
the path to you.
Your magnificent deeds are
words of strength and hope for us.
Open our hearts to listen to your
living word.

**Reader 1:** "You formed my inmost being;
you knit me in my mother's womb.
I praise you, so wonderfully you made me;
wonderful are your works!"
(Psalm 139:13–14)

**All:** Your word is a light to my path, O Lord.

**Reader 2:** "I raise my eyes toward the mountains.
From where will my help come?
My help comes from the LORD,
the maker of heaven and earth."
(Psalm 121:1–2)

**All:** Your word is a light to my path,
O Lord.

**Leader:** O God of creation, you made
all things good. Help us to see
the work of your hands in the
world and in our lives. May we
always praise you for your
wonderful deeds!

## 🎵 God, Creator, God Most High

Refrain:
God, Creator, God Most High,
be our ever present light.
Be among us, here before us, God
within us.

You are light for the world.
You are light for the lost to see.
Out of darkness we come to the
light of your love,
for your word is lamp unto our feet
to guide us. (Refrain)

You restored night to day.
You commanded the dark to cease.
By your promise of love we shall
not walk in fear.
We shall walk in the light of hope
and peace to guide us. (Refrain)

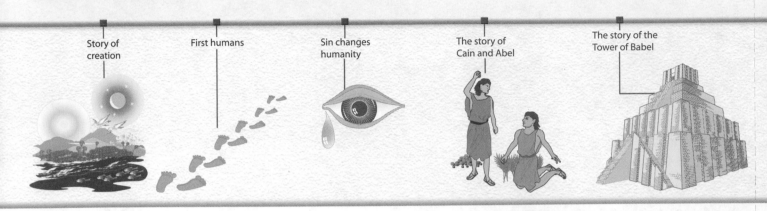

Story of creation

First humans

Sin changes humanity

The story of Cain and Abel

The story of the Tower of Babel

# We can know God through his creation.

## WE GATHER

✝ *O God, help us to know you.*

What are the ways that you discover new ideas or gather new information?

_____

_____

How do you use your senses—sight, hearing, taste, touch, and smell—to help you to gain information?

_____

_____

How does your own experience help you to learn about yourself and the world?

_____

_____

How does the experience of other people help you to learn things?

_____

_____

## WE BELIEVE

One very important factor in learning is thinking. When we think, we are using our natural ability to reason and to come to sound conclusions. These conclusions can even be tested logically and scientifically.

The ability to reason is a gift that all human beings have. And through reason humans have drawn many conclusions about God. For centuries, great thinkers have developed reasonable theories for God's existence. The simplest of these theories is based on the idea that a machine, such as a watch or a computer, does not make itself. It has a maker. The reasonable conclusion is that the same principle applies to the universe. The universe has a maker. We believe that the maker, or creator, of the universe is God.

God establishes covenant with Abraham

Abraham's faith is tested by God

Isaac becomes patriarch

Jacob tricks Esau

God renews covenant with Jacob

God changes Jacob's name to Israel

Joseph is sold into slavery

Joseph works for pharaoh

Joseph's brothers go to Egypt

Joseph and his brothers reconcile

**The World Around Us**   In his writings Saint Paul reminds us that the human mind can find God "in what he has made" (Romans 1:20). For example, by looking at the vast expanses of space through a telescope we get to know something of God's power. By discovering more about the universe we get to know about God's knowledge and wisdom. By smelling a flower on a cool summer morning we can experience God's beauty.

By noticing the great variety of plant and animal life in the world we can come to understand God's generosity. By appreciating how tenderly a mother sheep cares for her newborn lamb we can see a glimpse of God's loving kindness. And by observing human life, the greatest and most astounding creation in the universe, we get another glimpse into who God is. Learning about who we are, how we think and behave, and what we hope for helps us to think about what God must be like.

So by making use of all of our natural gifts, and those of other people, we get to know about our world, about ourselves, and about God. These are purely natural ways of coming to know God. They help us to believe in God and to understand that it is reasonable to believe in him. However, these natural means are all limited. We need something else to get to know God better. God has to tell us about himself.

**WE RESPOND**

Look at the photos on these pages. Which ones help you to know what God is like? Why?

Make a postcard of another scene that reminds you of God. In a caption on the card, explain why the scene makes you think of God. With your class decide on a special place to display all the cards.

**21**

# God makes himself known through Divine Revelation.

✝ *Loving God, teach us your ways.*

Think about a movie or television show about people who are friends. How do they trust one another? share with one another? know and care about one another?

### WE BELIEVE

God wants us to have a close friendship with him. He loves us so much that he confided in us. He told us about himself. He revealed himself to us. *Reveal* means "to make known." **Divine Revelation** is God's making himself known to us.

God did not reveal himself by writing us a letter or sending an e-mail. God has made himself known to us through his mighty deeds and by his interactions with his people throughout time.

Although God spoke to individual men and women about himself and his plan for his people, his message was for the whole community. God made it clear that he wanted to have a loving relationship with all people. In revealing himself, God answered all sorts of questions that human beings ask but cannot answer on their own. Revelation made it possible for humans to know God more deeply and to respond to him in a way that was otherwise not possible.

However, God did not reveal himself all at once. God has made himself known gradually over a long period of time. God's Revelation of himself began with the creation of the first human beings and their descendants. It continued through the ancient Israelites and the Jewish people.

God's Revelation is full and complete in his only Son, Jesus Christ. By sending his Son, God tells us what we need to know about himself. In the Gospel of John we read, "No one has ever seen God. The only Son, God, who is at the Father's side, has revealed him" (John 1:18).

Jesus Christ is the only Son of God who became man. Jesus shows us God his Father's love. In learning about Jesus Christ, we learn about the Father. When we follow Jesus' example of living, we grow closer to the Father. Together with the Father, he sends God the Holy Spirit to strengthen us. The Holy Spirit helps us respond to God's great love for us. God the Father, God the Son, and God the Holy Spirit are the Blessed Trinity. The **Blessed Trinity** is the three Persons in one God.

The Holy Spirit guides the Church—those who are baptized in Jesus Christ and follow him—to understand God's Revelation and to apply it in our lives. As the Church, we try to live by God's plan for us and by his laws. We hope for the clearer understanding of God's plan that comes to those who are with God forever in eternal life. Only then will God be completely known by us. As Saint John said, "Now this is eternal life, that they should know you, the only true God, and the one whom you sent, Jesus Christ" (John 17:3).

Reread pages 22 and 23. Highlight or underline ways God revealed himself.

**Key Words**

**Divine Revelation**  God's making himself known to us

**Blessed Trinity**  the three Persons in one God: God the Father, God the Son, and God the Holy Spirit

## WE RESPOND

God speaks to all of us every day. How is God speaking to you today?

Almighty God, thank you for revealing yourself to us in your only Son, Jesus Christ. Praise and glory to you! Amen.

## God's Revelation is handed down through the Bible and Tradition.

### WE GATHER

✝ *Loving God, guide us in truth.*

How do you know about your relatives who lived before you? How can you pass on memories of your family to the next generation?

### WE BELIEVE

To pass on memories about someone, we often write down things about that person so that later generations can read it. This gives us a written record. Another way of passing on memories about someone is by sharing our recollections of that person with others in our family or community. This keeps the person alive in our hearts and minds and helps us to pass our memories on to the next generation. This is called oral tradition.

God's Revelation of himself has been handed on in very much the same way. The **Bible**, also called *Sacred Scripture* or simply *Scripture*, is the written record of God's Revelation and his relationship with his people. **Tradition** is the Revelation of the good news of Jesus Christ as lived out in the Church, past and present.

God's Revelation of himself took place long before the Bible existed. The events and the recollections that people had of God were passed on from generation to generation. People's living experience of God helped to shape the form and content of the Bible.

**The Bible**   The Bible is a book of faith and is unlike any other book. It has a divine author, God, and many human authors, or biblical writers. These writers used their own words and expressions and chose the way to organize their writings. But as they worked, they were guided by God the Holy Spirit.

The special guidance that the Holy Spirit gave to the human authors of the Bible is called **divine inspiration**. This inspiration of God the Holy Spirit guaranteed that the human authors wrote without any error God's saving truth. For that reason God is the true author of the whole Bible. Thus, the Bible is the *word of God*. We treat the Bible with reverence because it is God's word to us today. From the Bible we learn of how to relate to God—Father, Son, and Holy Spirit.

**Tradition** Tradition, the good news of Jesus Christ as lived out in the Church, includes teachings and practices handed on orally from the time of Jesus and his apostles. It includes the creeds, or statements, of Christian beliefs. It also includes the teachings and documents of the Church, the Church's worship, and other practices. Tradition is the source of the Church's ongoing understanding of the meaning of Revelation and the ways to apply it to our lives.

The written message of Scripture and the spoken message of Tradition have been handed on by the apostles to the whole Church. The bishops are the successors of the apostles. With the pope as their head, they form the *Magisterium*, the living, teaching office of the Church. In Jesus' name and with the help of the Holy Spirit, the Magisterium interprets both Scripture and Tradition.

Through the centuries the Church has continued to share and build on the faith of the apostles. The Church community in every generation believes and lives this faith and passes it on to future generations.

How are the Bible and Tradition the same? How are they different?

## As Catholics...

The Church, primarily the bishops, has the task of interpreting and teaching Scripture. The bishops share this teaching responsibility with priests and laypeople. Many people help the bishops to interpret the meaning of Scripture. Some of these people are biblical scholars who find out the meanings of ancient words. They translate and study ancient scrolls. They visit places in the Middle East to find evidence of the Bible and how it was written.

Other scholars are archaeologists. They dig at sites in the Middle East to find artifacts—tablets, scrolls, jewelry, pots, and tools. They help us to understand how people lived in biblical times.

Who are some people who teach you about the Bible?

## Key Words

**Bible** the written record of God's Revelation and his relationship with his people

**Tradition** the Revelation of the good news of Jesus Christ as lived out in the Church, past and present

**divine inspiration** the special guidance that the Holy Spirit gave to the human authors of the Bible

## WE RESPOND

Imagine that you have to teach this truth to your class: God's Revelation is passed on through the Bible and Tradition. Design a visual (poster, chart, screensaver, or other object) that might help the class to understand this truth.

# The Bible is a collection of books.

## WE GATHER

✝ *Your word, Lord, lights my way.*

🧑 What different kinds of things can you learn about the ocean from each of these types of books?

From a **Poetry Book**

From a **Science Book**

From an **Adventure Book**

_____ (Add your own)

## WE BELIEVE

The word *bible* means "books." The Bible is not just one book but a small library of sacred, or holy, books. Each book uses literary forms to help us to learn about God in a unique way. A *literary form* is a type of writing used to get a message across.

Since it is a library, the Bible contains all kind of literary forms: ancient folktales, histories, novels, short stories, advice on living, codes of law, letters, prophecy, visions, poetry, hymns, and many other types of writing. Each book of the Bible is written in one or more of these literary forms.

The Bible is a collection of seventy-three separate books. The Bible is divided into two parts called *Testaments*.

The *Old Testament* contains forty-six books originally written in Hebrew, Aramaic, or Greek. In the Old Testament we learn about God's relationship with the people of Israel. The *New Testament* contains twenty-seven books originally written in Greek. The New Testament contains the story of Jesus, his mission, his first followers, and the beginning of the Church. Together these two testaments make up the complete Bible.

It took almost a thousand years to assemble all the books of the Old Testament. In the tenth century before Christ (B.C.), the Israelite people first began to write down the stories that had been handed down by word of mouth for generations. The last book of the Old Testament was probably written in the first century B.C.

The books of the New Testament, however, came into being more quickly. Only about sixty or seventy years passed between the death of Jesus and the completion of the last book of the New Testament.

Many of the biblical writers are completely unknown. Some have left us written clues about their lives and personalities. And there are just a few about whom much is written for example, Sirach, in the Old Testament, and Saint Paul, in the New Testament.

## WE RESPOND

When we refer to a citation from the Bible we refer to the name of the book, the chapter of the book, and verse(s) of the chapter. Thus, Genesis 1:1–2 refers to the Book of Genesis, chapter 1, verses 1 and 2.

🧑 Explain what the following citation means: Revelation 21:1–3.

Thank you, O God, for the gift of your word in the Bible. Amen.

# Books of the Bible

## The Old Testament

### Pentateuch ("Five Scrolls")

| These books tell about the formation of the covenant and describe basic laws and beliefs of the Israelites. | Genesis | Exodus | Leviticus | Numbers | Deuteronomy |
|---|---|---|---|---|---|

### Historical Books

| These books deal with the history of Israel. | Joshua | 1 Samuel | 1 Chronicles | Nehemiah | Esther |
|---|---|---|---|---|---|
| | Judges | 2 Samuel | 2 Chronicles | Tobit | 1 Maccabees |
| | Ruth | 1 Kings | Ezra | Judith | 2 Maccabees |
| | | 2 Kings | | | |

### Wisdom Books

| These books explain God's role in everyday life. | Job | Proverbs | Song of Songs | Wisdom | Sirach |
|---|---|---|---|---|---|
| | Psalms | Ecclesiastes | | | |

### Prophetic Books

| These books contain writings of the great prophets who spoke God's word to the people of Israel. | Isaiah | Ezekiel | Amos | Nahum | Haggai |
|---|---|---|---|---|---|
| | Jeremiah | Daniel | Obadiah | Habakkuk | Zechariah |
| | Lamentations | Hosea | Jonah | Zephaniah | Malachi |
| | Baruch | Joel | Micah | | |

## The New Testament

### Gospels

| These books contain the message and key events in the life of Jesus Christ. Because of this, the gospels hold a central place in the New Testament. | Matthew | Mark | Luke | John |
|---|---|---|---|---|

### Letters

| These books contain letters written by Saint Paul and other leaders to individual Christians or to early Christian communities. | Romans | Colossians | Titus | 2 Peter |
|---|---|---|---|---|
| | 1 Corinthians | 1 Thessalonians | Philemon | 1 John |
| | 2 Corinthians | 2 Thessalonians | Hebrews | 2 John |
| | Galatians | 1 Timothy | James | 3 John |
| | Ephesians | 2 Timothy | 1 Peter | Jude |
| | Philippians | | | |

### Other Writings

| | Acts of the Apostles | Revelation |
|---|---|---|

**Write the letter that best defines each term.**

1. _____ Divine Revelation

2. _____ Bible

3. _____ Tradition

4. _____ divine inspiration

**a.** written record of God's Revelation and his relationship with his people

**b.** a type of writing used to get a message across

**c.** the special guidance that the Holy Spirit gave to the human authors of the Bible

**d.** God's making himself known to us

**e.** the Revelation of the good news of Jesus Christ as lived out in the Church, past and present

**Write True or False next to the following sentences.
Then change the false sentences to make them true.**

5. _____ The Magisterium is the living, teaching office of the Church.

_____

6. _____ The Bible is the word of God.

_____

7. _____ We learn about God's relationship with the people of Israel in the New Testament.

_____

8. _____ Tradition is the written record of God's Revelation and relationship with his people.

_____

**Write a paragraph to answer this question.**

**9–10.** How has God revealed himself to us?

Design a computer screensaver that sends this message: God makes himself known to us.

# We Respond in Faith

## Reflect & Pray

When I read the Bible I

_____

_____

God, thank you for revealing yourself to me through

_____

_____

**Key Words**

**Divine Revelation** (p. 23)
**Blessed Trinity** (p. 23)
**Bible** (p. 25)
**divine inspiration** (p. 25)
**Tradition** (p. 25)

## Remember

- We can know God through his creation.
- God makes himself known through Divine Revelation.
- God's Revelation is handed down through the Bible and Tradition.
- The Bible is a collection of books.

## OUR CATHOLIC LIFE

### Saint Jerome

Saint Jerome was born during the fourth century. He studied in Rome and learned Greek and Latin. He became a monk, but he worried that his love for the lifestyle and writings of non-Christians would take away from his love for God. After several years he went to live in the desert to fast, pray, and focus on God. Jerome studied the writings of the Old Testament and the Hebrew language with another monk. With his skill in Hebrew and Greek, Jerome later translated the Bible into Latin. Because of his translation of the Bible, many people were able to read and study Scripture.

In his later years Jerome lived in Bethlehem where he studied the Bible, prayed, and wrote letters and books about the Bible. Saint Jerome is one of the Church's great biblical scholars, and we celebrate his feast day on September 30.

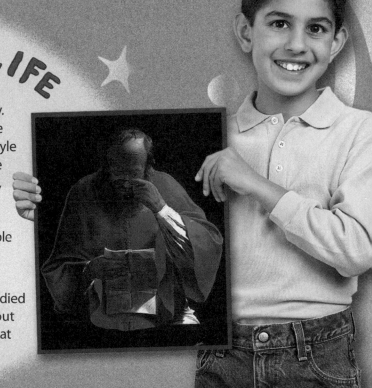

# SHARING FAITH
## with My Family

## Sharing What I Learned

Discuss the following with your family:

- Divine Revelation
- Scripture and Tradition
- divine inspiration
- the books of the Bible.

## "Finding God"

Saint Paul tells us that we can find God "in what he has made" (Romans 1:20). This week, encourage your family to "find God" in your home, school or work, and community. Make a family plan of action to live out what you have found.

THE BIBLE

The word *bible* means

_____

_____

The Old Testament contains

_____ books about the

_____

The New Testament contains

_____ books about the

_____

## We Believe Trading Cards

Complete the facts on the back of the trading card. Then share with your family what you have learned about the Bible.

Visit Sadlier's

**www.WEBELIEVEweb.com**

**Connect to the Catechism**
For adult background and reflection, see paragraphs 32, 38, 81, and 120.

# Creation

## ✝ We Gather in Prayer

**Leader:** O God of creation,
You have given us wonderful gifts!
We praise and thank you for all
that you have created.

**Reader:** "All good giving and every
perfect gift is from above, coming
down from the Father of lights."
(James 1:17)

**Leader:** We thank you for our gift of life.

**All:** We praise you God.

**Leader:** We thank you for our sense
of smell, hearing, and touch.

**All:** We praise you God.

**Leader:** We thank you for our
families and friends.

**All:** We praise you God.

**Leader:** We thank you for our
abilities and talents.

**All:** We praise you God.

## ♫ I Know You Are God

In the morning's first sunlight, I know you
are God.
In the gentle and starry night, I know you
are God.
I see in your majesty all that you are to me,
in each and ev'rything, I know you are God.

In your loving forgiveness I know you
are God.
In your kindness, compassion I know you
are God.
My trust rests in you alone, source of all
peace and hope;
bless the Lord, O my soul, I know you
are God.

# The Book of Genesis is about beginnings.

## WE GATHER

✝ *God, we thank you for being with us always.*

Think about the beginning years of your life. Describe your earliest memories or something your family has told you about your early life. What have they told you about events in your family that took place before you were born?

## WE BELIEVE

The history of God and his people covers over two thousand years. It is recorded in the Bible. Each part, or period, of this story connects in a special way with the covenant. The **covenant** is an agreement between God and his people.

This chart divides this lengthy history into smaller periods. The chart lists historical periods that are presented in the Bible and indicates some books of the Bible that describe each period.

| Historical Period | Books of the Bible |
| --- | --- |
| Prehistory | Genesis |
| The Patriarchs | Genesis |
| Israel in Egypt | Exodus |
| The Wilderness Experience | Exodus, Leviticus, Numbers, Deuteronomy |
| Settling the Land | Joshua, Judges, Ruth |
| The United Kingdom | 1–2 Samuel, 1–2 Kings, 1–2 Chronicles, Psalms |
| The Divided Kingdom | 2 Kings, 2 Chronicles, Amos, Hosea, Micah, Isaiah, Jeremiah, Nahum |
| The Babylonian Captivity | Lamentations, Ezekiel, Isaiah, Daniel, Esther |
| Return to the Homeland | Ezra, Nehemiah, Tobit, Judith, Jonah, Ecclesiastes |
| Israel Among the Nations | 1–2 Maccabees, Daniel, Sirach |
| Jesus' Earthly Ministry | Matthew, Mark, Luke, John |
| The Early Church | Acts of the Apostles, Letters, Revelation |

*Genesis* means beginning. The **Book of Genesis** is the first book in the Bible, and it is about beginnings. In the first eleven chapters of Genesis, we read about prehistory, the events from creation down to the time of Abraham. These chapters contain stories that describe the beginning of God's relationship with humanity. These stories are very old and are not necessarily about factual events. Instead the stories tell of actual religious truths about God and his actions and interactions with humanity.

The stories contained vivid descriptions and imagery, repeated details often, and had simple plots with not many characters. These features made it easy for people to understand the meaning of the stories, to remember them, and to pass the stories down through the ages.

The biblical writer used symbols to tell a realistic story and at the same time to give the deeper meaning of the story. The symbols used in the Bible express ideas and beliefs about God and his actions throughout history.

In the first eleven chapters of Genesis, the stories are sometimes separated from each other by genealogies, or family trees. The genealogies tell how people are related to one another and how they are part of God's family.

*The Gates of Paradise,* by Lorenzo Ghiberti (1378–1455), depict Old Testament scenes. Baptistery of the Duomo, Florence, Italy

## WE RESPOND

Think about all the "beginnings" that have taken place in your life. You might include the first time you rode a bicycle or the time when you first received Holy Communion.

Write a prayer asking God to continue to help you in all your "beginnings."

_____

_____

_____

_____

# God created the universe.

Genesis 1:1–31; 2:1–4

## WE GATHER

✝ *O God, how wonderful is your universe!*

Have you ever looked at the night sky filled with stars? What did you wonder about?

## WE BELIEVE

Through the ages people have wondered about the universe: Where did it come from? How did it begin? Who created it? Why was it created? When did it start?

Scientists have focused on the problems of *how* and *when* the universe and all of life came into being. They have discovered many facts and have come up with some very interesting theories. The Church recognizes the importance of these studies. However, science cannot answer the questions of *who* created the universe, *why* it was created, and *where* it is going. These questions can only be answered in faith. So we look to Scripture and Tradition for the answers to these questions.

The Book of Genesis contains two accounts of creation. In the first, Genesis 1:1—2:4, we find a beautiful and imaginative story of the creation of the universe. In simple but poetic language, the biblical writer tells us that God freely created the universe over a six-day period. A *day* in this story does not mean twenty-four hours. In fact, *day* does not represent any definite period of time. Scholars think the biblical writer showed God creating the universe in six days because that was the normal workweek of the Israelites who lived at the time the story was written.

In the creation story God spoke and everything was created: light, sun, moon, stars, sky, water, earth, sea, fish, plants, animals, and humans. By God's word the universe came into being. And at each stage God saw that what he created was good. Then on the seventh day God rested, just as the Israelites rested after their long workweek.

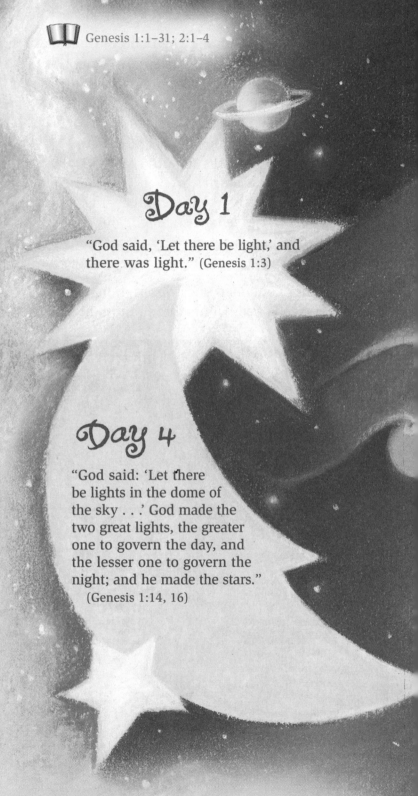

### Day 1

"God said, 'Let there be light,' and there was light." (Genesis 1:3)

### Day 4

"God said: 'Let there be lights in the dome of the sky . . .' God made the two great lights, the greater one to govern the day, and the lesser one to govern the night; and he made the stars." (Genesis 1:14, 16)

This creation account is not meant to be a scientific study of creation. It is not an exact recording of God's work within a certain time frame. However, it is the story that revealed to God's people the truths about creation: everything in existence is created by God, and everything that God created is good and depends on him.

# First Story of Creation

"In the beginning, when God created the heavens and the earth, the earth was a formless wasteland, and darkness covered the abyss, while a mighty wind swept over the waters."

(Genesis 1:1–2)

## Day 2

"God said, 'Let there be a dome in the middle of the waters, to separate one body of water from the other.' And so it happened." (Genesis 1:6)

## Day 3

"God said, 'Let the water under the sky be gathered into a single basin, so that the dry land may appear . . . ' Then God said, 'Let the earth bring forth vegetation: every kind of plant that bears seed and every kind of fruit tree on earth that bears fruit with its seed in it.' " (Genesis 1:9, 11)

## Day 5

"God said, 'Let the water teem with an abundance of living creatures, and on the earth let birds fly beneath the dome of the sky.' " (Genesis 1:20)

## Day 6

"God said, 'Let the earth bring forth all kinds of living creatures: cattle, creeping things, and wild animals of all kinds' . . . Then God said: 'Let us make man in our image, after our likeness' . . . male and female he created them.

God blessed them, saying: 'Be fertile and multiply; fill the earth and subdue it. Have dominion over the fish of the sea, the birds of the air, and all the living things that move on the earth.' . . . God looked at everything he had made, and he found it very good." (Genesis 1:24, 26, 27, 28, 31)

 In groups portray the events of creation in a dramatic representation.

### WE RESPOND

What does creation tell us about God's love? his wisdom? his power? his goodness?

Heavenly Father, thank you for your wonderful gift of creation.
Amen.

## Day 7

"Thus the heavens and the earth and all their array were completed. Since on the seventh day God was finished with the work he had been doing, he rested on the seventh day from all the work he had undertaken. So God blessed the seventh day and made it holy, because on it he rested from all the work he had done in creation.
Such is the story of the heavens and the earth at their creation." (Genesis 2:1–4)

# God is the source of all life.

## WE GATHER

✝ *God, there is nothing you cannot do.*

 Choose one of your favorite characters from a book, television show, or movie. Then with a partner describe two positive qualities about that character. How does the character show these qualities?

## WE BELIEVE

The first account of creation in Genesis 1:1—2:4 not only tells us about creation, it also tells us about God. To begin with, the account shows us that God is the one, true God. In other words, God is unique. There is no other God. This understanding of God is very different from the one held by other ancient peoples.

They believed that there were many gods and even thought of objects as gods. They often worshiped the sun or moon, other forces of nature like the weather, or ideas like fate or justice.

From the first account of creation we learn how the one true God was different from the many false gods or idols that were the focus of beliefs in ancient times. The first creation account makes it clear that the God we worship is a personal God, not an object or an idea. God is a living being, and is the source of all life. In fact, God is the greatest of all beings. God is the supreme being who creates all life and keeps it in existence.

Throughout history God has continued to reveal himself as the one who is the source of all creation. In the Bible we find many references to God as creator.

| Old Testament | New Testament |
|---|---|
| "Our help is in the name of the LORD, the maker of heaven and earth." (Psalm 124:8) | "The God who made the world and all that is in it, the Lord of heaven and earth, does not dwell in sanctuaries made by human hands, nor is he served by human hands because he needs anything. Rather it is he who gives to everyone life and breath and everything." (Acts of the Apostles 17:24–25) |

The first account of creation helps us to know some of God's attributes, or characteristics.

- **God is eternal.** This means that God always was and always will be. God is changeless and timeless. Change and time are part of creation, and God is *not* part of creation. The Israelites' view of God was very different from the one held by other ancient peoples. They worshiped false gods that they thought were a part of creation. They believed these gods were born, usually in some fantastic way, and could die.

- **God is all-powerful.** This means that God can do anything. God is perfect. Here again God differs from the false gods that people believed in. They believed that their gods made mistakes and sometimes failed. They often pictured these gods as guilty of terrible evils.

- **God is all-knowing.** This means that God knows everything—past, present, and future. Yet God's knowledge never keeps people from choosing and acting freely. Unlike the Israelites, other people believed in false gods that did not know everything, could not do everything, and often tried to keep the people from making their own decisions.

- **God is ever-present.** This means that God is everywhere at all times. Again the false gods that other people believed in did not have this quality. They could not be present everywhere and always. They were often described as traveling from place to place, just like human beings.

The first creation account tells us so much that we need to know about God. And there is still more that we can learn. However, human words and ideas can only explain so much. We will never have full and complete knowledge of God. That is why God will remain a mystery to us in this life.

To help you remember the attributes of God, use words and images to complete this diagram.

God is . . .

## WE RESPOND

Which of God's attributes best describes your own experience of God? Why?

# Human beings are created in God's image and likeness.

## WE GATHER

✝ *Loving Father, you are always by our side.*

> 🏃 In a group brainstorm words that can be used to describe the term *human beings*. Then write a definition of the term.
>
> _____
>
> _____

## WE BELIEVE

The account of creation that begins the Book of Genesis indicates that God created not only the universe but all the living things in it. However, there is something strikingly different in the description of the creation of humans.

"God created man in his image;
    in the divine image he created him;
    male and female he created them."
(Genesis 1:27)

The biblical writer is telling us that only human beings are made in the image and likeness of God. We are like God because as human beings each of us has been created as someone, not something.

Each one of us is a unique person who possesses a human dignity. **Human dignity** is the value and worth that comes from being made in God's image and likeness. Both males and females are created in God's image and likeness. God created humans different but equal. And God found that good. Girls and boys, women and men, have differences but we are equal because we all share the same human dignity.

Each one of us is created to be like God and to share in his friendship. Of all the creatures we alone are created by God with **free will**, the freedom and ability to choose, and with **conscience**, the ability to know the difference between good and evil, right and wrong. We alone are able to think and love and form relationships. We alone can know and love our creator. God calls us to be open to his love and to the love of others. He calls us to love as he loves and to live in his friendship.

Being made in the image and likeness of God carries with it serious responsibilities. We are called to respect and care for all that God has given us. And since our free will makes us responsible for our own thoughts and actions, we must make our choices carefully. We are called to choose what is good and right and to act in the image and likeness of our creator.

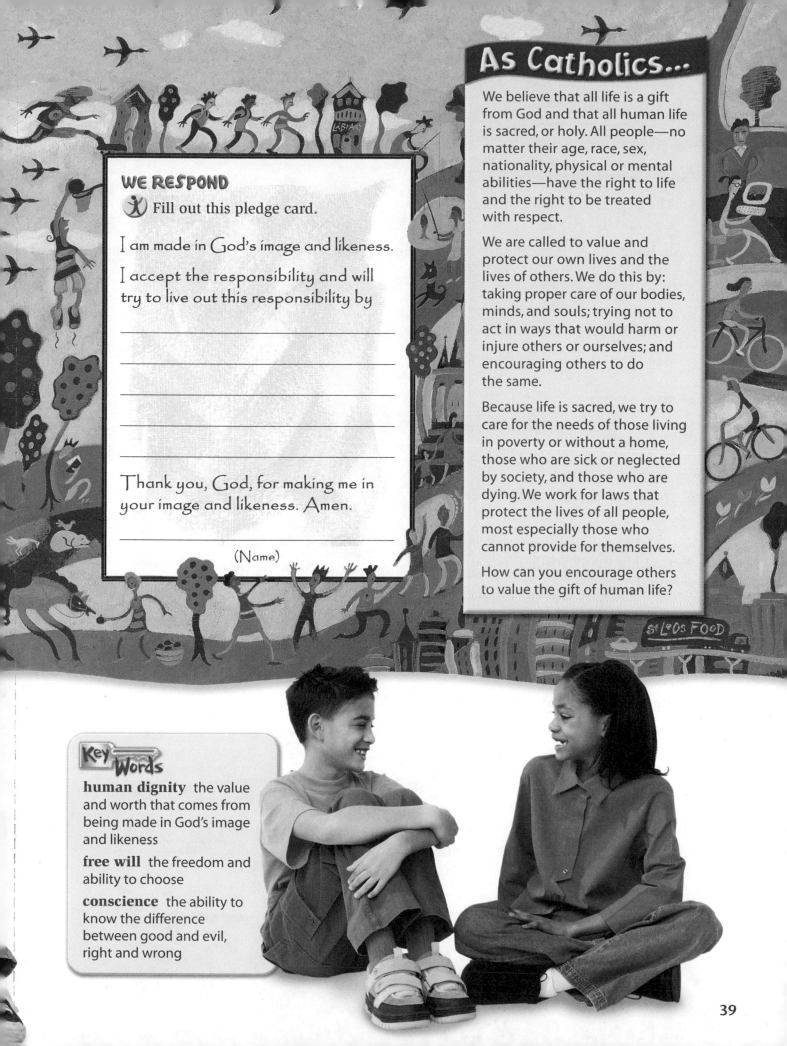

## WE RESPOND

Fill out this pledge card.

I am made in God's image and likeness.

I accept the responsibility and will try to live out this responsibility by

_____

_____

_____

_____

_____

Thank you, God, for making me in your image and likeness. Amen.

_____
(Name)

### Key Words

**human dignity** the value and worth that comes from being made in God's image and likeness

**free will** the freedom and ability to choose

**conscience** the ability to know the difference between good and evil, right and wrong

**Circle the letter of the correct answer.**

1. The _____ is an agreement between God and his people.

    **a.** Bible        **b.** creation        **c.** covenant

2. Biblical writers used _____ to tell a realistic story and at the same time to give the deeper meaning of the story.

    **a.** attributes     **b.** symbols     **c.** scholars

3. _____ is the freedom and ability to choose.

    **a.** Genesis     **b.** Free will     **c.** Conscience

4. _____ is the source of all life.

    **a.** The Bible     **b.** The Book of Genesis     **c.** God

**Short Answers**

5. Why is Genesis an appropriate name for the first book of the Bible?

    _____

6. What truths does the first creation story reveal to us?

    _____

7. God has many attributes; list three.

    _____

8. What is human dignity?

    _____

**Write a paragraph to answer this question.**

9–10. Because we were created in the image and likeness of God, what responsibilities do we have?

ASSESSMENT

Retell the first story of creation in your own way. Use pictures, make a video, or write and record it as a song. Share your creation story with your class or family.

# We Respond in Faith

## Reflect & Pray

God, you made people in your image and likeness, I

_____

Lord, help us to give you glory by

_____

_____

**Key Words**

**covenant** (p. 33)
**Book of Genesis** (p. 33)
**human dignity** (p. 39)
**free will** (p. 39)
**conscience** (p. 39)

## Remember

- The Book of Genesis is about beginnings.
- God created the universe.
- God is the source of all life.
- Human beings are created in God's image and likeness.

## OUR CATHOLIC LIFE
### The Vatican Observatory

The Vatican Observatory is one of the oldest astronomical institutes in the world. It was founded in 1582, and the Jesuit priests and brothers are responsible for it. Today the observatory has two research centers: one in Castel Gandolfo, Italy, and one in Tucson, Arizona. The Vatican Advanced Technology Telescope (VATT) in Tucson is the first optical-infrared telescope to be used to study light at the farthest points of the universe. The observatory center in Italy has a unique meteorite collection which is being used to study the history of the solar system.

Like the scientists who work at the Vatican Observatory, we grow closer to God and help others get closer to God by appreciating the wonders of his creation. Studying science—the stars, meteorites, and other solar systems of our universe— is one way to do this.

# SHARING FAITH
## with My Family

## Sharing What I Learned

Discuss the following with your family:

- the Book of Genesis
- creation
- God's attributes or characteristics
- human dignity.

## A Family Tree

Genealogies, or family trees, tell how people are related to one another and how they are part of God's family. Ask your family to help you make your family tree. List all members of your family who are now living and their relationship in the family. List those family members who have died and their relationship in the family. Do research as to how you can learn more about your family.

"GOD CREATED THE HEAVENS AND THE EARTH."
Genesis 1:1

The story of creation is found in the Book of _____

By God's _____ the universe came into being.

Human beings are made in the _____ and _____ of God.

## We Believe Trading Cards

Complete the facts on the back of the trading card. Then share with your family what you have learned about the creation story.

Visit Sadlier's

www.WEBELIEVEweb.com

**Connect to the Catechism**
For adult background and reflection, see paragraphs 289, 293, 301, and 357.

## ✝ We Gather in Prayer

**Leader:** Blessed be the God of creation who forms us like clay in the hands of a potter.

**All:** Blessed be God now and for ever.

**Reader 1:** "This word came to Jeremiah from the LORD: Rise up, be off to the potter's house; there I will give you my message.

**Reader 2:** I went down to the potter's house and there he was, working at the wheel. Whenever the object of clay which he was making turned out badly in his hand, he tried again, making of the clay another object of whatever sort he pleased.

**Reader 3:** Then the word of the Lord came to me: Can I not do to you, house of Israel, as this potter has done? says the LORD.

**Reader 4:** Indeed, like clay in the hand of the potter, so are you in my hand, house of Israel." (Jeremiah 18:1–6)

The word of the Lord.

**All:** Thanks be to God.

# God created human beings, body and soul.

## WE GATHER

✝ *Thank you, Lord, for the breath of life.*

🧑 With a group brainstorm some things that human beings do that other creatures cannot do.

## WE BELIEVE

After the opening story of creation, the Book of Genesis provides a second story of creation. We can read it in Genesis 2:5–25. In this second account of creation, the biblical writer describes that God created humans *before* he created plants and other creatures. Thus, the two creation stories differ. Yet both accounts make the same point: God created humanity as the high point of creation.

The following words from another book of Scripture make it clear that God gave great dignity and power to all humans.

"What are humans that you are mindful of
    them,
   mere mortals that you care for them?
Yet you have made them little less than a
    god,
   crowned them with glory and honor.
You have given them rule over the works of
    your hands,
   put all things at their feet." (Psalm 8:5–7)

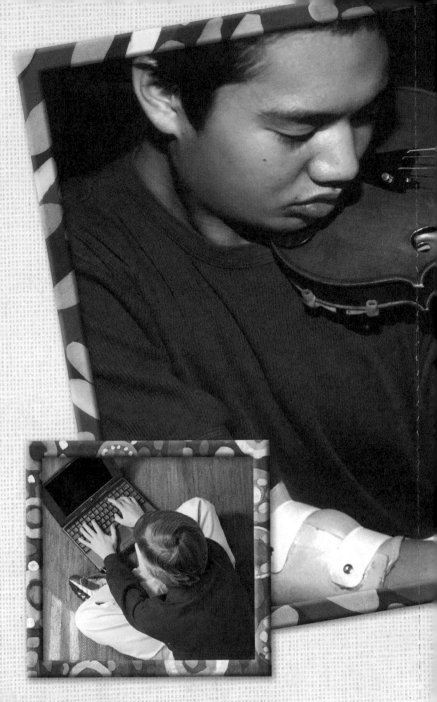

In the second creation story, the biblical writer tells us that God created humans by taking a lump of clay from the earth and using it to form the body of the first man. This creation account is very old, yet it agrees with the idea from today's modern scientific study: Our human bodies are made out of the same elements as the rest of the universe.

In this story we read "the Lord God formed man out of the clay of the ground and blew into his nostrils the breath of life, and so man became a living being" (Genesis 2:7). This symbolizes that God gave humanity life. This breath of life from God refers to our **soul**, the invisible spiritual reality that makes each of us human. The soul is immortal; it will never die.

This story makes it clear that humans are a union of a visible, physical body and an invisible, spiritual soul. Every human being is unique, yet each of us is made body and soul. And one day we will die and our bodies will turn to dust. But our souls, the breath of God in us, will live forever. At the end of time, our body and soul will be reunited when Christ comes again at the last judgment.

We also find in this second story of creation that God said, "It is not good for the man to be alone. I will make a suitable partner for him" (Genesis 2:18). So God created many wild animals and birds and then finally, while the man slept, God took one of his ribs and created the first woman. When the man woke up and saw this woman he said,

"This one, at last, is bone of my bones
and flesh of my flesh" (Genesis 2:23).

God's creation of woman from the rib of man symbolizes that females and males share the same human dignity and are equal. This also reminds us that all humans are united to one another. We all have one true Father—God. It is God who has created us and has breathed life into us. We are all created to share in God's own life, and to help one another to know and love God.

## WE RESPOND

We all have gifts and abilities. What are some of yours? How do you use your unique gifts and abilities to help others know and love God? How do they use their gifts to help you?

### 🎵 And It Was Good

Ev'rything was now in place,
earth and sky and sea;
then God blew a mighty breath
making you and me.

And it was good, good, very, very good,
and it was good, good, very, very good,
and it was good, good, very, very good,
it was very, very, very good.

# God called us to be stewards of creation.

## WE GATHER

✝ *God, help us to love all that you love.*

What are some things you do each day to show that you care for God's creation? How can these actions make a difference in the world?

## WE BELIEVE

In Genesis God told the first human beings, "Be fertile and multiply; fill the earth and subdue it. Have dominion over the fish of the sea, the birds of the air, and all the living things that move on the earth" (Genesis 1:28).

God created human beings and gave them life. Then God allowed humans to be partners with him and with one another in continuing his work of creation. God told the first man and woman to bring new life into the world and thus create the human family. He asked them to be responsible for the earth and all the living things in it.

God put the first man and woman in the beautiful garden in Eden and shared his own friendship and life with them. They also had use of all the gifts of creation. The garden was a symbol that the biblical writer used to show the happiness that human beings had in the presence of God.

The biblical writer tells us about another symbolic event: God gave humans authority over all the animals by allowing them to name the animals. To the ancient Israelites, people had authority over those whom they named. So humans were called by God to be the caretakers of creation.

Of all of God's creatures, humans alone have the ability to care for creation and make it prosper. In fact, that is exactly what stewardship involves—authority and responsibility. A **steward** is a person who is given both the authority over what he or she cares for and the responsibility for seeing that it lives and grows. Each of us is a steward of God's creation.

**Stewards Today** Today people around the world are trying to carry out their responsibilities as God's stewards of creation. Many people work to protect our environment by recycling and using resources wisely. Some plant new trees to maintain the world's forests. Other people work to stop air and water pollution, and to protect our wildlife. Scientists and farmers find ways for us to safely grow enough food to feed all the people in the world. By caring for creation, we show respect for the creator.

**Key Word**

**steward** a person who is given both the authority over what he or she cares for and the responsibility for seeing that it lives and grows

WE RESPOND

We are all called to take care of creation every day. What specific things can we do to:

use water wisely _____

recycle _____

take care of pets _____

protect the environment _____

other _____

Plan to do one of these things with your family next week.

Thank you, Lord, for making us the stewards of this beautiful world we live in.
Amen.

# Evil entered the world through a human act.

## WE GATHER

✝ *God, help us in our choices.*

What are some of the reasons that people make choices that lead them away from God and others?

## WE BELIEVE

In Chapter 3 of the Book of Genesis, the biblical writer uses a story with many symbols and other storytelling devices to teach important truths about sin and suffering. This story tells of a very real truth—the choice of the human race to turn away from God and lose its close friendship with him.

As the story opens, the first man and woman were living in a beautiful garden in Eden. They had everything they needed for a happy life. They were God's friends, and because of this friendship they had happiness and harmony in their lives. In fact, they were at one with God, each other, and the rest of creation. They were living in the original state of innocence, holiness, and justice for which God had created them. The first humans were free to do whatever they wanted except one thing: they could *not* eat the fruit of the tree of the knowledge of good and bad. God told the man that if he ate from it, he would die. This warning about the forbidden fruit symbolizes that friendship with God depends on complete trust in God and on following his will for us. It reminds us that, as created beings, we are limited and we must respect those limitations.

But we learn from the story that the first man and woman disobeyed God. A serpent spoke to the woman and said, "God knows well that the moment you eat of it [the fruit] your eyes will be opened and you will be like gods who know what is good and what is bad" (Genesis 3:5). She believed the serpent. So she picked some of the fruit and ate it. Then she offered some to the man, who also ate it.

This story is filled with symbols. The serpent represents the devil, who tempted the woman to do evil. The fact that the woman believed the serpent reminds us of just how attractive evil can be. Eating the fruit symbolizes a choice. It shows that because of our free will, humans have the power to make choices that can lead to good or to evil.

As the story continues the first man and woman realized the seriousness of their actions. They became frightened of God and hid from him. But God knew what they had done, and, as the story closes, God sent them out of the garden. They no longer had any right to be there.

Of their own free will, humans chose to turn from God. By their own actions, the first human beings broke their friendship with God and let evil into the world. And this is when pain, sorrow, and death also entered into human life.

## WE RESPOND

With a group discuss recent news stories that show people who are suffering in some way. How can they be comforted? Illustrate ways that you and your class can help people who are suffering in your own school and neighborhood.

Loving God, comfort us in our sufferings. Guide us, too, in helping others who are suffering and in need of comfort.

## All people suffer from the effects of original sin.

### WE GATHER

✝ *Lord, deliver us from evil.*

What might damage your relationship with a friend or a family member? Explain.

### WE BELIEVE

The story of the first human beings, whom we call Adam and Eve, shows how close the relationship between God and human beings originally was. It also shows how that relationship was broken by human actions.

The first humans disobeyed God. Instead of respecting God's warning and trusting his words, they turned away from him. They selfishly did what *they* wanted, rather than what God commanded. In other words, they committed a sin. **Sin** is a thought, word, deed, or omission against God's law.

This sin of the first humans took away their original innocence, holiness, and justice. They lost the harmony they felt with God, with each other, and with the rest of creation.

The first humans had committed personal sin because they personally chose to turn from God and failed to love and obey him. Their personal sin was the first sin and is called **original sin**. Original sin weakened human nature and brought ignorance, suffering, and death into the world. This wounded human nature was passed on to the rest of humanity. Thus, we all suffer from the effects of original sin, though it is not a sin for which we are personally responsible.

**sin** a thought, word, deed, or omission against God's law

**original sin** the first sin that weakened human nature and brought ignorance, suffering, and death into the world; we all suffer from its effects

**God's Mercy**   Even after the first human beings turned away from God, God did not turn away from them. God did not abandon humanity. Instead God showed them his mercy. In very symbolic language, the biblical writer tells us that God said a descendant of the first man and woman would rescue humanity from evil one day.

"He will strike at your head,
   while you strike at his heel." (Genesis 3:15)
God promised that sin and evil would one day be overcome.

So humanity was *not* completely lost. Human nature was wounded, but not totally destroyed. Humans were still a part of God's good creation, and God still loved all those he created. But because of original sin, human nature needed to be restored to its original relationship with God.

## As Catholics...

Our Lord and Savior Jesus Christ, as true God and true man, is free from all sin, including original sin. He died and rose to free us from sin. Because Mary was to be the mother of the Son of God, she was blessed by God in a special way. Mary was free from original sin from the moment she was conceived, and she did not commit sin during her entire life. We call this belief the Immaculate Conception.

Mary, under the title of the Immaculate Conception, is the patroness of the United States. The whole Church celebrates the Feast of the Immaculate Conception on December 8. In the United States this feast is a holy day of obligation.

How does your parish celebrate this feast?

## WE RESPOND

Write a prayer asking God to keep us close to him.

_____
_____
_____
_____
_____
_____
_____
_____
_____
_____

**Write True or False for the following sentences.**
**Then change the false sentences to make them true.**

1. _____ In the stories of creation in the Book of Genesis, we find out that God's greatest creation was humanity.

_____

2. _____ God calls each of us to be responsible for the earth and all the living things in it.

_____

3. _____ Friendship with God depends on complete trust in him and on following his will for us.

_____

4. _____ We are born with original sin and suffer from its effects because it is sin for which we are personally responsible.

_____

**Write the letter that best defines each term.**

5. _____ steward

6. _____ sin

7. _____ soul

8. _____ original sin

**a.** the first sin that weakened human nature and brought ignorance, suffering, and death into the world

**b.** a thought, word, deed, or ommission against God's law

**c.** the invisible spiritual reality that makes each of us human and that will never die

**d.** person who is given both the authority over what he or she cares for and the responsibility for seeing that it lives and grows

**e.** the original state of innocence, holiness, and justice for which humans were created

**Write a paragraph to answer this question.**

**9–10.** What messages do the symbols in the creation stories convey?

ASSESSMENT

Write a news article entitled, "The Relationship Between God and People." Describe how this relationship changed and the relationship before and after the change.

# We Respond in Faith

## Reflect & Pray

God calls us to be partners with one another in caring for creation.
Lord, thank you for your wonderful gift of creation, especially

_____

Help me to

_____

**Key Words**

soul (p. 45)
steward (p. 47)
sin (p. 50)
original sin (p. 50)

## Remember

- God created human beings, body and soul.
- God called us to be stewards of creation.
- Evil entered the world through a human act.
- All people suffer from the effects of original sin.

## OUR CATHOLIC LIFE

### National Catholic Rural Life Conference

In recent times, dangers such as pollution and land overuse have threatened the environment. The National Catholic Rural Life Conference is among the groups who are concerned about these problems. This group helps families in rural farm areas and reminds us of our call to the stewardship of all creation.

The National Catholic Rural Life Conference is concerned about scientific advances in growing food. The group speaks out to make sure that Catholic social teachings help us to make good decisions about these issues. This group calls all people to respect life, uphold human dignity, and show respect for creation.

# SHARING FAITH
## with My Family

## Sharing What I Learned

Discuss the following with your family:

- the creation of human beings: body and soul
- steward of creation
- the first humans turn from God
- original sin and personal sin.

## Being Stewards

Share with your family that God called humanity to be stewards of his creation. Discuss ways your family can care for God's creation in your home, school/work, and community. Make a family plan of action.

### STEWARD OF CREATION

Of all God's creatures humans alone have the ability to care

for _____

_____

By caring for creation, people

show _____

What are some responsibilities that stewards of creation share?

_____

_____

## We Believe Trading Cards

Complete the facts on the back of the trading card. Then share with your family what you have learned about being a steward of creation.

Visit Sadlier's

## www.WEBELIEVEweb.com

**Connect to the Catechism**
For adult background and reflection, see paragraphs 362, 373, 397, and 404.

# God Promises to Help People

✝ **We Gather in Prayer**

**Leader:** Sit quietly and think of a beautiful place. It might be a mountaintop, a park, a deep canyon, or the ocean's edge. Choose a place that makes you feel happy and peaceful.

Now imagine Jesus standing with you in your special place.

- What do you say to Jesus?
- What does he say to you?
- What do you want to ask Jesus?
- What do you want to thank him for?

Have a short conversation together, as friend with friend. Now let us pray together.

**Leader:** Jesus, Son of the living God,

**All:** have mercy on us.
(Response to all petitions.)

**Leader:** Jesus, splendor of the Father,
Jesus, king of glory,
Jesus, dawn of justice,
Jesus, Son of the Virgin Mary,
Jesus, worthy of our love,
Jesus, prince of peace,
Jesus, all-powerful,
Jesus, God of peace,
Jesus, our refuge,
Jesus, Good Shepherd,
Jesus, crown of all saints.

**Leader:** Christ hear us.

**All:** Christ hear us.

**Leader:** Lord Jesus, hear our prayer.

**All:** Lord Jesus, hear our prayer. Amen.

# God promised to send a Savior.

## WE GATHER

✝ *Glory be to the Father, and to the Son, and to the Holy Spirit.*

 With your group brainstorm stories from books or television shows that are about broken friendships. What are the various outcomes of these stories?

_____

_____

_____

What caused these outcomes?

_____

_____

_____

## WE BELIEVE

We learn from the Old Testament that original sin separated human beings from God. Thus, even though they would try to do the things God asked, human beings would continue to sin. It would be very hard for them to have a close friendship with God again. Yet God would never stop loving people and forgiving them.

Humanity could not undo the effects of original sin. To fully restore the friendship with God that was broken by the first humans' disobedience, humanity needed God's help. So God promised to send a Savior. God's people waited for the one who would bring humanity back to the perfect state of holiness in which God had created them. God's people believed that when the Savior came, he would completely restore their friendship with God.

Some of the most meaningful writings in the Old Testament are from the Book of Isaiah. As a prophet, Isaiah spoke to the people on God's behalf and reminded them of the way God wanted them to live. In his writings Isaiah told

of someone who would come to free humanity from sin and restore their friendship with God. Isaiah described this person as the *suffering servant*.

"Through his suffering, my servant shall
     justify many,
   and their guilt he shall bear."
(Isaiah 53:11)

Christians believe that the suffering servant referred to by Isaiah is God's own Son. In the fullness of time God the Father sent his only Son to restore our relationship with him. Through Mary's obedience and acceptance of God's will, the Son of God became man. Jesus Christ is the Son of God who became one of us. He is truly divine and truly human, and he fulfilled all that God promised. Jesus was obedient to his Father. For our sake Jesus died on the cross and rose from the dead to save all people from sin and to bring us the hope of new life. As Saint Paul wrote, "For just as in Adam all die, so too in Christ shall all be brought to life" (1 Corinthians 15:22).

The New Testament contains four separate books about Jesus. We call these the Gospels of Matthew, Mark, Luke, and John. The word *gospel* means "good news." The **gospel** is the good news about God at work in Jesus Christ.

In the gospels we read of Jesus' work to bring hope to the poor and suffering, freedom to those who are persecuted, and healing to those who are sick. From the gospels we learn that through his life, death, and Resurrection, Jesus Christ makes it possible for all humanity to again share in God's life.

**gospel** the good news about God at work in Jesus Christ

### WE RESPOND

How does the way you live show that you share in God's life and friendship?

Father in heaven, thank you for keeping your promise and sending your Son, Jesus Christ. Amen.

## The first human family struggled because of original sin.

### WE GATHER

✝ *Jesus, Savior, guide and protect all families.*

👤 What positive things can people do to handle the anger they might feel in certain situations?

_____

_____

_____

### WE BELIEVE

The story in the Book of Genesis continues by telling us about Adam and Eve's family. In the fourth chapter of Genesis we find out that Adam and Eve had two sons. The older son Cain was a farmer. His younger brother, Abel, was a shepherd.

By all appearances this family was loving and happy. Then something happened to set brother against brother. Both brothers made an offering of their goods to the Lord, but "the LORD looked with favor on Abel and his offering, but on Cain and his offering he did not" (Genesis 4:4–5).

The story does not explain why one offering was acceptable and the other was not. That was the biblical writer's way of indicating that we cannot always understand the ways of God and should not try to judge his ways. Yet Cain judged everything only from his own point of view. He felt that he had been treated unfairly, and he became very angry about it. Perhaps he was also envious of Abel's success.

In the story God saw what Cain was going through and offered him some good advice. God told Cain that he could do the right thing in this situation and feel good about it, or he could do the wrong thing and sin. God told Cain that he had the ability to overcome evil. But Cain could not rise above his anger. He took his resentment out on his innocent brother—Cain killed Abel. Murder, one of the worst effects of original sin, came into existence.

In the Genesis account, God asked Cain where Abel was. Cain replied, "I do not know. Am I my brother's keeper?" (Genesis 4:9). God was deeply offended and said to Cain, "What have you done! Listen: Your brother's blood cries out to me from the soil! Therefore you shall be banned from the soil that opened its mouth to receive your brother's blood from your hand" (Genesis 4:10–11).

Suddenly, Cain realized that he was being sent away and would lose God's protection. He feared that he himself would now be killed. Yet God came to Cain's aid. He put a mark on Cain. This showed that though he murdered Abel, Cain was protected by God. So even in this terrible circumstance God showed his great love for Cain.

The story of Cain and Abel can be understood on several levels. On one level it declares the sacredness of human life and prohibits murder of any kind. On another level it symbolizes the separation of human beings from one another. On a third level it is about accepting life as one finds it and respecting one another. And on a fourth level it is about the healing power of God's love.

Write a prayer for all families everywhere. Ask God to be with all families. Ask him to help families solve their problems in a loving and caring way.

_____

_____

_____

_____

_____

## WE RESPOND

How can you show love for your family this week?

59

# God made a covenant with Noah.

## WE GATHER

✝ *Father, help us to be just in all our ways.*

*Justice* means respecting the rights of others and giving them what is rightfully theirs. Just comes from the word *justice*.

Who in your neighborhood or school would you describe as a just person? Why?

## WE BELIEVE

As the Book of Genesis continues, we learn that God is greatly displeased with humankind. They were not being the faithful stewards of the world that they were created to be.

📖 Genesis 6:7—9:17

So to Noah, who was a just man, God said, "I have decided to put an end to all mortals on earth; the earth is full of lawlessness because of them. So I will destroy them and all life on earth" (Genesis 6:13). Then God commanded Noah to build a great ark, a kind of ship. Noah was to fill it with two of every living thing, male and female, along with his wife and family.

When Noah had everything ready, God sent forty days and forty nights of continual rain. God allowed the seas to spill over onto the land and the floodwaters to slowly rise above the highest mountains. All life outside the ark was lost.

Eventually the floodwaters went down, and God allowed Noah, his family, and all the animals to leave the ark. In gratitude, Noah built an altar and offered God a sacrifice on it. God was pleased with this sacrifice and made

a covenant, or agreement, with Noah. In this covenant God promised that even if humanity failed him again, he would never send another flood to destroy life on earth. The symbol of this promise was a rainbow. God told Noah, "This is the sign of the covenant I have established between me and all mortal creatures that are on earth" (Genesis 9:17).

This story, which is found in Chapters 6—9 of the Book of Genesis, revealed an important religious truth: God's forgiveness and love, and humanity's goodness, can overcome all evil. Through Noah God made an everlasting covenant with the whole of humanity. For that reason all people are called to friendship with God. All people are invited to enjoy God's love and forgiveness.

Yet humanity lost something because of its responsibility for the flood. It lost its unity with the rest of creation. It became more difficult for humanity to be stewards of God's creation.

To symbolize God's justice and his love and forgiveness, the biblical writer used the powerful symbol of water in the story of the great flood. Water is always a very meaningful symbol. Water can be forceful and even threatening, yet it can be cleansing and calming.

A story of a great flood that almost destroys all life is very common among the ancient peoples of the world. The Genesis account of Noah and the flood is perhaps the most famous of these stories, but it is not original. It goes back to a much more ancient tale of a great flood. A version of this tale is preserved in the Epic of Gilgamesh, which was written sometime between 2000 and 1000 B.C.

**Christian Symbolism: The Flood** There is great meaning in the symbols found in the story of Noah. Some Christian writers think that the ark is a symbol of the Church: just as the ark saved Noah and all who were with him, so through the Church we are saved.

In the Church, the flood is a symbol of the waters of the sacrament of Baptism. Through Baptism we are freed from original sin and all personal sins. Through Baptism God offers us his forgiveness and his love.

Just as Noah and his family were brought to a new life through the flood, in the waters of Baptism we are brought to a new life in Christ. Through the waters of Baptism, God begins a covenant relationship with each Christian. Just as the world was washed and made clean by the flood, we are washed and made clean in the baptismal water.

Design a stained-glass window that reminds you of God's friendship with all people.

## WE RESPOND

### Water of Life/Agua de Vida

Refrain:
Water of life, holy reminder;
touching, renewing the body of Christ.
Water of life, holy reminder;
touching, renewing the body of Christ.

All generations, come forth and receive
the blessing of this holy water;
making us one with the God who forgives,
the one who is faithful and just. (Refrain)

Refrain:
Agua de vida, santo recuerdo;
Une y renueva al cuerpo de Cristo.
Agua de vida, santo recuerdo;
Une y renueva al cuerpo de Cristo.

Vengan, reciban el agua de paz,
revivan su santo bautismo.
Dejen atrás los rencores de a yer
y vivan la nueva a lianza. (Refrain)

*Tower of Babel,* by Pieter the Elder Brueghel (1515–1569)

## The unity of the human race was lost.

### WE GATHER

✝ *Lord, help us to live as one world family.*

What are some of the causes of divisions in our world today? How can the world be more united?

### WE BELIEVE

We now come to the very last event that the Book of Genesis records for the period called prehistory. In Genesis 11:1–9 we read the story of the tower of Babel. This story symbolizes the separation among different groups of people. It symbolizes humanity's loss of unity and the development of different languages.

We read that at first "the whole world spoke the same language, using the same words" (Genesis 11:1). This symbolizes that all human beings were related. Because they were able to communicate, they could truly act as God's stewards of the earth. Part of God's plan for completing the work of creation involved humanity's spread across the face of the earth. However, human beings feared this. They feared being exposed to all sorts of dangers and weakening their ability to defend themselves. So they decided to resist God's plan: They would all settle in one place and build a great tower to live in. The tower that they tried to build looked very much like an ancient structure called a *ziggurat*.

A ziggurat is made of a series of smaller and smaller brick platforms, one on top of the other. On the top of the highest platform stood a temple. Long staircases led up to the various platforms and to the temple. The biblical writer called the city and the tower that the humans built *Babel*, the Hebrew name for Babylon. Babylon was an ancient city with the most famous ziggurat of all. In fact we think that this story might be about actual ancient people who built the great ziggurat.

In the story the tower was a symbol of human resistance to God's will. The people who were building it did not trust God. They preferred to do things their way. God saw what human beings were doing and decided to stop them. He did this by confusing their language. As a result, humans could not understand one another. They could not work together. To explain what happened the biblical writer used a Hebrew word that means *babble*. All people could do was babble helplessly at one another. The biblical writer was suggesting that the unity of the human race had been lost.

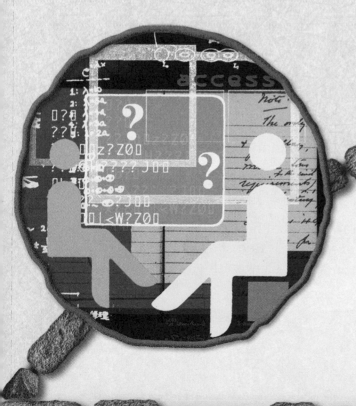

What do you think this expression means: "They don't speak the same language."

_____

_____

_____

_____

**Misunderstandings Begin** Sometimes the only reason people disagree is because they do not understand one another. This misunderstanding can lead to suspicion, mistrust, and even open hostility. According to the biblical writer, this began to happen to the human race after Babel. Humanity began to lose its unity and break up into rival groups.

As the story closes, the process of populating the earth continued as God had planned. Now, however, humans spoke many different languages and had developed different ways of living and communicating. Throughout history it has been necessary to respect these differences and to appreciate the dignity that all people possess.

## WE RESPOND

As a class produce a talk show. The topic of today's show is: Do the divisions symbolized by the story of the tower of Babel still affect our lives today? Why or why not?

Each person in the class is to participate in the talk show. Work together to decide who will be the moderator, interviewer, panelists, audience, and reporter.

**Circle the letter of the correct answer.**

1. The _____ are the books of the Bible in which the "good news" of Jesus' life and teachings are presented.

   **a.** covenants   **b.** Genesis   **c.** gospels

2. Isaiah was a _____ who spoke to the people on God's behalf and reminded them of the way God wanted them to live.

   **a.** prophet   **b.** shepherd   **c.** farmer

3. The story of the tower of Babel symbolizes the _____ among different groups of people.

   **a.** covenant   **b.** separation   **c.** love

4. God promised to send _____ who would restore humanity's friendship with God.

   **a.** Isaiah   **b.** Noah   **c.** a Savior

**Short Answers**

5. What does God do to help humanity after they have turned away from him?

   _____

6. The story of Cain and Abel can be understood on several levels. List two.

   _____

7. What important religious truth is revealed in the story of Noah?

   _____

8. In the story of the tower of Babel, what does the tower symbolize?

   _____

**Write a paragraph to answer this question.**

**9–10.** How did God keep his promise and restore his life and friendship to all humanity?

ASSESSMENT

Make a chart that lists the ways that humanity turned from God, and the ways that God showed mercy toward them. Discuss your chart with your class or family.

# We Respond in Faith

## Reflect & Pray

God promises to be with us always. God is with me when I

_____

_____

Dear God, help me to

_____

_____

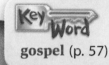

**gospel** (p. 57)

## Remember

- God promised to send a Savior.
- The first human family struggled because of original sin.
- God made a covenant with Noah.
- The unity of the human race was lost.

## OUR CATHOLIC LIFE

### Catholic News Service

How do we know what is affecting the Church in our world? The Catholic News Service is a news agency that provides news and photographs to newspapers and other news agencies around the world. This Catholic news agency was started in 1920. The bishops of the United States decided that it would be a good idea for people to get news about what Catholics were doing throughout the world. The agency lets people know what is going on in the world and in the Church today. The professional journalists and photographers who work for the agency write stories and take pictures that keep people informed about Catholics. The latest news is posted regularly on their Web site at www.catholicnews.com and is often printed in diocesan newspapers.

# SHARING FAITH
## with My Family

## Sharing What I Learned

Discuss the following with your family:

- Jesus as Savior
- the story of Cain and Abel
- the story of Noah
- the story of the tower of Babel.

## Finding the "Good News"

Share with your family that the word *gospel* means "good news." This week, be on the lookout for people and events that help to share the good news of Jesus Christ in your home, school/work, and community. Share your good news with the other members of your family.

Who is Noah?

_____

_____

What are the events of the story?

_____

_____

Why is this story important for us today?

_____

_____

THE STORY OF NOAH

## We Believe Trading Cards

Complete the facts on the back of the trading card. Then share with your family what you have learned about the story of Noah.

Visit Sadlier's

**www.WeBelieveweb.com**

**Connect to the Catechism**
For adult background and reflection, see paragraphs 410, 401, 58, and 57.

# The Patriarchs: God Chooses a People

## ✝ We Gather in Prayer

**Leader:** Loving God, your psalmist said, "Oh, that today you would hear his voice: Do not harden your hearts." (Psalm 95:7–8)

**All:** Help us to hear and follow your word with open hearts. Amen.

**Reader 1:** For the times when we have deliberately chosen to do what we know is wrong.

**All:** Lord, have mercy.

**Reader 2:** For the times we have excluded others because they are not like us.

**All:** Lord, have mercy.

**Reader 3:** For the times we have used words to hurt and harm rather than to heal.

**All:** Lord, have mercy.

**Reader 4:** For the times we have walked by someone in need.

**All:** Lord, have mercy.

**Leader:** Loving God, we believe in you and place our trust in you. Help us strengthen our faith each day.

**All:** Amen.

St. Theresa's Fall Harvest Drive

## The patriarchs are our ancestors in faith.

### WE GATHER

✝ *Lord, from generation to generation we praise you.*

What do you know about your ancestors? How can you find out more about them?

### WE BELIEVE

The last six verses of Chapter 11 of Genesis introduce us to a new stage in God's relationship with humanity. During this stage God formed a people for himself. We call this formative period *The Age of the Patriarchs*.

A **patriarch** is a father, or founder, of a clan, a group of related families. The four Old Testament patriarchs are Abraham, Isaac, Jacob, and Joseph. Through them God chose a special family for himself. This family is the people of God. Sarah, Rebekah, Rachel, and Leah were important women in God's family. They are called matriarchs. These men and women lived from approximately 1900 B.C. to about 1650 B.C. Their story is told in Chapters 12—50 of the Book of Genesis.

The families of these Old Testament patriarchs and matriarchs lived in tents and made their living primarily by raising flocks of sheep and goats. These people roamed the unoccupied territory between the towns and villages of Canaan and the desert. **Canaan** was an area in western Palestine that included most of present-day Israel.

Although the patriarchs owned no land and had no houses, they usually stayed in one place long enough to grow grain and raise a variety of fruits and vegetables. They also traded with other people for what they needed. They normally traveled on foot, but sometimes they used donkeys for transportation. Their life centered on their families and the clan.

During the period of the patriarchs, Canaan was made up of small independent city-states. A king ruled each city-state. Each city-state was made up of a walled city, usually built on a hill, and the surrounding countryside. Farms and villages dotted the countryside and provided food to the city-state. The walled city itself was the center of industry, crafts, and trade.

**Key Words**

**patriarch** a father, or founder, of a clan, a group of related families

**Canaan** an area in western Palestine that included most of present-day Israel

**faith** a gift from God that enables us to believe in him and accept all that he has revealed

The inhabitants of Canaan, or Canaanites, had the same background as the patriarchs and their families. They all spoke a similar language. That is why they treated one another as distant cousins rather than as complete strangers.

We, too, think of the families of the patriarchs and matriarchs as our family. They are our ancestors in faith. **Faith** is a gift from God that enables us to believe in him and accept all that he has revealed. "Faith is the realization of what is hoped for and evidence of things not seen." (Hebrews 11:1) Through the trusting relationship of faith, the patriarchs and their families learned what it meant to be a part of God's family. They lived their lives trying to follow God's commands and going where God led them.

These ancestors in faith are a good example of reliance on God during our own journey through life. Because of the gift of faith we, too, are able to believe all that God has revealed to us and to respond positively to it. Faith helps us to freely say yes to God with all our heart and strength. By our yes we follow God's will for us. Through the gift of faith we begin to see our lives and the world around us as God sees them. We start to live the way God wants us to live.

## WE RESPOND

One day you will be an ancestor of your family. How would you like to be remembered by future generations of your family?

How will the way you express your faith be a part of your family's memory of you?

# God chose Abraham to be the father of his people.

## WE GATHER

✝ *Lord, help us to know and do your will.*

👤 In small groups make a list of people who faced a challenge and never gave up. Their stories might be found in movies, television shows, in the news, on the Internet, or in your neighborhood.

## WE BELIEVE

The Book of Genesis describes how God decided to form a people for himself.

📖 Genesis 12:1–7

God looked about him and called Abram. God said, "Go forth from the land of your kinsfolk and from your father's house to a land that I will show you" (Genesis 12:1). This land was the land of Canaan, which God promised to give to Abram and his descendants forever.

As soon as Abram heard God's call, he and his wife, Sarai, gathered their family and property. They started out from the town of Haran in northern Mesopotamia on the long journey to Canaan. This journey symbolized the journey of faith that we make throughout our lives.

In Abram God chose a very unlikely person to begin his people. Abram was seventy-five years old; he was neither famous nor powerful; and, his wife, Sarai, could not have children. Yet when God spoke to him, Abram responded to God. He did not argue with God. Abram had great faith, and trusted completely in God's will. In fact, Abram is our most important Old Testament model of faith.

When Abram and Sarai arrived in Canaan, God tested their faith repeatedly. They went through many difficult situations, and they tried to make the decisions that God wanted them to make. By telling us about these tests, the biblical writer shows us that Abram and Sarai, though chosen by God, struggled like all humans to keep their faith in God.

This testing by God strengthened and purified their faith, and God decided to make a covenant with Abram. God said, "I am God the Almighty. Walk in my presence and be blameless. Between you and me I will establish my covenant, and I will multiply you exceedingly" (Genesis 17:1–2). By the terms of this agreement Abram and his descendants will serve God and follow his ways. In return, God will give Abram a son and make "a great nation" of him (Genesis 12:2). To indicate that they were beginning a new life as a new people, God changed Abram's name to Abraham and Sarai's name to Sarah.

Sometime later, God came to Abraham through three mysterious visitors who appeared at Abraham's tent. One of the visitors predicted that Abraham and Sarah would have a son. When Sarah laughed in disbelief, he asked, "Is anything too marvelous for the LORD to do?" (Genesis 18:14).

As predicted, Isaac, Abraham and Sarah's long-awaited son, was finally born. When Isaac was a young boy, Abraham was again tested by God.

📖 Genesis 22:2–18

God said to Abraham, "Take your son Isaac, your only one, whom you love, and go to the land of Moriah. There you shall offer him up as a holocaust on a height that I will point out to you" (Genesis 22:2).

This was a test of Abraham's faith in God. Abraham did what God asked. Early the next morning he took Isaac some way off, built an altar, and put the boy on it. He was about to sacrifice Isaac to God when a messenger from God called to him, "Do not do the least thing to him. I know now how devoted you are to God, since you did not withhold from me your own beloved son" (Genesis 22:12). Abraham showed his great faith in God, and God blessed him.

This example from Abraham's life shows us that God calls each of us to trust completely in him. We see in these Old Testament stories that God loved his people and wanted them to turn to him.

The Church sees a New Testament parallel in this story: God the Father offered his only Son, Jesus Christ, to save us.

## WE RESPOND

Think about the story of Abraham. How did the different parts of the story make you feel?

Do you think that you could listen to God if he told you to do something very difficult? Why or why not?

God our Father, we place our trust in you.

*The Story of Jacob and Esau,*
by Lorenzo Ghiberti (1378–1455)
Baptistery, Florence, Italy.

## God's people became known as the Israelites.

### WE GATHER

✝ *Father in heaven, bless what is good in us.*

Name the people in your family who are remembered as patriarchs or matriarchs. What do you know about them?

### WE BELIEVE

When Abraham died, his son, Isaac, inherited his father's position as patriarch of the family. Isaac married a woman named Rebekah, with whom he had twin sons: Esau, the elder, and Jacob, the younger. The birth of twin sons caused a problem. Which son would someday have Isaac's position in the family? It could not be divided. Only one of the twins could inherit it.

Esau was the first born. It seemed that he should by right inherit Isaac's role. But the matter was not that simple. Before the twins were born, God made it very clear that Jacob was to inherit Isaac's position. God had said to their mother, Rebekah,
"Two nations are in your womb,
    two peoples are quarreling while still
        within you;
But one shall surpass the other,
    and the older shall serve the younger"
(Genesis 25:23).

However, to inherit Isaac's position Jacob must overturn the man-made rules of inheritance. Thus, from the very beginning, the story of Jacob is a story of conflict.

If the choice of Abraham as patriarch was surprising, the choice of Jacob as his successor was even more surprising. Jacob grew up to be something of a trickster. We get our first hint of this side of Jacob's character in Genesis 25:27–34 when he tricked Esau into selling him his birthright for a bowl of lentil stew. A birthright is the natural right to inherit the father's property.

But this was not the end of Jacob's tricks. We read in Genesis 27:1–46 that with his mother's help Jacob pretended to be Esau and tricked his elderly and blind father into giving him the blessing that Esau had the right to. When his father Isaac discovered what had happened, he was outraged. And Esau vowed to get revenge. He wanted to kill his brother, Jacob. So Rebekah told Jacob to flee to the land of Haran.

Yet from all that we read about him, it is clear that Jacob possessed the one quality that was crucial to living out the covenant. This quality was determination, or perseverance. Jacob never gave up.

On his way to Haran Jacob had a dream in which he saw a great staircase reaching to heaven. In the dream God told Jacob what he told Abraham before him, "I, the LORD, am the God of your forefather Abraham and the God of Isaac; the land on which you are lying I will give to you and your descendants. These shall be as plentiful as the dust of the earth, and through them you shall spread out east and west, north and south. In you and your descendants all the nations of the earth shall find blessing. Know that I am with you; I will protect you wherever you go, and bring you back to this land. I will never leave you until I have done what I promised you" (Genesis 28:13–15).

With these words, God assured Jacob that he would inherit Canaan and that God would always protect him.

Though life in Haran was marked by constant conflict, Jacob prospered. He married, had many children, and grew very rich. This was the biblical writer's way of telling us that God's people were blessed and that they would continue to grow in number. After twenty years Jacob decided to return to Canaan, where he was finally reconciled to his brother and father.

In Genesis 35:9–15 we can read that God renewed the covenant with Jacob. He also changed Jacob's name to Israel. This was the symbolic way to show that God's people had grown to the point that they could actually be distinguished by name. God's people were now called the people of Israel, or the Israelites.

## WE RESPOND

Imagine you are an advice columnist. Answer this letter.

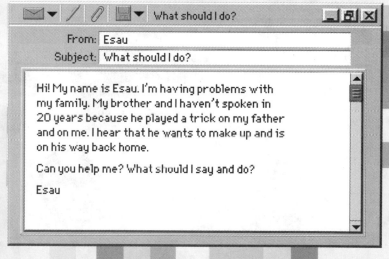

From: Esau
Subject: What should I do?

Hi! My name is Esau. I'm having problems with my family. My brother and I haven't spoken in 20 years because he played a trick on my father and on me. I hear that he wants to make up and is on his way back home.

Can you help me? What should I say and do?

Esau

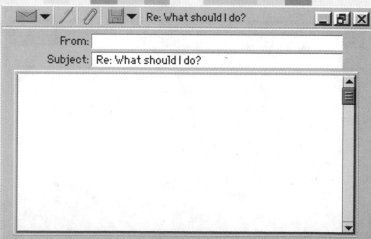

From:
Subject: Re: What should I do?

# God cared for the Israelites.

✝ *God, help me to discover your will for me.*

With small groups write a skit in which something negative is turned around into a positive outcome. Then act out your skit for the whole class. Ask the class to identify the negative that turned into a positive outcome.

## WE BELIEVE

The last of the Old Testament patriarchs is Joseph. His story is told in Genesis 37:1—50:26. Joseph's story is about the way that God's will is achieved. In Joseph's case, God's plan was to provide a temporary home for his people.

**Providence** is God's plan for and protection of all creation. Through providence God leads his creation toward the perfection for which it was made. In the story of Joseph, providence was symbolized by the fulfillment of dreams. Joseph's only contact with God was through dreams, and these dreams indicated God's plan.

Genesis 37:3–28; 39:1–23; 40:1—46:30

When we first meet Joseph, he and his brothers are on less than friendly terms. Joseph is the son of Rachel and Jacob, and is the favorite of Jacob's twelve sons. Jacob had given Joseph a special long robe such as a king might wear. The other brothers hated Joseph because their father, Jacob, loved him so much.

Joseph also had strange dreams. These dreams predicted that some day Joseph would have authority over his family. These dreams did not make Joseph's brothers very happy. So one day they grabbed him and took his robe. They sold Joseph as a slave to a passing caravan of merchants. The merchants sold Joseph to the chief steward of the **pharaoh**, the king of Egypt.

Twelve Sons of Jacob

1. Reuben
2. Simeon
3. Levi
4. Judah
5. Dan
6. Naphtali
7. Gad
8. Asher
9. Issachar
10. Zebulun
11. Joseph
12. Benjamin

At first Joseph did well in the steward's service, but eventually he was thrown into prison on false charges. In prison Joseph discovered his ability to interpret dreams. This skill brought him to the attention of the pharaoh himself, who had been disturbed by strange dreams. Joseph told the pharaoh that his dreams meant that a period of great abundance would be followed by a time of terrible famine. The pharaoh was delighted by Joseph's explanation of his dreams, and put Joseph in charge of the management of his kingdom. Joseph prepared Egypt for the famine.

When the famine arrived, Jacob and his family in Canaan suffered greatly from hunger. Hearing that there was food in Egypt, Joseph's brothers traveled there to buy grain. This brought them face-to-face with Joseph. They did not recognize Joseph at first and bowed down to him when he entered the room. So Joseph's dreams had come true. Joseph now had authority over his family.

Joseph was eventually reconciled to his brothers. He invited his whole family to move to Egypt. His father, Jacob, accepted the invitation, and, as the story continues, Jacob made the long journey to Egypt. God's purpose had been fulfilled. God's people found a temporary home in Egypt.

## WE RESPOND

Think of times when God acted in your life in an unexpected way. Talk with a partner about one of these times.

Thank God for his care and providence.

75

**Review**

**Write the letter that best defines each term.**

1. _____ faith

2. _____ providence

3. _____ patriarch

4. _____ Canaan

a. an area in western Palestine that included most of present-day Israel

b. a gift from God that enables us to believe in him and accept all that he has revealed

c. the natural right to inherit the father's property

d. a father, or founder, of a clan, a group of related families

e. God's plan for and protection of all creation

**Short Answers**

5. Who are the patriarchs of the Old Testament?

_____

6. How is providence symbolized in the story of Joseph?

_____

7. What is it about Jacob that makes him able to live out the covenant?

_____

8. How was Abraham's faith tested?

_____

**Write a paragraph to answer this question.**

9–10. What does the story of each patriarch show about our relationship with God?

ASSESSMENT

Using your knowledge of the patriarchs and matriarchs, design a genealogy. Include a description of each patriarch's story. Present your project in the form of a chart, a poster, or a sculpture.

# We Respond in Faith

## Reflect & Pray

God acted in the lives of many people to make the descendants of Abraham a great people.

Lord, we know you are still with us, acting in our lives

_____

_____

**Key Words**

**patriarch** (p. 69)
**Canaan** (p. 69)
**faith** (p. 69)
**providence** (p. 75)
**pharaoh** (p. 75)

## Remember

- The patriarchs are our ancestors in faith.

- God chose Abraham to be the father of his people.

- God's people became known as the Israelites.

- God cared for the Israelites.

## OUR CATHOLIC LIFE

### Family Blessings

Blessings are a large part of our daily prayer. This is a custom we received from and share with the Jewish people. We ask God to bless our food before we eat. We can always ask God to bless us in our everyday lives. There are blessings for families, children, homes, animals, workplaces, times of joy, and times of sorrow. Here is one blessing you might like to pray:

Protect us, Lord, as we stay awake;
watch over us as we sleep,
that awake, we may keep watch with Christ,
and asleep, rest in his peace. Amen.

# SHARING FAITH
## with My Family

## Sharing What I Learned

Discuss the following with your family:

- the patriarchs of the Old Testament
- God's covenant with his people
- faith and providence
- the story of Joseph.

## Going Where God Leads Us

This week, encourage your family members to go where God leads them. Take a few moments to talk and listen to God in private prayer. Ask God to lead you and your family to the people and places where your love and care are needed.

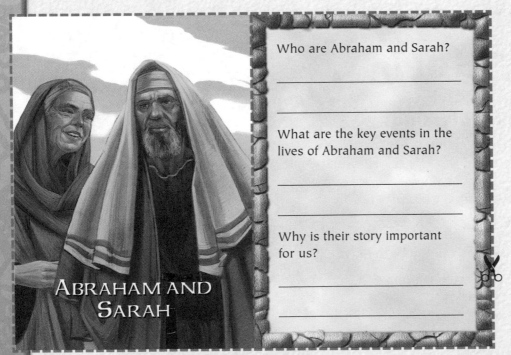

ABRAHAM AND SARAH

Who are Abraham and Sarah?

_____

_____

What are the key events in the lives of Abraham and Sarah?

_____

_____

Why is their story important for us?

_____

_____

## We Believe Trading Cards

Complete the facts on the back of the trading card. Then share with your family what you have learned about the story of Abraham and Sarah.

Visit Sadlier's

www.WeBelieveweb.com

**Connect to the Catechism**
For adult background and reflection, see paragraphs 61, 59, 63, and 303.

# The Liturgical Year

"Rejoice in the Lord always.
I shall say it again: rejoice!"

Philippians 4:4

# Throughout the liturgical year we celebrate the entire mystery of Christ.

## WE GATHER

✝ *Lord, you create all things to give you glory.*

What are some days of the year that are very important to you? Why? How do you show others that these days and times are special to you?

## WE BELIEVE

As the Church we have special days and times of the year that are very important to us. One special way we remember these times is in the celebration of the liturgy. The liturgy is the official public prayer of the Church. It includes the celebration of the Eucharist, or Mass, and the other sacraments. The liturgy also includes the Liturgy of the Hours, a prayer, parts of which the Church prays at various times during the day and night.

In the liturgy throughout the year, we remember and rejoice in the saving actions of Jesus Christ. So we call the Church year the *liturgical year*. During the liturgical year we recall and celebrate the whole mystery of Christ. We celebrate the birth of the Son of God, his younger years, his public ministry, his suffering, death, Resurrection, and Ascension into heaven. During this year we also venerate, or show devotion to, Mary, the Mother of God, and all the saints.

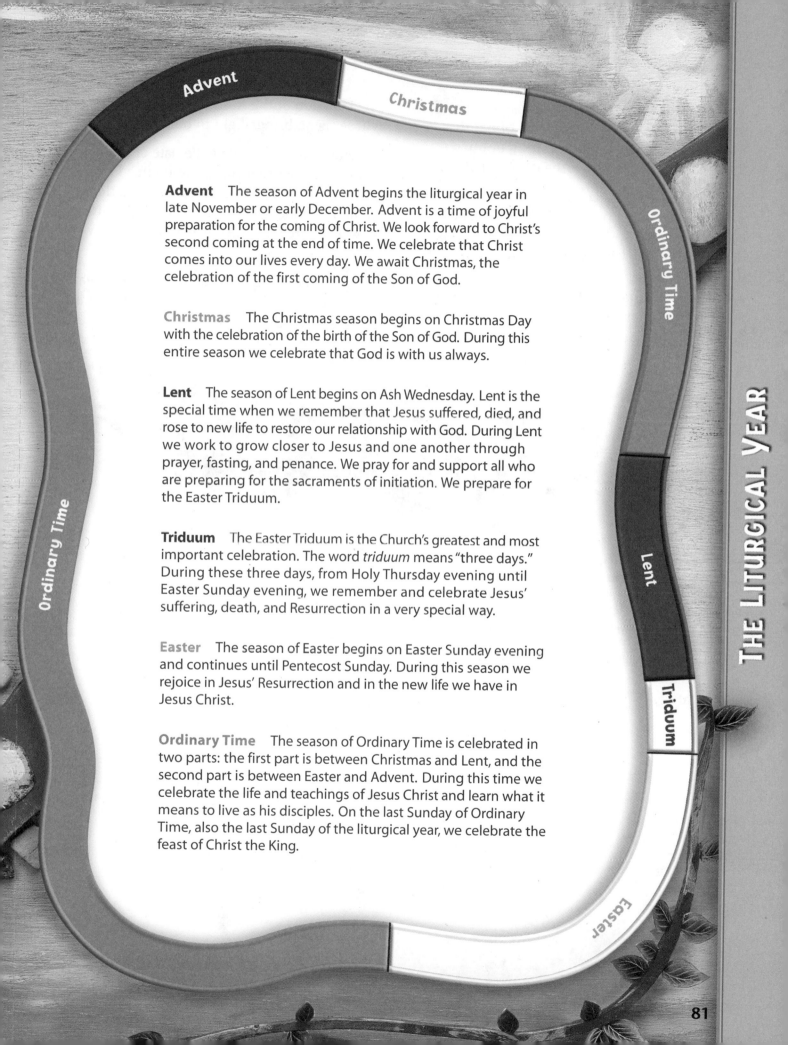

**Advent**   The season of Advent begins the liturgical year in late November or early December. Advent is a time of joyful preparation for the coming of Christ. We look forward to Christ's second coming at the end of time. We celebrate that Christ comes into our lives every day. We await Christmas, the celebration of the first coming of the Son of God.

**Christmas**   The Christmas season begins on Christmas Day with the celebration of the birth of the Son of God. During this entire season we celebrate that God is with us always.

**Lent**   The season of Lent begins on Ash Wednesday. Lent is the special time when we remember that Jesus suffered, died, and rose to new life to restore our relationship with God. During Lent we work to grow closer to Jesus and one another through prayer, fasting, and penance. We pray for and support all who are preparing for the sacraments of initiation. We prepare for the Easter Triduum.

**Triduum**   The Easter Triduum is the Church's greatest and most important celebration. The word *triduum* means "three days." During these three days, from Holy Thursday evening until Easter Sunday evening, we remember and celebrate Jesus' suffering, death, and Resurrection in a very special way.

**Easter**   The season of Easter begins on Easter Sunday evening and continues until Pentecost Sunday. During this season we rejoice in Jesus' Resurrection and in the new life we have in Jesus Christ.

**Ordinary Time**   The season of Ordinary Time is celebrated in two parts: the first part is between Christmas and Lent, and the second part is between Easter and Advent. During this time we celebrate the life and teachings of Jesus Christ and learn what it means to live as his disciples. On the last Sunday of Ordinary Time, also the last Sunday of the liturgical year, we celebrate the feast of Christ the King.

**The calendar** Our calendar of years, months, and days depends upon elements of nature, like the sun and the moon. Many of our liturgical feasts also reflect the cycle of nature.

Our liturgical year is constructed around the dates of the Easter Triduum, which depend each year on the spring equinox and the rising of the full moon. The spring equinox is the day the sun crosses the equator, making day and night of equal length everywhere. Easter Sunday follows the full moon after the spring equinox. This fact alone is a beautiful proclamation of the Resurrection of Christ, whose rising brings light to our darkness.

Astronomers can calculate the date of the spring equinox. They use formulas to do this for years into the future. Looking at their calculations we find that the date of Easter Sunday is always between March 22 and April 25.

Using the date for Easter Sunday, we can construct the liturgical calendar for each year. We can work backward six weeks to determine the beginning of Lent, and forward seven weeks to find the date of Pentecost.

## WE RESPOND

The readings we hear, the songs we sing, the colors we see, and the ways we worship, help us to celebrate each liturgical season.

In groups describe some of the ways your parish celebrates each of these seasons of the liturgical year.

**Advent**

_____

_____

**Christmas**

_____

_____

**Lent**

_____

_____

**Triduum**

_____

_____

**Easter**

_____

_____

**Ordinary Time**

_____

_____

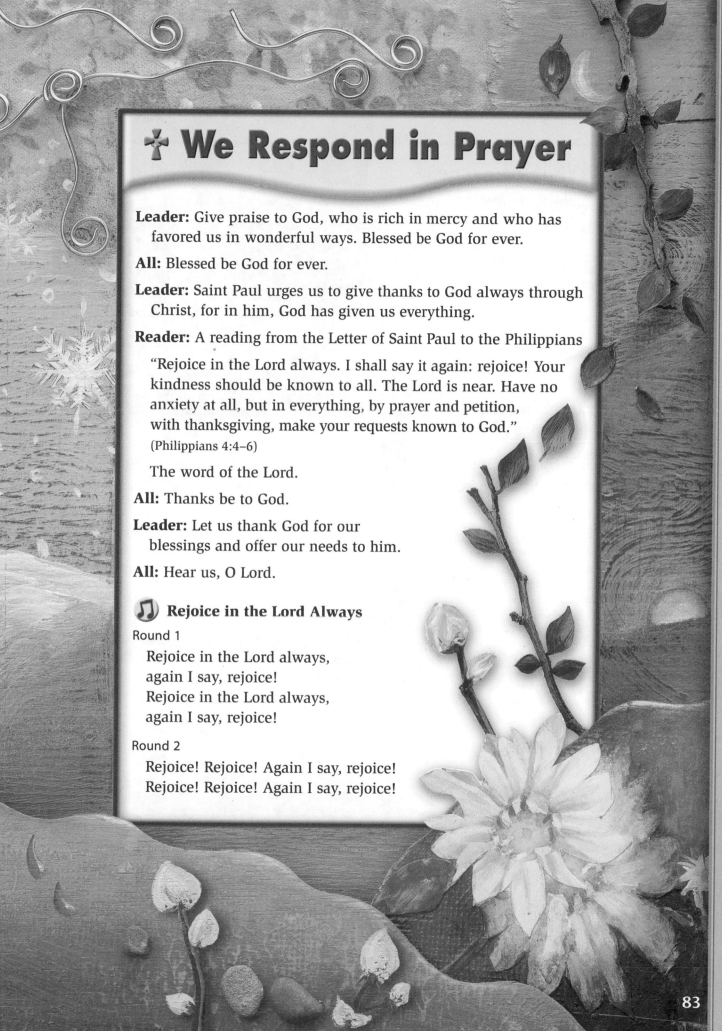

# ✝ We Respond in Prayer

**Leader:** Give praise to God, who is rich in mercy and who has favored us in wonderful ways. Blessed be God for ever.

**All:** Blessed be God for ever.

**Leader:** Saint Paul urges us to give thanks to God always through Christ, for in him, God has given us everything.

**Reader:** A reading from the Letter of Saint Paul to the Philippians

"Rejoice in the Lord always. I shall say it again: rejoice! Your kindness should be known to all. The Lord is near. Have no anxiety at all, but in everything, by prayer and petition, with thanksgiving, make your requests known to God."
(Philippians 4:4–6)

The word of the Lord.

**All:** Thanks be to God.

**Leader:** Let us thank God for our blessings and offer our needs to him.

**All:** Hear us, O Lord.

### 🎵 Rejoice in the Lord Always

Round 1

Rejoice in the Lord always,
again I say, rejoice!
Rejoice in the Lord always,
again I say, rejoice!

Round 2

Rejoice! Rejoice! Again I say, rejoice!
Rejoice! Rejoice! Again I say, rejoice!

THE LITURGICAL YEAR

# SHARING FAITH with My Family

## Sharing What I Learned

Discuss the following with your family:

- the liturgical year
- the liturgical seasons of the year
- the liturgical calendar.

## Around the Table

Use a calendar to find the dates on which each of these liturgical seasons begins this year.

Advent _____

Christmas _____

Ordinary Time (1st part) _____

Lent _____

Triduum _____

Easter _____

Ordinary Time (2nd part) _____

### A Family Prayer

This prayer is from the Liturgy of the Hours. It is from Compline, or Night Prayer. Pray it together tonight.

Lord, bless us as we are awake
and guard us as we sleep,
that, awake or asleep, we
may trust in your goodness
and give you glory. Amen.

Visit Sadlier's

www.WeBelieve.web.com

**Connect to the Catechism**
For adult background and reflection, see paragraph 1168.

# Ordinary Time

"This is the day the LORD has made;
let us rejoice in it and be glad."

Psalm 118:24

## During the season of Ordinary Time, we celebrate the life and teachings of Jesus Christ.

### WE GATHER

✝ *Jesus, help us to keep Sunday holy.*

What is your attitude toward Sunday? Do you look forward to it? Why or why not? How is it the same as other days of the week? How is it different?

### WE BELIEVE

Ordinary Time is a season of life and hope. We learn what it means to live as Christ's disciples and we grow as members of the Church. The color green, which we use during this season, reminds us of the life and hope that come from Christ.

Other seasons during the liturgical year focus on a particular event or period in Jesus' life. During the season of Ordinary Time, we celebrate all that Christ does for us through his birth, life, death, Resurrection, and Ascension. We recall the life of Jesus Christ and focus on his teachings in a special way.

The season of Ordinary Time lasts thirty three to thirty four weeks. It is called Ordinary Time because the weeks are "ordered," or named in number order. For example, the first week in Ordinary Time is followed by the second week in Ordinary Time, and so on.

We celebrate Ordinary Time twice during the liturgical year. We celebrate first for a short time between the seasons of Christmas and Lent. The first part of Ordinary Time begins in early January and lasts until the Tuesday before Ash Wednesday. The second part of Ordinary Time is between the seasons of Easter and Advent. So it begins in late May or June after Pentecost Sunday, which ends the Easter season, and lasts several months until the evening before the first Sunday of Advent in late November or early December.

**The Lord's Day** In the Jewish calendar, Saturday was and still is the Sabbath, the day of rest set apart to honor God in a special way. The Sabbath is a special day to praise God for giving us his creation and for acting in the lives of his people. Saturday is the last day of the week, and the Jewish people rest as God rested on the seventh day after completing his creation. It is Jewish tradition to observe that Sabbath from sundown on Friday to sundown on Saturday.

The early Christians followed many of the Jewish customs of prayer and worship. They prayed the psalms and they kept the Sabbath. Gradually, because Jesus Christ rose on a Sunday, Sunday became the Christian Sabbath. Because Christ rose on a Sunday, the Christians called it "the Lord's Day." On this day they gathered to recall Christ's death and Resurrection by celebrating the Eucharist.

Today the Church keeps Sunday as our first holy day. We keep the Lord's Day holy by participating in the celebration of the Eucharist, by resting from work and enjoying our families, by remembering our relationship with God and by serving the needs of the community.

Sunday is the most important day to gather with our parishes for the celebration of the Eucharist, also called the Mass. In the Mass, we

- praise and thank God for his many gifts

- listen to God's word

- remember Jesus' life, death, and Resurrection and celebrate Jesus' gift of himself in the Eucharist

Receiving the Eucharist

- receive the Body and Blood of Christ in Holy Communion

- are joined more closely to Christ and one another in the Church

- are sent out to share Jesus' love, serve others, and work for justice and peace.

In observing the Lord's Day we follow the Jewish custom of celebrating from sundown to sundown. So we begin our celebration on Saturday evening and complete it on Sunday evening. This is why some people participate in the Sunday Mass on Saturday evening.

**A Procession** On the Feast of the Body and Blood of Christ, we celebrate the presence of Jesus Christ with us in the Eucharist in a special way. Many parishes have a procession in honor of Christ's presence in the Eucharist, the Blessed Sacrament. The priest carries the Blessed Sacrament in a special holder called a monstrance. People carry banners and flowers and worship together as they process, or walk, through the city streets or around the area of the parish. In some places flowers are strewn on the streets as the community processes with the Blessed Sacrament. In the church a carpet made of flowers is sometimes laid in the center aisle as a sign of respect and reverence to Jesus in the Blessed Sacrament. There Mass is usually celebrated.

**Sundays during Ordinary Time** Sundays are the foundation of our liturgical year, and we use them to mark the passing of the weeks of Ordinary Time and the other seasons. Sunday's importance comes from the fact that Jesus' Resurrection was on a Sunday.

During Ordinary Time there are three very important Sundays.

- Trinity Sunday, the first Sunday after Pentecost, is the first Sunday in the second part of Ordinary Time. On this Sunday we celebrate in a special way our belief in the Blessed Trinity: God the Father, God the Son, and God the Holy Spirit.

- The Body and Blood of Christ is the Sunday after Trinity Sunday. This is sometimes called "Corpus Christi Sunday" because the term *Body of Christ* comes from these two Latin words.

- Christ the King is the last Sunday in Ordinary Time. On this day we rejoice that Christ is the King of the universe. He saves us from evil and brings us new life. Through him the Kingdom of God has begun on earth.

**WE RESPOND**

In groups list some ways that you celebrate the Lord's Day.

_____

_____

_____

_____

_____

_____

Have the rest of the class guess what you listed by acting out some of the ways.

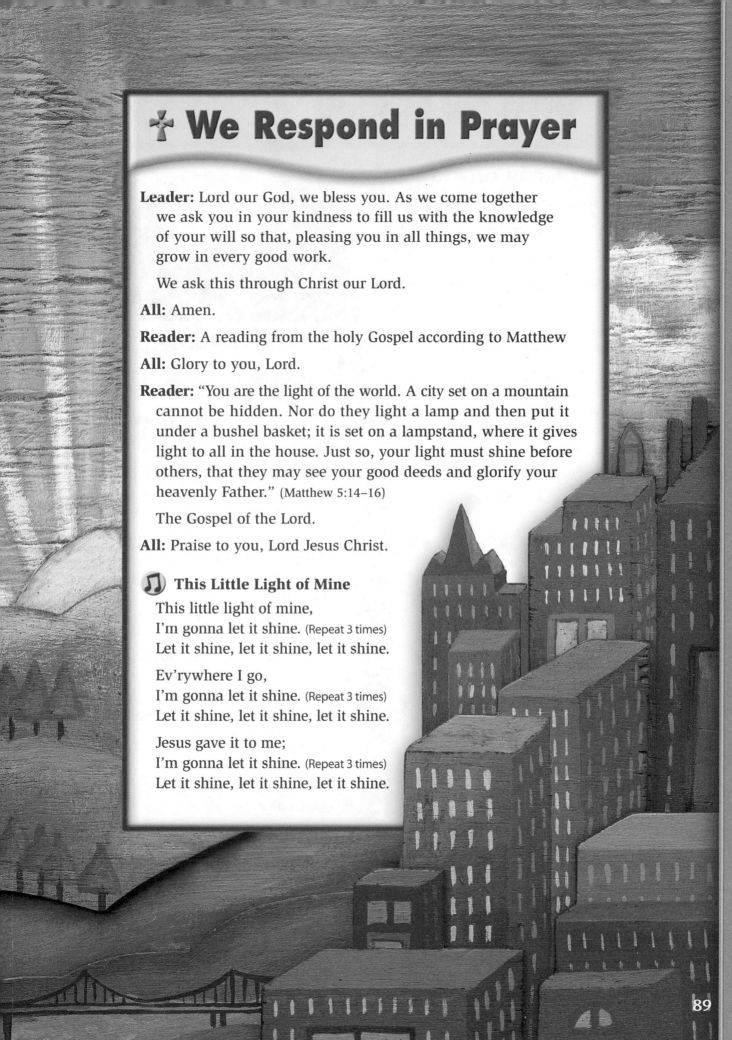

# ✝ We Respond in Prayer

**Leader:** Lord our God, we bless you. As we come together we ask you in your kindness to fill us with the knowledge of your will so that, pleasing you in all things, we may grow in every good work.

We ask this through Christ our Lord.

**All:** Amen.

**Reader:** A reading from the holy Gospel according to Matthew

**All:** Glory to you, Lord.

**Reader:** "You are the light of the world. A city set on a mountain cannot be hidden. Nor do they light a lamp and then put it under a bushel basket; it is set on a lampstand, where it gives light to all in the house. Just so, your light must shine before others, that they may see your good deeds and glorify your heavenly Father." (Matthew 5:14–16)

The Gospel of the Lord.

**All:** Praise to you, Lord Jesus Christ.

## 🎵 This Little Light of Mine

This little light of mine,
I'm gonna let it shine. (Repeat 3 times)
Let it shine, let it shine, let it shine.

Ev'rywhere I go,
I'm gonna let it shine. (Repeat 3 times)
Let it shine, let it shine, let it shine.

Jesus gave it to me;
I'm gonna let it shine. (Repeat 3 times)
Let it shine, let it shine, let it shine.

# SHARING FAITH
## with My Family

## Sharing What I Learned

Discuss the following with your family:

* the season of Ordinary Time
* the importance of Sunday
* the feasts of the Lord during Ordinary Time.

## Around the Table

Discuss these questions as a family:
How can we celebrate the Lord's Day as a day of rest and prayer?
What can make Sunday more special in our home?

## A Family Prayer

Begin your Sunday meal with this prayer.

*One person lights a candle and says:*
Jesus Christ is the light of the world.
*All:* A light no darkness can overpower.
*The leader lifts up the bread and prays:*
We thank you, Father,
for the life and knowledge you
    have revealed to us
through your child Jesus.
Glory be yours through all ages.
As grain once scattered on the hillside
was in this broken bread made one,
so from all lands may we be gathered
into your kingdom by your Son.

The Lord bless us and keep us.
*All:* Amen.
The Lord's face shine upon us and be
    gracious to us.
*All:* Amen.
The Lord look upon us with kindness
    and give us peace.
*All:* Amen.

*(Catholic Household Blessings and Prayers)*

Visit Sadlier's
www.WeBelieveweb.com

 **Connect to the Catechism**
For adult background and reflection,
see paragraph 1163.

**Fill in the circle beside the correct answer.**

1. God's making himself known to us is called _____.

   ○ personal sin          ○ Divine Revelation          ○ free will

2. Evil entered the world through a human act that we call _____.

   ○ original sin          ○ Genesis          ○ suffering

3. The first book of the Bible is called *Genesis*, a word meaning _____.

   ○ Scripture          ○ beginning          ○ covenant

4. A _____ is a person who has both the authority over what he or she cares for and the responsibility for seeing that it lives and grows.

   ○ patriarch          ○ prophet          ○ steward

5. Among the _____, or characteristics, of God are that he is eternal, all knowing, and ever present.

   ○ attributes          ○ symbols          ○ genealogies

6. To fully restore the friendship with God that was broken by the first humans' disobedience, God promised to send a _____.

   ○ prophet          ○ Savior          ○ covenant

7. God renewed his covenant with Jacob, and changed that patriarch's name to _____.

   ○ Israel          ○ Isaac          ○ Abram

8. In the Old Testament story of _____ the Church sees a parallel to God the Father's offering his only Son, Jesus Christ, to save us.

   ○ Esau and Jacob          ○ Cain and Abel          ○ Abraham and Isaac

**Write True or False for the following sentences. Then change the false sentences to make them true.**

9. _____ Tradition is the Revelation of the good news of Jesus Christ as lived out in the Church, past and present

10. _____ Agreement between God and his people is called grace.

11. _____ The special guidance that the Holy Spirit gave to the human authors of the Bible is called divine inspiration.

12. _____ Every human being has an invisible spiritual reality that will never die. This breath of life from God refers to the body.

13. _____ In the story of Joseph, God's plan for and protection of all creation, which we call providence, is symbolized by the fulfillment of dreams.

14. _____ The prophet Isaac described a person as the suffering servant who would come to free us from sin.

15. _____ The flood is the sign God gave to Noah to symbolize the covenant between God and all mortal creatures on earth.

16. _____ The four patriarchs of the Old Testament are Abraham, Isaac, Jacob, and Joseph.

**Answer the questions.**

17–18. Among all the creatures made by God to dwell on earth, humans alone are created with free will. What does this mean and why is it important?

19–20. The patriarchs of the Old Testament are our ancestors in faith. They freely said yes to God with all their hearts. How can we follow their example?

# Building the Covenant Nation

# UNIT 2 SHARING FAITH as a Family

## Three Psalms for Families

A psalm is a poetic prayer or poem. The psalms in the Bible run the gamut of human emotion—from terror to trust, from happiness to heartache, from anger to adoration. There seems to be a psalm for every occasion. Here are three examples of how psalms can be used for family prayer.

"The LORD is my shepherd,
    there is nothing I lack."
(Psalm 23:1)

The beauty of this psalm of David has consoled people for centuries. Read it together in its entirety when your family is going through a time of loss, change, or anxiety.

"LORD, you have probed me,
    you know me."
(Psalm 139:1)

This psalm describes how intimately God knows each one of us. Pray it on birthdays as a way to celebrate the uniqueness of each individual in your family.

"Praise the LORD from the heavens;
    give praise in the heights."
(Psalm 148:1)

Celebrate God's greatness and creativity by praying this psalm together to express the joy that fills your household.

## Plant a Biblical Herb Garden

There are many references in the Old and New Testaments to herbs such as rosemary, mint, dill, anise, parsley, and mustard. Start a biblical herb garden. Use a plant tray or small planting pots to start. Some suggestions before planting: dill, parsley, and mustard are best sowed from seed; mint, rosemary, and anise are best planted from a cutting of a plant. Invite the entire family to have fun tending to your biblical herb garden!

## From the Catechism

"The importance of the family for the life and well-being of society entails a particular responsibility for society to support and strengthen marriage and the family."
(Catechism of the Catholic Church, 2210)

## What Your Child Will Learn in Unit 2

In this unit, the children will be introduced to the development of God's people. They will read about the enslavement of the Israelites in Egypt, the Exodus from Egypt under the leadership of Moses, and the journey in the wilderness of Sinai. The children will learn about the covenant God makes with his people through Moses, the Ten Commandments, and the prophecy of the new covenant in Christ. The children will follow the journey of the Israelites to the promised land of Canaan and their conquest of the area. The children will study the period of history known as the time of the Judges and will learn about Deborah and Samson. Through the story of Ruth, the children will be more aware of the meaning of being faithful to God.

Unit 2 continues the saga of God's people and their efforts to establish the nation of Israel. The children read stories about the wisdom of Solomon and the building of the Temple in Jerusalem. The unit closes with an examination of the different kinds of psalms in the Book of Psalms and of the literary style contained in the Song of Songs.

## Plan & Preview

▶ Scissors should be on hand to cut out the *We Believe* Trading Card (*Chapters 8–12*).

▶ Pieces of cardboard or stiff paper can be used for the trading cards. The front and back of the cards can be glued to the cardboard to form a sturdy trading card.

## A Story in Faith

**Denise Lenore Benedetto**

Like Ruth of the Old Testament, Denise was faithful to her family, to her friends, and to her God. She was a devoted mother. Like Ruth, she put God first in her life as well. Her faith in God was put to the test when it was discovered she was suffering from a very serious spinal condition. There was a good chance she would be paralyzed. But Denise never lost faith in God's plan for her.

It took six months in a full body cast, but she recovered fully and went on being the wonderful person she had always been. She went back to work as an office professional at the World Trade Center in New York City. And she was there on September 11, 2001 when the towers at this site were destroyed by terrorists. Denise Lenore Benedetto lost her life with thousands of others. But her example of love of God and family will not be lost as long as one person remembers her faithfulness!

# An Enslaved People

## ✝ We Gather in Prayer

**Leader:** For followers of Christ, freedom is a gift of love and goodness, and comes from Christ. Let us pray for all those who are not free, who are enslaved, in our world today.

**Reader 1:** "For freedom Christ set us free; so stand firm and do not submit again to the yoke of slavery." (Galatians 5:1)

**Reader 2:** For all who are enslaved by the habit of sin and selfishness, let us pray:

**All:** Lord Jesus Christ, set them free.
(Response to all petitions.)

**Reader 3:** For all who are enslaved by unsafe working conditions and low pay, let us pray:

**Reader 4:** For all who are enslaved by addiction, let us pray:

**Reader 5:** For all who are enslaved by disease and chronic illness, let us pray:

**Reader 6:** For all who are enslaved by poverty and hunger, let us pray:

**Reader 7:** For all who are unjustly denied their freedom, let us pray:

### ♫ Go Down, Moses

When Israel was in Egypt's land,
Let my people go;
Oppressed so hard they could not stand,
Let my people go.

Refrain:
Go down, Moses,
Way down in Egypt's land;
Tell old Pharaoh: Let my people go.

Oh, let us all from bondage flee,
Let my people go;
And let us all in Christ be free,
Let my people go. (Refrain)

Israelites grow and prosper in Egypt

Moses is born and raised by pharaoh's daughter

God reveals himself to Moses

Oppression of the Israelites increases

The first Passover: God leads the Israelites out of Egypt

God speaks with Moses on Mt. Sinai/ Israel is a holy nation

Israelites journey for many years

Pharaoh begins oppression of Israelites

Moses flees Egypt

Moses returns to Egypt to lead the Israelites

Egypt suffers many plagues

Miriam leads rejoicing

Moses dies

God gives Moses the Ten Commandments

# Egypt became the home of the Israelites.

## WE GATHER

✝ *Loving God, protect us.*

What does someone have to do to feel at home in a new town? What difficulties might he or she face? What are some ways we can help people to feel at home?

## WE BELIEVE

God led the family of Jacob, or as God had named him, Israel, into Egypt. All twelve of Israel's sons, including Joseph, were reunited. In Egypt they were saved from famine and protected from hardships that they may not have been able to survive. God had provided for his people through Joseph.

Joseph informed the pharaoh, "My father and my brothers have come from the land of Canaan, with their flocks and herds and everything else they own; and they are now in the region of Goshen" (Genesis 47:1). The pharaoh told Joseph that his family could settle there. He said, "the land of Egypt is at your disposal" (Genesis 47:6).

So Jacob's family became honored guests in Egypt. They were given the best land in Goshen, a fertile area in northern Egypt. At the time Egypt was divided into two kingdoms. The southern part of the country was ruled by Egyptian kings. A separate kingdom in northern Egypt was ruled by people who came from regions to the east of Egypt.

**Change in Egypt** In Goshen, in northern Egypt, Jacob's family prospered and God's people grew in number. At first they lived there in safety and comfort. But in time the Egyptians gained control of the northern kingdom. Two Egyptian kings, who were also brothers, united Egypt. They drove away many rulers and people from foreign countries and kept other people as slaves. Egypt entered a period of tremendous wealth and power. This period is usually called the New Kingdom. It lasted for hundreds of years.

As time passed, Joseph and his generation died. The pharaoh who welcomed the family of Jacob also died, and a new pharaoh came into power. He did not know of Joseph and did not look upon the Israelites as honored guests. In fact, he feared them, saying, "Look how numerous and powerful the Israelite people are growing, more so than we ourselves! Come, let us deal shrewdly with them to stop their increase; otherwise, in time of war they too may join our enemies to fight against us, and so leave our country" (Exodus 1:9–10).

In the Book of Exodus, the second book of the Bible, we find out that eventually the Egyptians made the Israelites their slaves.

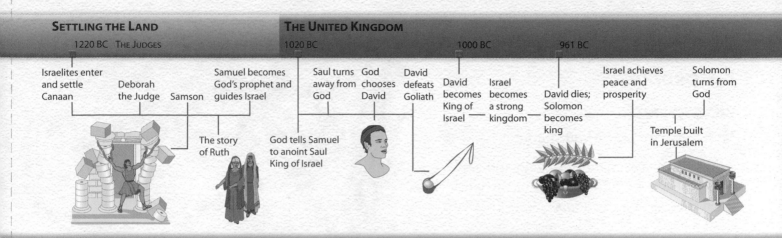

**SETTLING THE LAND**

1220 BC   THE JUDGES

**THE UNITED KINGDOM**

1020 BC                    1000 BC                    961 BC

Israelites enter and settle Canaan

Deborah the Judge    Samson

Samuel becomes God's prophet and guides Israel

The story of Ruth

Saul turns away from God    God chooses David

David defeats Goliath

God tells Samuel to anoint Saul King of Israel

David becomes King of Israel    Israel becomes a strong kingdom

David dies; Solomon becomes king

Israel achieves peace and prosperity

Solomon turns from God

Temple built in Jerusalem

The pharaoh forced them to build monuments and buildings. He also made some Israelites work long hours in the fields. They were no longer free to worship the one true God and to follow his laws. And their lives became so unbearable that they cried out to God to be rescued from Egypt.

## As Catholics...

Throughout history slavery has not only required people to work against their will. It has devalued their human dignity and taken away their freedom. Fortunately most countries have changed their laws and policies to protect people from slavery and forced labor. However, the need to protect the rights of workers remains. The Church teaches us that the opportunity to be employed, to have safe working conditions, and to earn a fair wage are issues of justice.

The work of social justice is to protect the rights and dignity of each person and to make sure that all people have or are given what is due to them. The Church speaks out against any system, private organization, or government that focuses on making a profit at the expense of human dignity and freedom. Instead the Church encourages individuals and groups to bring the good news of Jesus Christ into society and to work for change in policies and laws so that each person is respected.

What can you do to respect the dignity of workers?

## WE RESPOND

Today there are people who need to be rescued from slavery, poverty, homelessness, and hunger.

List some other things from which people need to be rescued.

_____

_____

_____

What can you do with your parish to help these people?

_____

_____

_____

# God chose Moses to lead his people.

## WE GATHER

✝ *O Lord, we praise your name.*

In what ways are you free to do and say things? Do people in all parts of the world have these same freedoms?

## WE BELIEVE

In the Book of Exodus we find the story of what happened to Jacob's descendants in Egypt. We read of the terrible suffering of the Israelites as slaves of the pharaoh. We learn that out of that suffering God brought freedom and hope. More importantly, in the Book of Exodus we learn about God carrying out his plan to bring his people back to Canaan. The word *exodus* comes from the Greek word for "departure." **Exodus** is the biblical word describing the Israelites' departure from slavery to freedom.

The Israelites were also called Hebrews, since their language was known as Hebrew. The pharaoh noticed that despite all the difficulties in their lives, the number of Hebrews was still growing. He told some of the Hebrew women that all the newly born sons of the Israelites must be killed. But these women did not listen to the pharaoh. They followed God's laws instead. So the pharaoh gave a new command: "Throw into the river every boy that is born to the Hebrews" (Exodus 1:22). Now it was even more difficult for the Hebrew women to protect their baby boys.

In the second chapter of Exodus we read about one woman who saved her son. She made a basket out of reeds from the river. She coated it with tar to prevent it from sinking and then put her son in it. She placed the basket in the shallow water near one of the riverbanks. The pharaoh's daughter found the child and took him home with her. She named the child Moses and raised him as an Egyptian.

This is another biblical story that is filled with symbolism. The same Hebrew word is used for *basket* and *ark*. Moses was saved in the basket just as Noah's family was saved in the ark. As Christians we are saved in the Church through the waters of Baptism.

**Life in Midian** When Moses was an adult, he visited his fellow Hebrews. One day he saw a Hebrew slave being beaten by an Egyptian, and Moses killed the Egyptian. The pharaoh heard about what Moses had done and wanted him put to death. Moses had to run away to the desert region of Midian. Moses settled there and he married a woman named Zipporah, with whom he had children. There Moses lived the life of a shepherd.

One day while Moses was tending his flocks, God appeared to him in a burning bush. The fire was flaming from the bush but not destroying it. So Moses went over to look more closely. God called out to Moses from the bush and Moses answered, "Here I am" (Exodus 3:4).

> ### Key Word
> **Exodus** the biblical word describing the Israelites' departure from slavery to freedom

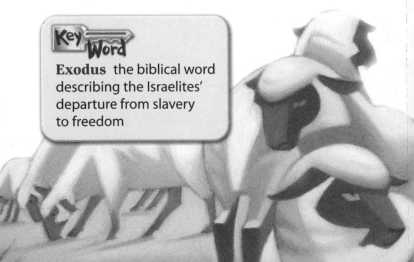

God told Moses that this place was holy. God also told Moses that he wanted him to return to Egypt and lead the Hebrews out of slavery. Moses asked God how he would be able to do this, and God told Moses that he would be with him.

Moses asked God what he should say when the Israelites asked him who sent him to them. "God replied, 'I am who am.' Then he added, 'This is what you shall tell the Israelites: I AM sent me to you'" (Exodus 3:14).

This name that God gave was the source of the word *Yahweh*. "I AM" was a name that described God as ever-present to his people. This name was so holy that out of reverence the Israelites did not even speak it. Instead they used the title *Adonai*, which means "my Lord."

In the third chapter of Exodus we read that God once again spoke to Moses. "Go and assemble the elders of the Israelites, and tell them: The LORD, the God of your fathers, the God of Abraham, Isaac and Jacob, has appeared to me and said: I am concerned about you and about the way you are being treated in Egypt; so I have decided to lead you up out of the misery of Egypt into the land of the Canaanites, . . . a land flowing with milk and honey." (Exodus 3:16–17) Moses did as God commanded.

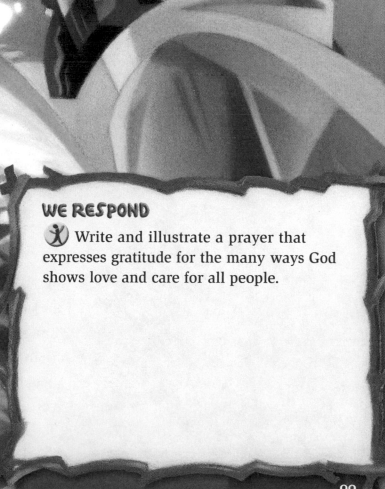

## WE RESPOND

Write and illustrate a prayer that expresses gratitude for the many ways God shows love and care for all people.

# God helped his people.

## WE GATHER

✝ *Lord, help us to remember that without you we can do nothing.*

🏃 List some tasks that you and your classmates might be put in charge of completing. How would you convince others to help you to complete these tasks?

_____

_____

## WE BELIEVE

After God appeared to Moses in the burning bush, Moses returned to Egypt. Moses' brother, Aaron, helped him to explain God's message to the Israelites. Gradually, Moses gained the support of the people.

Moses and Aaron met face-to-face with the pharaoh. They said, "Thus says the LORD, the God of Israel: Let my people go, that they may celebrate a feast to me in the desert" (Exodus 5:1). But the pharaoh refused their request. Worse still, the pharaoh did not give the Israelite slaves the materials they needed for their work.

Soon it became almost impossible for the Israelites to complete their required work. They began to blame Moses for this hardship.

Moses told God how the people were suffering, and God replied, "Now you shall see what I will do to Pharaoh. Forced by my mighty hand, he will send them away; compelled by my outstretched arm, he will drive them from his land" (Exodus 6:1). When Moses told the Israelites what God would do for them, they did not believe him. They were too weary.

God knew that it would be difficult to convince the pharaoh to let the Israelites leave Egypt. So God said to Moses, "I will lay my hand on Egypt and by great acts of judgment I will bring the hosts of my people, the Israelites, out of the land of Egypt, so that the Egyptians may learn that I am the LORD, as I stretch out my hand against Egypt and lead the Israelites out of their midst" (Exodus 7:4–5).

These "great acts of judgment" that God spoke of were the plagues. During biblical times, a major disaster or catastrophe was considered a plague. We read about the plagues in Chapters 7—11 of the Book of Exodus.

Egyptian clay figure (14th Century BC) highlights the terrible destruction of the plague of the frogs.

## THE TEN PLAGUES

| | |
|---|---|
| the river of blood | Exodus 7:17 |
| frogs | Exodus 7:27–28 |
| gnats | Exodus 8:12 |
| flies | Exodus 8:16–17 |
| disease | Exodus 9:1–3 |
| boils | Exodus 9:8–9 |
| hail | Exodus 9:18–19 |
| locusts | Exodus 10:4–5 |
| darkness | Exodus 10:21 |
| death of first born | Exodus 11:4–5 |

**The Plagues** A conflict began when Moses and Aaron went to the pharaoh to demand freedom for the Israelites. Moses and Aaron showed the pharaoh a sign of God's power, but the pharaoh and the Egyptians disregarded this sign. A great struggle over the Israelites then began between God and the pharaoh. The ten plagues symbolize this struggle.

The story recounts that at first the pharaoh's magicians were able to duplicate each plague, and the pharaoh refused to recognize Moses' request for the Israelite's freedom. As time went by, however, the pharaoh's magicians could no longer reproduce the plagues. When the Israelites saw the effects of the plagues, they knew that God was protecting them. Their faith in God was strengthened.

The pharaoh considered letting the Israelites leave. He even began to negotiate with Moses and to agree to some of Moses' demands. Yet the pharaoh never completely gave in. Through Moses God continually called the Egyptians to listen to him. However, the pharaoh did not listen to God's warnings and refused to free the Israelites from slavery. Because of his actions the pharaoh was responsible for the suffering of the Egyptian people.

At the end of the ninth plague, the pharaoh seemed to give in to Moses' requests. But again the pharaoh changed his mind. He even refused to see Moses and Aaron. "Then the Lord told Moses, 'One more plague will I bring upon Pharaoh and upon Egypt. After that he will let you depart. In fact, he will not merely let you go; he will drive you away.'" (Exodus 11:1)

## WE RESPOND

Imagine that you have been asked to design a banner advertisement for a Web site devoted to people throughout the world whose freedoms are being denied. Design a banner ad that will make people want to visit the Web site and assist in the work of freedom for all.

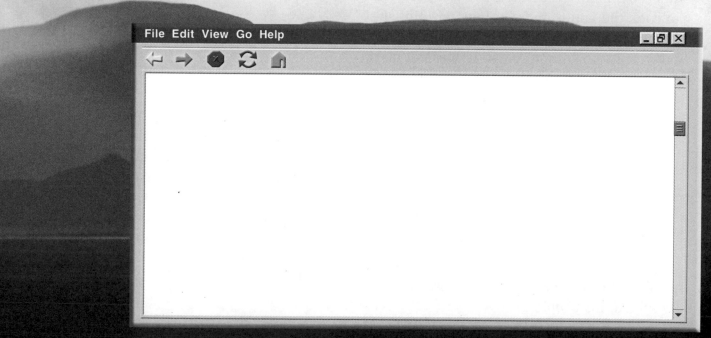

File Edit View Go Help

**101**

# God guided his people to freedom.

## WE GATHER

✝ *God, we are your people.*

🧍 What are some ways that these signs protect us:

• traffic signs

_____

• signs on appliances

_____

• signs in school

_____

(Add some other signs)

• _____

## WE BELIEVE

When Moses left the pharaoh's presence after the ninth plague, God told him to have every Israelite family prepare for their escape from Egypt. They were to get a lamb and kill it. Then they were to mark the doorframes of their houses with blood from the lamb. This would be a sign that the people inside the house were Israelites, not Egyptians.

After marking the doorframes, the Israelites were to remain inside their houses. They were to cook the lambs and eat them with bitter herbs and unleavened bread. Unleavened bread is made without yeast. It does not need to rise and therefore takes less time to prepare. This unleavened bread symbolized the Israelites' rush to escape.

The Israelites obeyed God's instructions. At midnight God passed over all of Egypt, taking the lives of every firstborn Egyptian, including the son of the pharaoh. This plague even caused the death of all the firstborn animals belonging to the Egyptians. Only the Israelites and their animals were spared. This event was called the **Passover**, since God passed over, or spared, his people.

Every year Jews remember this special night. During the feast of Passover they celebrate a seder by eating the same meal that their ancestors ate on the first Passover. They follow God's command that all descendants of the Israelites observe the feast of Passover. By celebrating this feast, Jews today recall how God spared the lives of their ancestors and brought them out of slavery in Egypt.

**Leaving Egypt** Horrified by what had happened, the pharaoh summoned Moses and Aaron during the night. He told them to take the Israelites and their possessions out of Egypt immediately. Fearing that the pharaoh would again change his mind, Moses and the Israelites left quickly. The Exodus was finally underway.

Moses led the Israelites toward the Red Sea, the water that separated Egypt from the Arabian Peninsula. During their escape, "The LORD preceded them, in the daytime by means of a column of cloud to show them the way, and at night by means of a column of fire to give them light. Thus they could travel both day and night. Neither the column of cloud by day nor the column of fire by night ever left its place in front of the people" (Exodus 13:21–22).

As soon as the Israelites were gone, the pharaoh changed his mind and sent his army to recapture them. By this time, the Israelites were at the Red Sea, and God again caused a wonder that saved his people.

 Exodus 14:10–28

The Egyptian army closed in on the Israelites. God parted the Red Sea, and the Israelites escaped over the dry path God had made through it. But when the Egyptians tried to follow, the waters closed over them, and they drowned.

In this way God brought his people from slavery into freedom. It was the great turning point in the history of God's relationship with his people. As the biblical writer showed us in the story of Noah, God used water to save the people. For the Israelites the salvation of the nation came about as they passed through the waters of the Red Sea. As Christians the waters of the Red Sea symbolize the saving waters of our own Baptism.

## WE RESPOND

 **Be Not Afraid**

Refrain:
>    Be not afraid.
>    I go before you always.
>    Come, follow me,
>    and I will give you rest.

>    If you pass through raging waters
>            in the sea,
>        you shall not drown.
>    If you walk amid the burning flames,
>        you shall not be harmed.
>    If you stand before the pow'r of hell
>            and death is at your side,
>        know that I am with you through it all.

(Refrain)

**Passover** the event in which God passed over the whole of Egypt, taking the lives of every firstborn Egyptian and sparing the Israelites

**Complete the following.**

1. When Israel's family first entered Egypt, they were treated as honored guests and given

_____

2. The child Moses was saved from

_____

3. While Moses was living in Midian and tending his flocks,

_____

4. The pharaoh would not let the Israelites leave Egypt, so God

_____

**Write True or False for the following sentences.
Then change the false sentences to make them true.**

5. _____ Goshen was the period of tremendous wealth and power of Egypt.

_____

6. _____ The Israelites suffered terribly as slaves of the pharaoh.

_____

7. _____ God revealed his name to the pharaoh.

_____

8. _____ After the Passover the Israelites were able to escape from the pharaoh's army.

_____

**Write a paragraph to answer this question.**

9–10. Why did God free the Israelites from slavery in Egypt?

ASSESSMENT

The word *exodus* comes from the Greek word for "departure." Design a mural or a photo display with captions to portray the importance of the Israelites' exodus from Egypt.

# We Respond in Faith

## Reflect & Pray

For those people whose lives seem unbearable, I pray

_____

_____

Holy Spirit, help me to love and care for all of God's people.
Amen.

**Key Words**

**Exodus** (p. 98)
**Passover** (p. 103)

## Remember

- Egypt became the home of the Israelites.
- God chose Moses to lead his people.
- God helped his people.
- God guided his people to freedom.

## OUR CATHOLIC LIFE

### Blessed Pierre Toussaint

Pierre Toussaint, born in 1778 in Haiti, was a slave. He came to New York with the Catholic couple who owned him. They taught him to read and write which was unusual at the time. They allowed him to become a hairdresser. He encouraged his clients to pray, to trust in God, and to live according to the gospel. When the husband died, the wife offered to free Pierre, but he refused. He used his earnings to support her, and he eventually became a free man. Pierre married a Haitian woman, and together they helped the poor and worked to free slaves. In New York Pierre and his wife helped to found one of the first orphanages and the first Catholic school for children of color. Pierre Toussaint died in 1853, and in 1996 Pope John Paul II recognized Pierre Toussaint as having lived an outstanding Christian life.

# SHARING FAITH
## with My Family

## Sharing What I Learned

Discuss the following with your family:

- the Israelites' life in Egypt
- Moses
- Passover
- the exodus from Egypt.

## Questions About Judaism

**Q:** What is the Jewish seder?

**A:** Passover is a Jewish festival which celebrates liberation from slavery. The seder is a symbolic meal during the festival. The symbols used include matzoh, bitter herbs, salt water, the paschal lamb, and parsley. They represent the conditions of slavery and the events leading to the deliverance of the Jews from Egypt as recounted in the Old Testament. The aim of the seder is to make the participants understand that they are a part of the Jewish people and that this history and redemption applies to them.

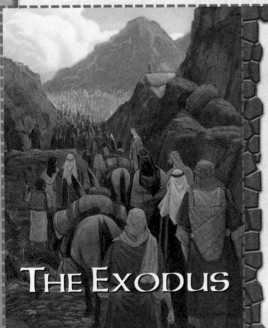

THE EXODUS

Why did the Israelites want to leave Egypt?

_____

_____

What are the important parts of the story of the exodus from Egypt?

_____

_____

How is this event remembered today?

_____

_____

## We Believe Trading Cards

Complete the facts on the back of the trading card. Then share with your family what you have learned about the Israelites' exodus from Egypt.

Visit Sadlier's
**www.WEBELIEVEweb.com**

**Connect to the Catechism**
For adult background and reflection, see paragraphs 312, 2575, 207, and 1363.

# A Free People

## ✝ We Gather in Prayer

**Leader:** Like the Israelites, we are on a journey with God. Along the way, there are difficulties, obstacles, and hardships that test our faith and courage. But we follow Jesus, who tells us, "Do not be afraid"(Matthew 14:27).

**Side 1:** "Send your light and fidelity, that they may be my guide

**Side 2:** And bring me to your holy mountain, to the place of your dwelling,

**Side 1:** That I may come to the altar of God, to God, my joy, my delight."

(Psalm 43:3–4)

**Side 2:** Glory to the Father, and to the Son, and to the Holy Spirit.

**All:** As it was in the beginning, is now, and will be for ever. Amen.

## 🎵 Be Not Afraid

You shall cross the barren desert,
　but you shall not die of thirst.
You shall wander far in safety,
　though you do not know the way.
You shall speak your words in foreign
　lands and all will understand.
You shall see the face of God and live.

Refrain:
Be not afraid.
I go before you always.
Come, follow me,
and I will give you rest.

# Moses led God's people through the wilderness.

## WE GATHER

✝ *God, help us to follow you.*

Can you remember a very long trip you took with your family? Describe some of the events that might have happened along the way.

## WE BELIEVE

As we read in Chapter 15 of the Book of Exodus, the Israelites had escaped from Egypt. They were overjoyed that God had saved them. They were beginning their journey to the land of Canaan, the land that God had promised them. Moses and the Israelites sang a song of praise to God. Miriam, the sister of Moses and Aaron, took a tambourine and led a dance of victory. She sang,

"Sing to the Lord, for he is gloriously
        triumphant;
    horse and chariot he has cast into the sea"
(Exodus 15:21).

Write the lyrics to your own song or poem praising God for something he has done for you.

_____

_____

_____

_____

_____

_____

The Israelites faced a long journey through the wilderness of the Sinai Peninsula. The Sinai Peninsula was the triangle of land that connected northeastern Egypt with southern Palestine and northwestern Arabia. The story of the Israelites' wanderings in the wilderness is mainly told in Chapters 16—18 of the Book of Exodus. The Israelites spent many years in the wilderness. It was during this period of wandering that the Israelites made the difficult transition from being slaves under the pharaoh to living as a free people in service of God.

**Toward Mount Sinai** God was with his people during their time in the wilderness. With God's help Moses led the Israelites toward **Mount Sinai**. This was a mountain peak in the rocky southern part of the Sinai Peninsula. During this journey God tested his people's faithfulness again and again. As we saw in the story of Abraham, God asked his people to show their faith and trust in him. He asked them to stay close to him and to follow his plan. God often asked them to do things that at first did not seem reasonable to them. Yet when they followed God's will, they saw the wisdom of God's plan for them.

The Israelites, however, did not always follow God's will for them. At times they forgot that God had taken them out of slavery. They grumbled against Moses for the hardships of this journey through the wilderness.

Even though the Israelites sometimes doubted God, God demonstrated his faithfulness to his people. He watched over them and worked many miracles. A **miracle** is an extraordinary event that is beyond human power and brought about by God.

For instance, when the people complained that they could not drink the bitter water at Marah, God had Moses change it into drinkable water. When they complained that they had no food, God sent small birds called quail. All through their journey God also provided a bread-like substance called **manna**. This manna, a sweet food that tastes like honey, fell from the desert shrubs. And when the Israelites again grumbled that they had no water, God instructed Moses to strike a certain rock and water miraculously gushed out.

In all of these ways, God listened to his people. He made sure they had what they needed to live and to follow his plan for them. Throughout history God has continued to care for the needs of his people. God listens to us today, helping us to be strong and guiding us to follow his ways.

Along the way to Mount Sinai, Moses was reunited with his family. They had remained in Midian when Moses returned to Egypt. Now with God's help Moses, his family, and all of God's people continued their journey together.

The Exodus and the journey through the desert are clearly signs of God leading his people. We, too, are called by God to follow his plan for us. We may not cross seas and deserts, and we may not lack bread and water. But we do need God's love and guidance on our journey through this life. Just like the Israelites in the desert, we, too, need to trust in God and to believe in his love for us.

The rugged mountain landscape of Mount Sinai, Egypt.

## Key Words

**Mount Sinai** a mountain peak in the rocky southern part of the Sinai peninsula

**miracle** an extraordinary event that is beyond human power and brought about by God

**manna** a sweet bread-like food that God provided for the Israelites in the desert

## WE RESPOND

Look back at the song or poem that you wrote praising God. Reflect on the words and their meaning for you. Share this with a partner.

Now praise God together.
"Give praise with tambourines and dance,
    praise him with flutes and strings.
Give praise with crashing cymbals,
    praise him with sounding cymbals.
Let everything that has breath
    give praise to the LORD!
Hallelujah!" (Psalm 150:4–6)

# God gave his people the law.

## WE GATHER

✝ *O God, help us to be faithful to your covenant.*

What do friends need to do to keep their friendship strong?

## WE BELIEVE

When the Israelites arrived at Mount Sinai, they made their camp. Moses went up to the mountain to pray to God. There God reminded Moses that the Israelites were God's people, special to him. Because of this covenant relationship, the people of Israel "shall be to me a kingdom of priests, a holy nation" (Exodus 19:6). The Israelite people were consecrated to God in a special way. As his people, all of them were to take part in worshiping God and offering sacrifice to him.

When Moses told the Israelites what God had said, they answered together, "Everything the LORD has said, we will do" (Exodus 19:8). On the third day of their stay at Mount Sinai, God appeared to the whole people. Clouds and smoke surrounded Mount Sinai. There was thunder and lightning and the sound of trumpets. The mountain trembled, and God made his presence known.

Then God called Moses to come back up to the top of the mountain. There God gave the Ten Commandments to Moses. The **Ten Commandments** are the laws of God's covenant. If God's people would live by the Ten Commandments, they would keep their covenant relationship with God. He would be their God, and they would be his people. We can find the Ten Commandments in Chapter 20 of the Book of Exodus.

Growing up in a Jewish family, Jesus learned these commandments. He lived by God's laws, and called his followers to obey them, too. As disciples of Christ, we try to show our love for God and for one another by following the Ten Commandments. We try to live in God's love.

## THE TEN COMMANDMENTS

1. I am the LORD your God: you shall not have strange gods before me.
2. You shall not take the name of the LORD your God in vain.
3. Remember to keep holy the LORD's Day.
4. Honor your father and your mother.
5. You shall not kill.
6. You shall not commit adultery.
7. You shall not steal.
8. You shall not bear false witness against your neighbor.
9. You shall not covet your neighbor's wife.
10. You shall not covet your neighbor's goods.

God also gave Moses many other laws to help the people live out the covenant. These laws are explained in the final chapters of the Book of Exodus and in the Book of Leviticus, the third book of the Bible.

**Sealing the Covenant** Moses came down from the mountain and shared with the people all the laws that God had given him. The Israelites agreed to follow these laws. So Moses wrote the laws down. He then set up a stone altar with twelve pillars. The pillars represented the twelve tribes of Israel, the descendants of the twelve sons of Jacob.

Moses then sacrificed some young bulls as a peace offering to God and sealed the covenant. Moses sprinkled some of the blood from the bulls, saying "This is the blood of the covenant which the LORD has made with you in accordance with all these words of his" (Exodus 24:8).

**Key Word**

**Ten Commandments** the laws of God's covenant given to Moses on Mount Sinai

After Moses celebrated this ritual with the Israelites, he went back up on the mountain. There he spent forty days and forty nights praying to God. The biblical writer used this number as a reminder of God's covenant with Noah. Throughout Scripture forty was a symbolic number. Noah had spent forty days and forty nights on the ark. And after his baptism at the Jordan River, Jesus spent forty days in the desert. There he prayed and fasted as preparation for his public ministry.

Another symbolic number used throughout Scripture was twelve. There were twelve pillars of the stone altar that Moses set up. And according to Christian interpretation, besides referring to the twelve tribes of Israel, these pillars also symbolized the twelve apostles. The apostles were the twelve men with whom Jesus shared his ministry in a special way. Jesus Christ would send them out to spread the good news that he was the Son of God, sent to save all people.

**The New Covenant**  Before his death Jesus had a last meal with his apostles and some disciples. They were celebrating the Passover meal together. At this meal, which Christians call the Last Supper, Jesus said, "This cup is the new covenant in my blood, which will be shed for you" (Luke 22:20).

As Christians we know that the *new* covenant between God and his people has also been sealed. It has been sealed with Jesus' blood. Jesus Christ offered his own life to save us and to free us from sin. Through this new covenant it is possible for us to share in God's life and friendship. We celebrate the new covenant at each celebration of the Eucharist.

## WE RESPOND

What is one way that you can show your love for God and others by following the Ten Commandments? Make a commitment to do so this week.

# The people built God a dwelling place.

🧍 When people let other people and things take the place of God, we say they are worshiping a false god. What are some of the false gods in today's world?

_____

_____

## WE BELIEVE

While Moses was on Mount Sinai, God gave him two tablets on which the Ten Commandments were written. God reminded Moses that the Israelites were to worship the one true God, not the false gods that other people thought existed. God gave Moses instructions on the ways the people should worship the one true God. These instructions included plans to make different things that the Israelites needed to use in their worship. Everything they were to make had to be portable because the Israelites still had the long journey to the promised land ahead of them.

Since Moses had been on the mountain for a very long time, the Israelites became restless. They went to Aaron and said, "Come, make us a god who will be our leader; as for the man Moses who brought us out of the land of Egypt, we do not know what has happened to him" (Exodus 32:1). So they constructed a statue of a calf out of their gold jewelry. When it was finished, they set it up in the center of the camp and began to worship it as if it were a god.

When Moses came down from the mountain, he saw the people celebrating around the calf. He was angry because the people were worshiping a false god. They had gone against God's commandment by building an idol. Moses threw down the tablets of the Ten Commandments and they broke. Moses then punished those who were unfaithful to God and begged God to forgive the people.

God called Moses to the mountain one last time. "Then the LORD said to Moses, 'Write down these words, for in accordance with them I have made a covenant with you and with Israel.' So Moses stayed there with the LORD for forty days and forty nights, . . . and he wrote on the tablets the words of the covenant, the ten commandments" (Exodus 34:27–28).

When Moses returned from the mountain with the two new tablets of the commandments, his face was shining from being in God's presence. Moses' face was so bright that the Israelites could not look at Moses. For that reason, Moses wore a veil over his face from then on. He only took it off when he spoke to God.

**Building the Dwelling Place**  Now as God had instructed them through Moses, the Israelites began the great work of making the "dwelling place" for God. They contributed their personal belongings, and made:

- a meeting tent, God's dwelling place, which served as a movable place of worship

- the **ark of the covenant**, a wooden box in which the tablets of the Ten Commandments were kept

- several altars

- various pieces of furniture needed for worship

- vestments for the priests.

Artist interpretation of the way the ark of the covenant might have looked.

## The Dwelling Place

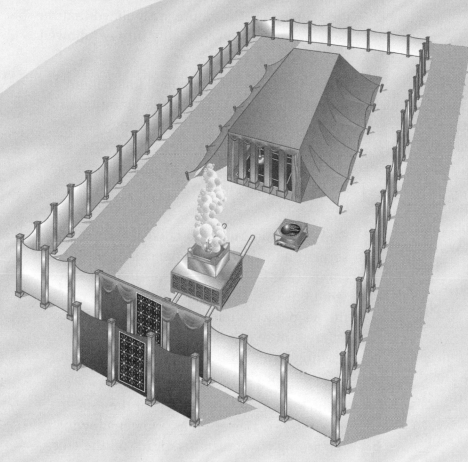

And on the first day of the first month, almost a year after the Israelites had left Egypt, God entered this "dwelling place." The biblical writer symbolized the presence of God by the thunder and lightning that appeared over the tent.

God no longer seemed far away. The Israelites realized that God was always with them, and they were comforted by the visible reminder of his presence. Confident that God was among them, the Israelites continued the long journey to the promised land.

**ark of the covenant**
a wooden box in which the tablets of the Ten Commandments were kept

## As Catholics...

In our churches, the tabernacle is a beautifully crafted box in which the Blessed Sacrament, or the Eucharist, is reserved for distribution to those who are sick, and also for adoration. *Tabernacle* comes from the Latin word for "tent." The Israelites covered the ark of the covenant with a tent as it traveled with the people. This dwelling place was a sign of God's presence with his people. For us the Blessed Sacrament kept in the tabernacle is more than a sign of the presence of God with us. Christ is really and truly present in the Eucharist.

We genuflect, or kneel briefly on one knee, before the tabernacle as a sign of reverence and worship for Jesus, the Son of God.

Plan to visit your parish church or chapel where the tabernacle is located. Spend time there in prayer before the Blessed Sacrament.

# God led his people toward the promised land.

## WE GATHER

✝ *God, help us as we journey to you.*

How is your life different now from when you were in fourth grade? What are some of the things that have changed?

## WE BELIEVE

The journey of the Israelites to the promised land of Canaan took many years. On this journey God's people grew and changed. From the time that they left Egypt, the biblical writer counted the Israelites' journey as taking forty years. The story of these years is mainly told in the Book of Numbers, the fourth book of the Bible. The Hebrew name for this book means "in the desert." The English meaning refers to two censuses, or head counts of all the people, that took place during the journey to Canaan.

On their journey God made his presence known to the Israelites by the huge cloud that hung over the meeting tent during the day. At night the cloud became fiery, so that the Israelites could see it. When the cloud moved, they followed it. When it did not move, the Israelites remained where they were. The guiding cloud symbolized that God himself was directing their journey.

**A Just and Forgiving God**   As soon as the journey began, the Israelites complained that they had no meat. Out of love for his people, God provided all the food that they needed.

Next the Israelites tried to conquer Canaan without God's consent, and they failed in their attempt. This failure symbolized that the Israelites would succeed only if they followed God's commands.

When the people again complained about the quality of their food—the manna that God provided every day—poisonous snakes appeared among them. Then the people were suddenly sorry for their grumbling and asked Moses to plead with God to remove the snakes.

God then told Moses to make a bronze serpent and set it up in the center of the camp. God said that whoever looked at it would recover from snakebite. In this way the people were reminded to turn to God for safety and to ask his forgiveness for not trusting in him. God was not only just but also all-forgiving.

Saint John, the writer of one of the four gospels, saw this event as a foreshadowing of the saving effect of Jesus' death on the cross. "And just as Moses lifted up the serpent in the desert, so must the Son of Man be lifted up, so that everyone who believes in him may have eternal life." (John 3:14–15)

**On the Plains of Moab** God used the experience in the desert to help his people grow to be more loving and faithful. The Israelites faced many difficult situations during their journey. From these situations they learned more about God and about themselves. Finally the Israelites arrived on the plains of Moab, east of Canaan. Here they met a prophet named Balaam, who predicted the greatness of Israel in the centuries to come.

"I see him, though not now;
  I behold him, though not near:
A star shall advance from Jacob,
  and a staff shall rise from Israel"
(Numbers 24:17).

Though the Israelites had not yet entered Canaan, the time was coming for Moses, who was a very old man, to die. So Moses asked God, "May the LORD, the God of the spirits of all mankind, set over the community a man who shall act as their leader in all things, to guide them in all their actions; that the LORD's community may not be like sheep without a shepherd" (Numbers 27:16–17).

God told Moses to lay his hand on Joshua, one of his trusted generals, and commission him to lead God's people into Canaan. God's promise would be fulfilled.

Look back over pages 114–115. Highlight the ways God acted in the lives of the Israelites.

### WE RESPOND

Look back at your own life. What are some of the ways God has acted in your life?

**Write the letter that best defines each term.**

1. _____ miracle

2. _____ manna

3. _____ Ten Commandments

4. _____ ark of the covenant

a. the laws of God's covenant given to Moses on Mount Sinai

b. an extraordinary event that is beyond human power and brought about by God

c. a wooden box in which the tablets of the Ten Commandments were kept

d. sweet bread-like food that God provided for the Israelites in the desert

e. a meeting tent that served as a movable place of worship

**Short Answers**

5. How did God demonstrate his faithfulness to his people on their journey to Mount Sinai?

_____

6. Why did the people need the Ten Commandments?

_____

7. List three things that the Israelites made for the "dwelling place" of God.

_____

8. How was God's presence made known to his people during their journey to the promised land?

_____

**Write a paragraph to answer this question.**

9–10. What does the story of the journey of God's people to the promised land tell us about our relationship with God?

On the Israelites' journey to the promised land, they went through many difficult situations. Imagine that you are one of the Israelites. Make a travel journal of your experiences that will be placed in a time capsule and shared with others in the future.

# We Respond in Faith

## Reflect & Pray

During the journey through the desert, the Israelites found it difficult to remain faithful to God. The next time I doubt God's loving action in my life, I will

_____

_____

## Remember

- Moses led God's people through the wilderness.

- God gave his people the law.

- The people built God a dwelling place.

- God led his people toward the promised land.

# OUR CATHOLIC LIFE

## Music and Song

We inherited some of our customs of worship from the Jewish people. Music and song are important parts of these customs. Miriam played a tambourine and danced for joy when the people gained their freedom. Jews often praise God with pipes and cymbals, trumpets and horns, lyres and harps. Today, we still celebrate with these instruments and many others. Organ, piano, drums, guitar—all can help us to "Sing to the LORD a new song" (Psalm 149:1).

We still sing the ancient Jewish psalms today, often in chant-like form. Gregorian chant is an ancient form of liturgical singing in Latin, and it has an honored place in our liturgy. You are probably more familiar with the many other musical styles we use in the liturgy. In our country, Latino music and spirituals of African-American origin are often used in the liturgy, as well as traditional music and songs from around the world.

# SHARING FAITH
## with My Family

## Sharing What I Learned

Discuss the following with your family:

- the journey to Mount Sinai
- miracles in the desert
- the Ten Commandments
- the ark of the covenant.

## Questions About Judaism

**Q:** What is the Torah?

**A:** In its narrowest sense, the Torah consists of the first five books of the Bible: Genesis, Exodus, Leviticus, Numbers, and Deuteronomy. In the broadest meaning of the word, the Torah is the entire body of Jewish law and teachings. The Jewish scriptures (the written Torah) are hand-written on parchment scrolls and kept in a large cabinet called an "ark." These scrolls are holy and out of reverence are not to be touched. Readers follow the text with a "Yad," a pointer often in the shape of a hand.

### MOSES AND THE TEN COMMANDMENTS

Who is Moses?

_____

_____

What are the Ten Commandments?

_____

_____

How does following the Ten Commandments help your family?

_____

_____

## We Believe Trading Cards

Complete the facts on the back of the trading card. Then share with your family what you have learned about the story of Moses and the Ten Commandments.

**Connect to the Catechism**
For adult background and reflection, see paragraphs 1334, 2057, 2578, and 697.

# A Conquering People

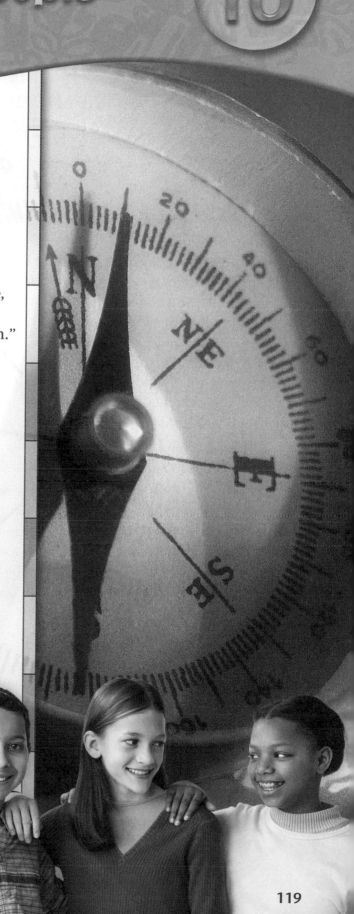

## ✝ We Gather in Prayer

**Leader:** Blessed be our God who has shown his people great love. Blessed be God for ever.

**All:** Blessed be God for ever.

**Reader 1:** "'Give thanks to the LORD who is good,
whose love endures forever!'
Let that be the prayer of the LORD's redeemed,
those redeemed from the hand of the foe,
Those gathered from foreign lands,
from east and west, from north and south."

**Reader 2:** "Some had lost their way in a barren desert;
found no path toward a city to live in.
They were hungry and thirsty;
their life was ebbing away."

**Reader 3:** "In their distress they cried to the LORD,
who rescued them in their peril,
Guided them by a direct path
so they reached a city to live in."

**Reader 4:** "Let them thank the LORD for such kindness,
such wondrous deeds for mere mortals.
For he satisfied the thirsty,
filled the hungry with good things."

(Psalm 107:1–9)

**Leader:** Let us pray that all cities
and towns, may be true cities of God.

## 🎵 City of God

O comfort my people; make gentle your words.
Proclaim to my city the day of her birth.

Refrain:

Let us build the city of God.
May our tears be turned into dancing!
For the Lord, our light and our love,
has turned the night into day!

# God's people conquered Canaan.

## WE GATHER

✝ *Lord, you alone are our God.*

Imagine that this year your class has moved to a different school building with the seventh and eighth graders. With a partner decide what you would tell the fifth graders to prepare them for their move up to the new school building next year.

## WE BELIEVE

The theme of the Book of Deuteronomy, the fifth book of the Bible, is that God's people must love God and be obedient to him when they enter into and live in the promised land. In Deuteronomy Moses not only said farewell to God's people, but passed his wisdom on to them. Moses told the people: "Hear, O Israel! The LORD is our God, the LORD alone! Therefore, you shall love the LORD, your God, with all your heart, and with all your soul, and with all your strength" (Deuteronomy 6:4–5). These words of Moses became an important prayer which is known as the Shema.

Moses told the Israelites, "Take to heart these words which I enjoin on you today. Drill them into your children. Speak of them at home and abroad, whether you are busy or at rest. Bind them at your wrist as a sign and let them be as a pendant on your forehead. Write them on the doorposts of your houses and on your gates" (Deuteronomy 6:6–9).

The Israelites followed Moses' instructions. And through the ages, the Jewish people have continued to make this prayer a part of their everyday lives. God's covenant relationship with the Jewish people remains strong today.

Ancient ram's horn

**Bringing the People into Canaan** As the Book of Deuteronomy ends, we learn that Moses saw the promised land from a mountain top but did not live to enter it.

We read in the beginning of the Book of Joshua, the sixth book of the Bible, that God called Joshua to bring the Israelites into their own land. God said to Joshua, "My servant Moses is dead. So prepare to cross the Jordan here, with all the people, into the land I will give the Israelites . . . I command you: be firm and steadfast! Do not fear nor be dismayed, for the LORD, your God, is with you wherever you go" (Joshua 1:2, 9).

The Book of Joshua deals with the Israelites' entry into Canaan. The details are greatly simplified, and the account of conquering and entering Canaan is relatively short. The Book of Joshua is not a day-by-day account of events, but rather the biblical writer's interpretation of the religious significance of these events. According to this book, the Israelites sometimes had to struggle with the Canaanites. In Chapters 1—6 of the Book of Joshua, we find one very famous event in the conquest of Canaan—the fall of Jericho.

**The Fall of Jericho**   Jericho was a well-known city in the center of Canaan, about twenty-three miles northeast of Jerusalem. What was so unusual about this event was the way in which the city was captured. The Israelites did not act like any other army. They did not attempt to batter down the city's walls with special machines. They did not attack the people who were defending the city. And they did not defeat the city's army in battle. Instead, the Israelites followed God's instructions and carried out an unusual plan outside the city walls.

Here is the story of the fall of Jericho.

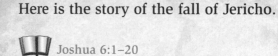 Joshua 6:1–20

God told Joshua not to attack the city directly but to march around it with his troops. Joshua had his troops do all that God commanded him. They carried the ark of the covenant before them. Seven priests using rams' horns as trumpets led the march. Joshua and his troops did this for six days. On the seventh day they marched around the city seven times. Then the priests blew their horns, and the Israelites shouted loudly. And the walls of Jericho fell down! Then Joshua and the Israelites took over the city of Jericho.

What do you think Joshua thought when he heard God's instructions about Jericho? What would you have thought?

The Israelites conquered this city because they followed the plan of God. In the story God was pictured as a kind of divine warrior who fought on the side of his people and who would bring them victory only if they obeyed him. Even though Joshua was the military leader, it was God who was the real hero in the capture of Jericho. The biblical writer used this story to show that the Israelites believed that God was with them in every part of their lives.

## WE RESPOND

The Book of Joshua emphasizes that God is with his people. Write and illustrate a story that will tell others that God is with them in every part of their lives. Plan your story here.

# God's people settled in Canaan.

## WE GATHER

✝ *Loving God, help us to see your plan for us.*

✗ In groups, discuss the different types of decisions people your age have to make at home, among friends, and at school. List some ways that you decide how to make these decisions.

_____

_____

_____

_____

## WE BELIEVE

After the Israelites conquered Canaan, the land was distributed among the twelve tribes of Israel. These tribes were the descendants of the twelve sons of Jacob, or Israel. The land was parceled out to each tribe by casting lots. The Hebrews often made decisions by following the ancient practice of casting lots. Lots were coins, sets of specially marked stones, or sticks wrapped in paper. Before the lots were cast, or thrown down, rules about the lots were agreed upon. The rules stated what the lots or the various positions of the lots would represent. The people believed that the outcome of the lots was an expression of God's will.

In the Book of Joshua the biblical writer used the casting of lots to show us that God alone was responsible for the distribution of the land. The land was a gift from God rather than a reward or a human achievement. The Israelites believed that no one except God could ever take the land away from them.

Once the land had been distributed, the tribes met at Shechem, a religious shrine in central Canaan. Here they thanked God for the great blessings he had bestowed on them and renewed their covenant with him. As soon as the ceremonies at Shechem were completed, the Israelites began to settle in Canaan. The story of their settlement in Canaan, which lasted for almost 200 years, can be found in the Book of Judges, the seventh book of the Bible.

As in the Book of Joshua, the biblical writer of the Book of Judges recorded events in a way that helped readers to understand important religious truths. In particular, the writer called attention to the following pattern:

- The Israelites turned away from the one true God and began to worship false gods.

- God allowed other tribes and nations to rule over the Israelites.

- The Israelites cried out to God for help.

- God remembered his covenant and sent a deliverer, in this case a judge, to save the Israelites. This judge was not an officer of the court as in modern times. However, he or she was often a military leader.

- The judge defeated the enemy, often in a great battle, and ruled the land as God directed. Only then did peace return.

This pattern was repeated over and over again during the time of the judges.

**Deborah, the Judge** One of the first judges the biblical writer described was Deborah. She was one of the great women of the Old Testament. God chose Deborah to remind the Israelites to keep the covenant. She settled legal disputes and offered advice to the people. "She used to sit under Deborah's palm tree, situated between Ramah and Bethel in the mountain region of Ephraim, and there the Israelites came up to her for judgment." (Judges 4:5)

During Deborah's lifetime the Israelites once again began to worship false gods. Due to this failure on their part, Israelite territory was taken over by a Canaanite king and his general. Deborah called on the Israelite commander Barak. Barak had been battling unsuccessfully against the Canaanite general. Deborah ordered Barak to call his troops together at Mount Tabor in the north. She told him that God would give the Israelites a great victory there.

Bible engraving of Deborah, by Gustave Dore, France

Barak doubted Deborah, but she insisted. Barak told Deborah that he would follow her order as long as she accompanied him and his army to Mount Tabor. So Deborah went with Barak and the army to meet the army of the Canaanites at Mount Tabor. God sent a great thunderstorm that caused the chariots of the Canaanites to get stuck in the mud, and they were defeated. Through God's actions and Deborah's firm faith in him, the land was again free of enemies. And Deborah prayed a great hymn, a canticle, in praise of God.

Here is the ending of the Canticle of Deborah: "May all your enemies perish thus, O LORD! but your friends be as the sun rising in its might!" (Judges 5:31).

## WE RESPOND

There are people in our lives who help us to stay focused on loving God and one another. Who are some of these people in your life? How do they help you? Let them know that you appreciate all they do for you.

# Samson was the most famous judge.

## WE GATHER

✝ *Loving God, give us the strength to do your will.*

What are the gifts and talents that people sometimes call their strengths?

How do you use your strengths to help others?

## WE BELIEVE

Even though the Israelites had won at Mount Tabor, they again turned from God. Some of God's people found themselves under the rule of the Philistines, who were their enemies. So God sent a special judge to his people. This judge was the only one whose birth was foretold in a very extraordinary way.

An angel of the Lord appeared to a woman in Zorah who had been unable to have any children. The angel said, "Though you are barren and have had no children, yet you will conceive and bear a son" (Judges 13:3). This woman was also told "As for the son you will conceive and bear, no razor shall touch his head, for this boy is to be consecrated to God from the womb. It is he who will begin the deliverance of Israel from the power of the Philistines" (Judges 13:5).

When the baby was born he was given the name Samson. Samson was blessed by God with great strength. Throughout his life Samson was a **Nazirite**, a person consecrated to God. As a Nazirite, Samson was supposed to keep special promises, or vows. He was not to drink wine or strong drink, touch anyone or anything that had died, or cut or shave his hair. The spirit of the Lord was with Samson. And as long as Samson kept his vows, God continued to make him strong.

Samson married a Philistine woman, but the Philistines mistreated him and his wife. So a very personal struggle began between Samson and the Philistines. The Philistines went so far as to kill Samson's wife and her family. Samson was enraged by this and took revenge on the Philistines. They began to fear Samson's strength and wanted to capture him. But they were not successful.

**Samson and Delilah**   Samson then fell in love with another Philistine woman, Delilah. Since the Philistine leaders still wanted to capture Samson, they paid Delilah to find out the secret of Samson's great strength.

At first Samson lied about the key to his strength. This made Delilah very angry. Samson became so afraid of losing her that he told her the truth. He told her that God gave him strength as long as he kept his Nazirite vows. If his hair was shaved, he would no longer have his great strength.

So while Samson was asleep, Delilah had a man shave off Samson's hair. Then she called in the waiting Philistines who blinded Samson. They then took Samson to a prison in one of their cities where they kept him chained and forced him to turn a great stone that ground grain.

While in prison, Samson's hair grew back. One day while the Philistines were having one of their religious festivals to the god of grain, they decided to bring Samson out to mock him. They placed Samson between two columns of their temple. Samson prayed and asked God to give him his strength once again. Then Samson pushed down the columns that were holding up the temple, killing himself and everyone else in it.

The story of Samson symbolized the Israelite nation of his time. Samson's birth, like the birth of Israel, was the result of God's guiding hand.

Samson was dedicated to God, and God was with him, just as God was with the Israelites. Yet instead of using his strength for God, Samson used his strength to take revenge on those who had personally hurt him. But God turned Samson's defeat into the beginning of the downfall of the Philistines. God again allowed the Israelites to be victorious against those who tried to defeat them.

## As Catholics...

The vows of a Nazirite play a large part in the story of Samson. Vows are serious promises that people make to God or to each other. The purpose of a vow is usually to help the person who makes the vow to live a life of holiness. For example, during the sacrament of Matrimony a man and a woman promise to love and honor each other. Similarly, women and men in religious life take vows of chastity, poverty, and obedience. In both cases, the vows help those who make them to focus on living lives dedicated to God and others.

Do you know anyone who has taken vows?

## WE RESPOND

Being strong is more than having physical strength. God makes us strong by sharing his life and love with us. What are some ways God does this in our lives?

Write a sentence using each letter of the word *strong* to tell how God shares his life and love with us.

_____ S _____

_____ T _____

In **Reconciliation** we receive God's forgiveness.

_____ O _____

_____ N _____

_____ G _____

# Ruth lived a life of self-sacrifice.

## WE GATHER

✝ *God, we are your faithful people.*

🧍 In a small group brainstorm synonyms for the word *faithful*. List some synonyms.

_____

_____

_____

_____

_____

_____

Discuss some ways people are faithful.

## WE BELIEVE

The Book of Ruth is the eighth book of the Bible. It is one of the Bible's most beautiful short stories. The biblical writer shows God's presence in the events of daily life. Even though it is only a few pages long, the story of Ruth teaches us that even in difficult times people can faithfully live out the covenant. They can be good, loyal, and kind. They can follow God's will for them.

The story begins in a time of famine in Israel. An Israelite named Elimelech, his wife Naomi, and their two sons needed to find food. So they traveled eastward from Bethlehem of Judah and crossed the Jordan River into Moab, where people did not believe in the one true God. Elimelech's family settled in Moab because there was no famine there.

Sometime after that, Elimelech died, and each of his sons married a Moabite woman. Then the unexpected happened: the two sons also died. This left Naomi and her daughters-in-law, Orpah and Ruth, sad and in financial trouble. They had no money and Naomi had no relatives in Moab who could help them.

Naomi decided to go back to her homeland. Naomi told her daughters-in-law that they should go back to their own mothers' houses. She prayed that they would marry again and have homes of their own. But Ruth refused to leave her mother-in-law. She said, "Do not ask me to abandon or forsake you! for wherever you go I will go, wherever you lodge I will lodge, your people shall be my people, and your God my God" (Ruth 1:16). Ruth's loyalty and her acceptance of the God of Israel impressed Naomi. The two women went together to Bethlehem.

**Wherever You Go**

Wherever you go I shall go.
Wherever you live so shall I live.
Your people will be my people,
and your God will be my God, too.

When it was time for the harvest, Ruth went into a field to gather up grain left behind from the harvest. People without money were allowed to do this, and Ruth needed to feed Naomi and herself. Boaz, who owned the field, noticed her. Boaz was a relative of Naomi's deceased husband, and he had been told about Ruth's devotion to Naomi. So Boaz told his servants to help and protect Ruth. He even shared some of his own food with her.

When Naomi heard this, she was overjoyed. She hoped that Boaz, as her relative by marriage, would claim some land that she was selling. If he did, then by the law of the Israelites, Boaz would also have the responsibility of taking Ruth as his wife.

Boaz did claim the land and married Ruth. God blessed Boaz and Ruth with a son, who was given the name Obed. "He was the father of Jesse, the father of David" (Ruth 4:17).

In the story of Ruth, the biblical writer shows us that sadness can be turned into joy. We learn that when we bring God's love to one another, God's will is accomplished by our actions. Like Naomi, Ruth, and Boaz, we are called to be part of God's plan by living lives of faithfulness and kindness.

## WE RESPOND

Imagine that you have been asked to produce a music CD about faithfulness. What would you name your CD? What songs would you include? Illustrate your CD cover.

## Review

**Write True or False for the following sentences.**
**Then change the false sentences to make them true.**

1. _____ The Israelites conquered the city of Jericho with special machines.

_____

2. _____ The land of Canaan was distributed to the twelve tribes of Israel by casting lots.

_____

3. _____ Delilah was chosen by God to remind the Israelites to keep God's covenant, settle legal disputes, and offer other advice.

_____

4. _____ During the times of the judges, the Israelites stayed faithful to the one true God.

_____

**Circle the letter of the correct answer.**

5. The book of _____ teaches that in difficult times people can live out the covenant.

   **a.** Deborah   **b.** Naomi   **c.** Ruth

6. A _____ was a person consecrated to God who promised vows.

   **a.** Nazirite   **b.** Philistine   **c.** Moabite

7. The book of _____ emphasizes God's role in the people's entry into the promised land.

   **a.** Joshua   **b.** Ruth   **c.** Judges

8. God blessed Samson with great _____.

   **a.** wisdom   **b.** strength   **c.** hair

**Write a paragraph to answer this question.**

**9–10.** How does the story of Samson symbolize the Israelite nation of his time?

ASSESSMENT

In what ways do the stories of Joshua, Deborah, Samson, and Ruth symbolize our relationship to God? Design a poster that illustrates your ideas.

# We Respond in Faith

## Reflect & Pray

How can you show love for God in your daily life?

_____

_____

_____

Dear God, help us to show our love for you in what we do each day. Amen.

**Nazirite** (p. 125)

## Remember

- God's people conquered Canaan.
- God's people settled in Canaan.
- Samson was the most famous judge.
- Ruth lived a life of self-sacrifice.

## OUR CATHOLIC LIFE

### Saint Catherine of Siena

Catherine was born in 1347 in Siena, Italy. From a very young age she lived a life of prayer focused on Christ. Gradually, people began to realize that she had the gift of good judgment. People went to her when they had disputes within their families or among their neighbors. Catherine's influence spread throughout the Church. She was concerned about current events and politics, and she tried to help the Church as much as she could. She visited kings and queens and asked them to avoid war with one another and to be at peace with the Church. Her writings are some of the most brilliant in the Church. While in Rome working for peace in the Church, Catherine died at the age of thirty-three. Her feast day is April 29.

# SHARING FAITH
## with My Family

## Sharing What I Learned

Discuss the following with your family:

- Joshua and the fall of Jericho
- Deborah and the time of the judges
- Samson and the Philistines
- Ruth and Naomi.

## Questions About Judaism

**Q:** What is a mezuzah?

**A:** A mezuzah is a case attached to the doorposts of Jewish homes. It contains a small scroll with passages of scripture written on it. The command for the mezuzah comes from Deuteronomy 6:4–9, a passage referred to as the "Shema." The words of the Shema are written on the tiny parchment scroll. Every time a person passes through a door with a mezuzah on it, he or she touches the mezuzah and then kisses the fingers that touched it, expressing love and respect for God and his commandments.

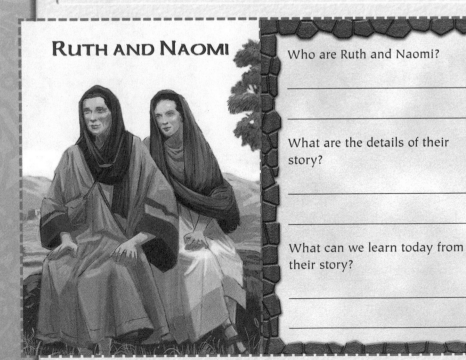

### RUTH AND NAOMI

Who are Ruth and Naomi?

_____

_____

What are the details of their story?

_____

_____

What can we learn today from their story?

_____

_____

## We Believe Trading Cards

Complete the facts on the back of the trading card. Then share with your family what you have learned about the story of Ruth and Naomi.

Visit Sadlier's
**www.WeBelieveweb.com**

**Connect to the Catechism**
For adult background and reflection, see paragraph 1611.

## 11

# A Royal People

## ✝ We Gather in Prayer

**Leader:** Jesus, you are the Good Shepherd. Help us to follow you in all that we say and do. Be with us as we pray.

**Reader 1:** "The LORD is my shepherd;
   there is nothing I lack.
   In green pastures you let me graze;
   to safe waters you lead me;
   you restore my strength."

**All:** Jesus, Good Shepherd, lead us in paths of peace.

**Reader 2:** "You guide me along the right path
   for the sake of your name.
   Even when I walk through a dark valley,
   I fear no harm for you are at my side;
   your rod and your staff give me courage."

**All:** Jesus, Good Shepherd, keep us from darkness and evil.

**Reader 3:** "You set a table before me
   as my enemies watch;
   You anoint my head with oil;
   my cup overflows."

**All:** Jesus, Good Shepherd, thank you for your Bread of Life.

**Reader 4:** "Only goodness and love will pursue me
   all the days of my life;
   I will dwell in the house of the LORD
   for years to come."
   (Psalm 23:1–6)

**All:** Jesus, Good Shepherd, show us your goodness and love!

## ♫ The King of Love My Shepherd Is

The King of love my shepherd is,
Whose goodness fails me never;
I nothing lack if I am his,
And he is mine forever.

Where streams of living water flow
With gentle care he leads me,
And where the verdant pastures grow,
With heav'nly food he feeds me.

# God called Samuel to serve him.

## WE GATHER

✝ *Speak Lord, we are listening.*

What are some events in the history of our country that are often retold?

_____

Why do you think we retell them?

_____

What can we learn from these stories?

_____

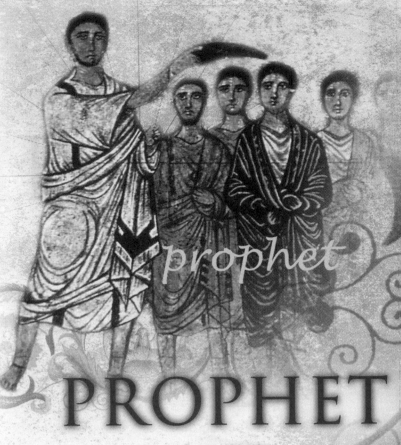

PROPHET

## WE BELIEVE

The Bible contains many literary forms, or types of writing used to get a message across. Whatever literary form the biblical writer uses, we get to know and encounter God through the events being retold.

As the events being recorded in Scripture changed, so did the literary forms. As Israel grew to become a nation, historical writing began. Historical writing gives an account of a historical event or period in history. The First and Second Books of Samuel, along with some other books in the Bible, represent Scripture's historical books. (See chart, page 27.)

As the First Book of Samuel opens, we read the prayer of a woman named Hannah. Hannah had no children and was praying for a son. She promised God that if he blessed her with a son, she would dedicate the child to God. Hannah did have a son, and she called him Samuel.

To thank God for the gift of her son, Hannah dedicated Samuel to God's service. Samuel was brought to the shrine at Shiloh, which is in central Israel. There he grew up under the watchful eye of an old priest named Eli.

When Samuel was still very young, God called to him while he was sleeping. At first Samuel thought Eli was calling him. However, after this happened three times, Eli realized that it was God who was calling Samuel. Eli told Samuel, "Go to sleep, and if you are called, reply, 'Speak, LORD, for your servant is listening'" (1 Samuel 3:9). When God called once more, Samuel answered him in the way Eli had instructed him. Then God spoke to Samuel and told him about the things that he, the Lord, would do.

God was with Samuel, and did not permit "any word of his to be without effect . . . The LORD continued to appear at Shiloh; he manifested himself to Samuel at Shiloh through his word, and Samuel spoke to all Israel" (1 Samuel 3:19, 21). Samuel became God's prophet. A **prophet** is someone who speaks on behalf of God, defends the truth, and works for justice.

**Key Word**

**prophet** someone who speaks on behalf of God, defends the truth, and works for justice

**Desperate Times** At this time the situation in Israel was desperate. Many people continued to turn away from God. Israel's enemy, the Philistines, took advantage of Israel's disunity and tried to conquer all of Israel. The Philistines were so successful that they threatened Israel's very existence. The Philistines took so much land from the tribe of Dan that the tribe was forced to find a new home elsewhere. The Philistines even captured the ark of the covenant and paraded it triumphantly through their towns. The ark of the covenant was only given back to the Israelites after those who kept it away from its rightful home experienced terrible hardships.

Besides having enemies, the Israelites were themselves in a state of chaos. For example, the tribe of Benjamin refused to acknowledge that some of their men were criminals and so a civil war broke out. The tribe of Benjamin was almost destroyed.

Worse yet, God himself seemed to have abandoned his people. In the last verse of the Book of Judges we read, "In those days there was no king in Israel; everyone did what he thought best" (Judges 21:25). The biblical writer meant that God, who was considered to be the only king of Israel at this time, did not seem to be with the people.

It was during this time that Samuel was called to gradually take over the leadership of Israel. He brought the ark of the covenant back to a proper resting place. And Samuel offered sacrifice to God, praying for Israel's victory over the Philistines. Indeed, God would never abandon his people. His love for them would never end.

prophet

PROPHET

## WE RESPOND

We are called to love and serve God in different ways. What do you think God is calling you to do? What can you do to answer God's call now and in the future?

# Saul became Israel's first king.

## WE GATHER

 *Lord, help us lead others to you.*

In a small group discuss the reasons why we need leaders. List some characteristics of a good leader.

_____

_____

## WE BELIEVE

As Samuel grew older, the Israelites cried out to him for a king. They wanted someone to lead and protect them from their enemies.

For about two hundred years, the twelve tribes of Israel had lived in Canaan. Israel's only king had been the Lord. As God's servants the judges protected the Israelites and led them in loving, obeying, and worshiping God. Now the people wanted to be like other nations. They wanted to be a monarchy. A **monarchy** is a kingdom or empire ruled by one person, either a king or a queen.

At first Samuel was displeased that the people were asking for a king. He believed only God was Israel's king. Although God was also displeased, he told Samuel to let the people have their way. So Israel would now have an earthly king and would become a monarchy.

**The First King**   God revealed his choice of the new king to Samuel. Samuel was told by God to anoint Saul, from the tribe of Benjamin, to govern the people of Israel. This anointing would be a symbol of Saul's consecration to God's service. Samuel poured oil on Saul's head and kissed him. As he anointed Saul, Samuel said, "The LORD anoints you commander over his heritage. You are to govern the LORD's people Israel, and to save them from the grasp of their enemies roundabout" (1 Samuel 10:1). Saul became Israel's first king. In the presence of the Lord, the people rejoiced and celebrated.

God spoke to Saul through Samuel. At first Saul followed Samuel's advice and led the people in following God's law. As commander of the Israelite army, Saul won battles against the Philistines. The Israelites were happy that they had a king.

**monarchy**  a kingdom or empire ruled by one person, either a king or a queen

Gradually, however, Saul stopped listening to Samuel. He was more concerned with his own interests than those of God's people. Saul began to act on his own, and once he even told his army to stop fighting. This error allowed the Philistines time to regroup, and Israel lost the battle.

As a result of Saul's actions, he no longer ruled with God's blessing. God said to Samuel, "I regret having made Saul king, for he has turned from me and has not kept my command" (1 Samuel 15:11). Therefore God would choose another king. Because God was displeased with Saul, none of Saul's sons would succeed him as king.

Imagine that you have traveled back in time and find yourself living during Saul's reign. You are able to give him advice about being king. What would you tell Saul? With a partner, role-play this scene.

### WE RESPOND

Take a moment to listen quietly to God. What is he saying to you today? How will you follow him?

135

# God chose David to lead Israel.

## WE GATHER

✝ *Thank you God, for loving me for who I am.*

👤 What does the expression "You cannot judge a book by its cover" mean to you? Give some examples that illustrate this expression.

## WE BELIEVE

The story of the way God chose Israel's second king is told in Chapter 16 of the First Book of Samuel. God sent Samuel to a man named Jesse who lived in Bethlehem. God told Samuel that he had chosen the next king from among Jesse's sons. So Samuel went to Bethlehem and offered sacrifice there. Then he invited Jesse and his family to the feast that followed the sacrifice.

Jesse and seven of his sons entered the feast, and each of these sons was presented to Samuel. Samuel thought that surely one of these would be the new king. But none of these were acceptable to God. God said to Samuel, "Not as man sees does God see, because man sees the appearance but the LORD looks into the heart" (1 Samuel 16:7).

Then Samuel asked Jesse whether he had any more sons. Jesse told him that he had one more son, David. David was the youngest and was in the fields tending the sheep. Samuel told Jesse to send for David.

David came before Samuel, "then Samuel, with the horn of oil in hand, anointed him in the midst of his brothers; and from that day on, the spirit of the LORD rushed upon David" (1 Samuel 16:13). God had chosen David to eventually replace Saul as Israel's king.

Meanwhile, the spirit of the Lord had left Saul, and he was tormented. So his servants told him about Jesse's son, David, who played the harp. Saul called for David. David played the harp, and his music soothed Saul's spirit. Soon after this, David entered into Saul's service.

**David and Goliath**   Around this time the Philistines were again trying to overcome the Israelites. The Philistine army was gathered on a hill in Judah, and the Israelite army was on a neighboring hill. The Israelites, however, were afraid to attack because the Philistine army was led by a giant of a man named Goliath. Goliath was much taller than all the other men and wore heavy bronze armor. His spear and shield were too heavy for most men to lift. Every day Goliath walked along the valley between the two hills shouting insults at the Israelites and challenging them to come and fight him. But no one accepted Goliath's challenge.

David's three oldest brothers were among the soldiers in the Israelite army. David himself was too young to be in the army. One day Jesse sent David with supplies for his brothers. As David entered the Israelite camp, Goliath began to shout his usual insults. When the Israelites saw Goliath, they fled. David asked, "What will be done for the man who kills this Philistine and frees Israel of the disgrace?" (1 Samuel 17:26).

David's words were reported to Saul, who sent for David. When David arrived, he assured King Saul that he was prepared to fight Goliath. Saul said that David was too young. But David told him that he had often killed a lion or bear when protecting his father's sheep. David said, "The Lord, who delivered me from the claws of the lion and the bear, will also keep me safe from the clutches of this Philistine" (1 Samuel 17:37). Saul then agreed to let David fight Goliath.

When David answered Goliath's challenge, Goliath took one look at him and cursed him. David, however, told Goliath that he came against him in the name of the God of the armies of Israel. David took a smooth stone from his knapsack, put it in his sling, and hurled the stone at Goliath. The stone hit Goliath in the forehead with such force that it knocked him down, and David was able to kill Goliath. When the Philistines saw their leader fall, they ran away. God had indeed saved David and the rest of Israel!

Unlike Saul, David relied on the Lord completely. David's courage came from trusting in God. His faithfulness and military skill would be very important when he became king.

🏃 In groups dramatize a TV news segment in which David, Goliath, and Saul are interviewed about the upcoming battle between David and Goliath. Ask each of them the following questions:

- What happened here?

- What is your role in this event?

- What do you think will happen next?

### WE RESPOND

What can you learn from the events in the lives of Saul, David, and Goliath?

# David was declared the king of Israel.

✝ *God, guide the leaders of the world.*

Name a person you consider to be successful. What qualities does this person have that led to his or her success?

## WE BELIEVE

David was from the tribe of Judah, which was a large southern tribe of Israel. After the death of Saul, the people of Judah proclaimed David as their king. Meanwhile, the rest of Israel accepted one of Saul's sons as their king. Saul's son, however, was weak and soon lost his title. Then the elders of the tribes went to David and agreed to make him the king over all of Israel. In around 1000 B.C. David was declared king of Israel by all of the people.

Michaelangelo (1475–1564), *David*

From events we read about in the Bible, David seemed to be an extremely energetic man. He immediately set out to solve Israel's problems. As soon as he became king, he began to plan his attack against the Philistines, the Israelites' main enemy. A born warrior, David soon drove the Philistines from central Israel once and for all. In later battles David forced them out of the rest of the country. He even captured large parts of the Philistines' territory for Israel.

Having conquered the Philistines, David dealt with another important task: taking over the areas in Israel that were still under Canaanite control. In a series of short battles, David captured most of these areas. The rest of the Canaanites simply surrendered to him. As a result, the Israelite takeover of Canaan, begun centuries before under Joshua, was finally completed. Israel became a nation united.

One of the Canaanite cities that David conquered was Jerusalem. The city became the king's private property because he had captured it with his own soldiers. Thus, in biblical writings Jerusalem became known as the City of David.

**The City of David** David decided to make Jerusalem the capital of all Israel. All the tribes agreed with David's choice because the city was centrally located and was not part of any territory that belonged to the tribes. Jerusalem was to be both the political and religious capital of all of Israel. David brought the ark of the covenant to Jerusalem. As it was brought into the city, David " . . . came dancing before the LORD with abandon, as he and all the Israelites were bringing up the ark of the LORD with shouts of joy and to the sound of the horn" (2 Samuel 6:14–15).

David also set up a government in Jerusalem. He appointed royal officials to run the country. However, he did not burden the people with new taxes. This won him great support from the people.

As a leader, David proved to be brilliant. He was full of ideas. God was with David. Under David's guidance Israel was transformed from a group of weak and disunited tribes into a strong kingdom. And through everything God was present in the lives of the people and in the life of the nation.

Throughout his years, David had been a shepherd, a storyteller, a poet, a musician, a warrior, and a great king. Although David was the greatest king of Israel, he also had weaknesses.

David's love for a beautiful woman named Bathsheba led him to displease God. Bathsheba was the wife of Uriah, one of David's army officers. David wanted to marry Bathsheba, but she was already married. So David arranged to have her husband killed in battle.

The prophet Nathan told David that Uriah's murder had displeased God. And David asked God's forgiveness saying, "I have sinned against the LORD" (2 Samuel 12:13). Then David, who was truly sorry, prayed for God's forgiveness. He did penance before the Lord, and God forgave David.

Once again in learning about the events in the life of God's people, we learn of God's great mercy. God always forgives those who are sorry for their sins.

Complete this profile to describe why you think David is chosen for person of the year in 999 B.C. Then pretend you are person of the year. Design your own profile.

| **David** | _____ |
| Person of the Year 999 B.C. | (name) |
|  | Person of the Year A.D. _____ |
| Major Accomplishments | Major Accomplishments |
| _____ | _____ |
| _____ | _____ |
| Ways he showed love for God | Ways you showed love for God |
| _____ | _____ |
| _____ | _____ |
| Other interesting facts | Other interesting facts |
| _____ | _____ |
| _____ | _____ |

## WE RESPOND

How did David use his gifts and talents to give glory to God?

How can you use your gifts and talents to give glory to God this week?

**Write the letter that best identifies the biblical character.**

1. _____ Saul

2. _____ Samuel

3. _____ Hannah

4. _____ David

   **a.** prayed for a child whom she promised to dedicate to God

   **b.** a leader and prophet of God who felt that only God should be considered Israel's king

   **c.** the father of David

   **d.** the first anointed king of Israel

   **e.** the king of Israel who united and transformed the nation of Israel

## Short Answers

5. How did Israel's enemy, the Philistines, take advantage of Israel's disunity?

_____

6. What was used to symbolize the consecration of Saul to God's service?

_____

7. What is the importance of the story of David and Goliath?

_____

8. What happened to the nation of Israel during King David's rule?

_____

**Write a paragraph to answer this question.**

9–10. What meaning do these words have in the story of David?
"Not as man sees does God see, because man sees the appearance but the LORD looks into the heart." (1 Samuel 16:7)

**ASSESSMENT**

Think about the biblical stories of Samuel, Saul, and David. Write a modern version of their stories in the literary form of your choice. Present your versions to your class or family.

# We Respond in Faith

## Reflect & Pray

David was a great king. I would like to model my life on his life by

_____

_____

_____

_____

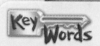

**Key Words**

**prophet** (p. 132)
**monarchy** (p. 134)

## Remember

- God called Samuel to serve him.
- Saul became Israel's first king.
- God chose David to lead Israel.
- David was declared the king of Israel.

## OUR CATHOLIC LIFE

### Spiritual Growth

Ignatius Loyola was a courageous and adventurous Spanish soldier who lived during the sixteenth century. Once in a battle his leg was badly broken. During his long recovery the only book he had to read was one on the lives of the saints. Ignatius realized that, like the saints, he could be courageous and adventurous for Christ. He eventually became a priest. He founded the Society of Jesus, also known as Jesuits, to help serve Christ and the Church.

Ignatius also wrote a book called *The Spiritual Exercises*. It is a training manual for spiritual growth, and people everywhere have used it to become more like Christ. His book includes these important questions: "What have I done for Christ? What am I doing for Christ? What am I going to do for Christ?" We honor Saint Ignatius Loyola on his feast day, July 31.

# SHARING FAITH
## with My Family

## Sharing What I Learned

Discuss the following with your family:

- Samuel, God's prophet
- the Israelites' need for a king
- Saul, David, and Goliath
- David as king of Israel.

*prophet*

## Questions About Judaism

**Q:** What are Rosh Hashanah and Yom Kippur?

**A:** Rosh Hashanah is commonly known as the Jewish New Year. It is a time to begin to look back at the mistakes of the past year and plan the changes that are needed in the new year. This week-long celebration ends with Yom Kippur, the day of atonement. This is a day set aside to atone for the sins of the past year. It is the chance to demonstrate repentance, to show sorrow, and restore relationships with others.

### DAVID AND GOLIATH

Who are David and Goliath?

_____

_____

What is their story?

_____

_____

How can we learn today from their story?

_____

_____

## We Believe Trading Cards

Complete the facts on the back of the trading card. Then share with your family what you have learned about the story of David and Goliath.

Visit Sadlier's

**www.WEBELIEVEweb.com**

**Connect to the Catechism**
For adult background and reflection, see paragraphs 2578, 1150, 2579, and 695.

# A Prosperous People

## 12

## ✝ We Gather in Prayer

**Leader:** Jesus called the apostle James a "son of thunder" because of his quick temper! But James became a wise man and taught the meaning of wisdom. Let us listen to his words.

**Reader:** A reading from the Letter of James

"Who among you is wise and understanding? Let him show his works by a good life in the humility that comes from wisdom. . . . But the wisdom from above is first of all pure, then peaceable, gentle, compliant, full of mercy and good fruits, without inconstancy or insincerity. And the fruit of righteousness is sown in peace for those who cultivate peace." (James 3:13, 17–18)

The word of the Lord.

**All:** Thanks be to God.

**Leader:** Let us pray for wisdom in our lives and in the lives of all people. We will respond, "Lord, hear our prayer."

**Reader:** For the wisdom to follow the path of goodness,

For the wisdom to be gentle and peaceful with others,

For the wisdom to care for the earth and its creatures,

For the wisdom to be merciful toward those in need,

For the wisdom to be faithful and sincere with our friends,

For the wisdom to include and not exclude others,

For the wisdom to walk the way of peace and righteousness,

**Leader:** We ask this in your name, Lord Jesus.

**All:** Amen.

# Solomon's reign was a time of peace and prosperity.

## WE GATHER

✝ *Christ, help us bring your peace to others.*

Who are some peacemakers you know or know about? How do they work for peace?

## WE BELIEVE

After forty years as king, David died and was buried in Jerusalem, the City of David. David's son Solomon succeeded him as king. Under Solomon's rule Israel achieved its greatest peace and prosperity. The story of Solomon's reign as king, which lasted for about forty years, is told in the first eleven chapters of the First Book of Kings and in the first nine chapters of the Second Book of Chronicles.

Solomon did not rule the way his father had. While David was remembered chiefly as a mighty warrior, Solomon was a diplomat.

Solomon's reign was a time of peace. Unlike his father, Solomon did not wage any wars. Rather, he made treaties, or agreements, with other kings and queens. These alliances kept Israel safe from attack and gave the country new business opportunities.

Solomon helped Israel to prosper by his success in overseas trade. During Solomon's time as king, Israel was richer than it had ever been before. For the first time in Israel's history, some of the common people—not just the powerful—began to enjoy a life of plenty.

To showcase Israel's power and success, Solomon began a great building program. This program was designed to strengthen the country's defenses and to beautify its cities, especially Jerusalem.

16th century depiction of the prosperity of Solomon's time.
*Solomon with the Treasure of the Temple*, Frans Francken II, Flemish, (1581–1642)

The most important of these building projects involved the construction of the Temple in Jerusalem. Other projects included a magnificent palace for the king and another residence for the daughter of the Egyptian pharaoh, whom Solomon married.

With the new emphasis on building, many forms of art began to flourish in Israel. Among the most important were ivory carving, carpentry, stonework, and jewelry making.

Literature was also very important during Solomon's reign. During this time the historical books of the Bible began to be written and compiled. Psalms, proverbs, and other kinds of poetry were also written. In fact, the first steps toward assembling the Bible were taken when Solomon was king.

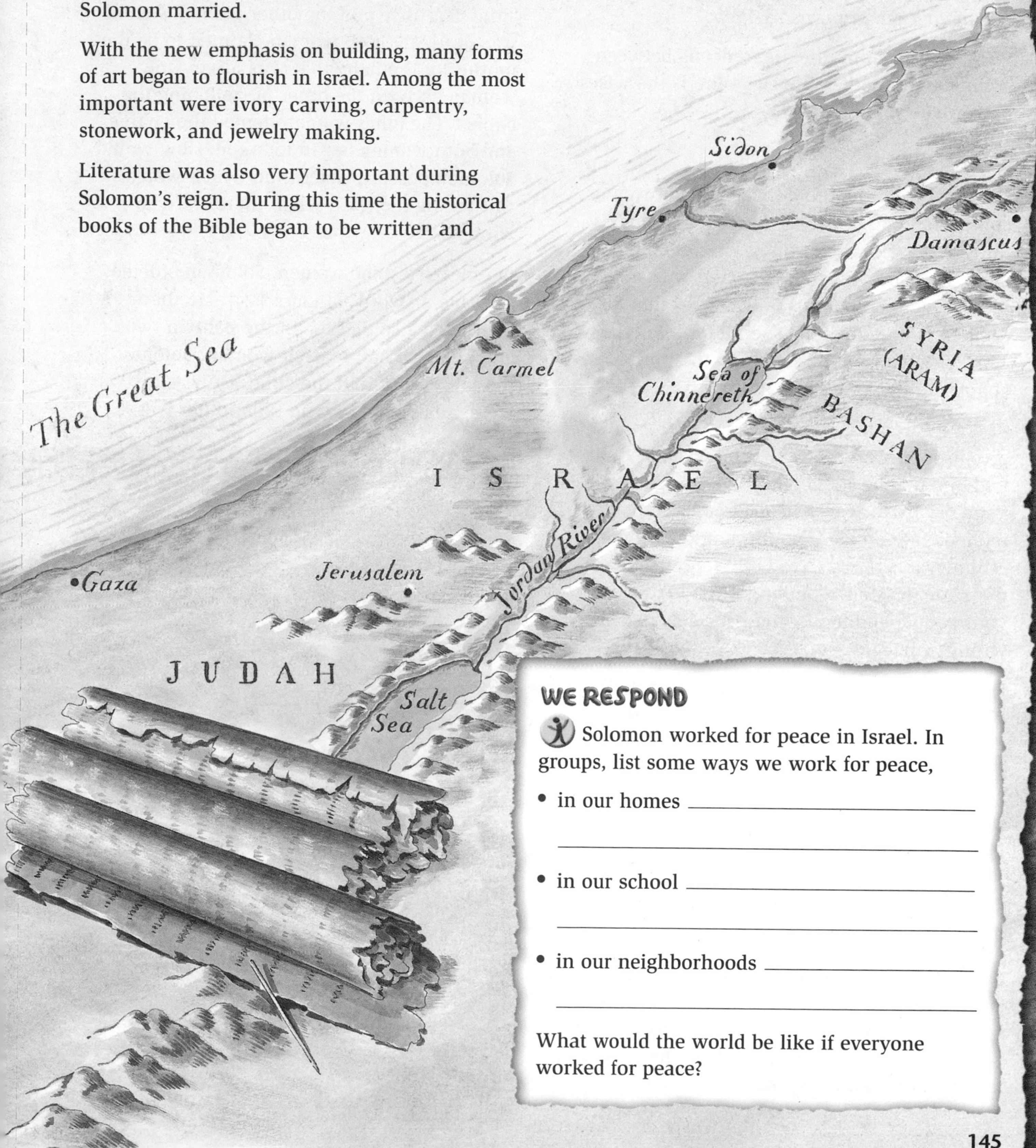

*The Great Sea*

*Sidon*

*Tyre*

*Damascus*

*Mt. Carmel*

*Sea of Chinnereth*

*SYRIA (ARAM)*

*BASHAN*

*ISRAEL*

*Jordan River*

*Gaza*

*Jerusalem*

*JUDAH*

*Salt Sea*

## WE RESPOND

Solomon worked for peace in Israel. In groups, list some ways we work for peace,

- in our homes _____

  _____

- in our school _____

  _____

- in our neighborhoods _____

  _____

What would the world be like if everyone worked for peace?

145

## Solomon gained fame for his wisdom.

### WE GATHER

✝ *Loving God, grant us wisdom.*

What do you think the difference is between being smart and being wise? Who is the wisest person you know?

### WE BELIEVE

We learn from the Bible that Solomon was considered one of the wisest people of his time. When he was a young king, Solomon prayed to God for guidance. God was so pleased with Solomon's faithfulness that he decided to do something special for him. The story of what God did is told in the third chapter of the First Book of Kings.

God appeared to Solomon in a dream and promised him anything that he wished. God told him that he could have riches or power or fame or anything else he desired. Solomon replied, "I am a mere youth, not knowing at all how to act. . . . Give your servant, therefore, an understanding heart to judge your people and to distinguish right from wrong" (1 Kings 3:7, 9).

Delighted by Solomon's reply, God said: "I give you a heart so wise and understanding that there has never been anyone like you up to now, and after you there will come no one to equal you" (1 Kings 3:12). God also promised to give Solomon riches and glory, for which Solomon had not asked. Then God concluded, "And if you follow me by keeping my statutes and commandments, as your father David did, I will give you a long life" (1 Kings 3:14).

Solomon was so grateful that he went to Jerusalem and stood before the ark of the covenant of the Lord. There he offered sacrifice and peace offerings. Then he gave a banquet for all his servants.

**Solomon's Wisdom** Soon after God granted Solomon wisdom, it was tested by a real-life event. Two women, each having had a child recently, came to Solomon. One woman's child was alive and the other woman's child was dead. Yet both women claimed to be the mother of the baby that was alive. One woman accused the other of switching the babies. The other woman denied the charge, and both women began to argue. How would Solomon possibly determine which woman was telling the truth when there were no witnesses?

In order to test the women, Solomon ordered, "Get me a sword" (1 Kings 3:24). He then instructed a soldier to cut the baby in two and give one half to each woman. Solomon did not want to kill the child. He was just trying to determine who the mother was.

The mother who truly gave birth to this baby pleaded with Solomon not to kill the child but to give the child to the other woman. The mother who had lied told the soldier to divide the child as Solomon had commanded.

Then Solomon ordered the baby to be given to the woman who had pleaded for its life. He saw that she was clearly the mother. All Israel was amazed by Solomon's ability to determine the truth in this case. In fact, they saw God's own wisdom behind Solomon's decision.

Solomon's story helps us understand the importance of wisdom. Wisdom is a gift from God. **Wisdom** is the knowledge and ability to recognize and follow God's will in our lives.

**wisdom** the knowledge and ability to recognize and follow God's will in our lives

It enables us to see as God sees and to act as God wants us to act. We need God's gift of wisdom to live a good life and to be faithful to our covenant with God.

## As Catholics...

God the Holy Spirit is our guide and helper, our advocate who acts on our behalf. The Holy Spirit is always close to us, and we can turn to the Holy Spirit for comfort and guidance. The Holy Spirit strengthens us to live as Christ's disciples and shares seven spiritual gifts with us. The gifts of the Holy Spirit are wisdom, understanding, right judgment, courage, knowledge, reverence, and wonder and awe. In the sacrament of Confirmation, we receive the gifts of the Holy Spirit in a special way. These gifts help us to follow Christ's teachings and to give witness to our faith.

What is one gift of the Holy Spirit that you would ask for right now?

## WE RESPOND

Wisdom is one of the gifts of the Holy Spirit. It helps us to see and follow God's plan for us. Identify some situations in which people call upon God for wisdom.

_____

_____

_____

This week ask God for wisdom in everything you do.

# The Temple was built in Jerusalem.

### WE GATHER

✝ *Holy God, we glorify you.*

Name some national monuments and memorial buildings. Why are they important to people of our country? What meanings do they have for us?

### WE BELIEVE

To show his love for God and his desire to be faithful to the covenant, Solomon decided to build a great stone Temple in Jerusalem. This Temple was meant to be the center of worship of the one true God. It was meant to bind all the people to God and to Israel.

The Temple that Solomon built in Jerusalem was a large stone rectangle sitting on an even larger walled stone platform. To create the platform, thousands of workers flattened part of a hill just to the north of Jerusalem.

The Temple itself consisted of two main rooms: the sanctuary, or holy of holies, and the nave. The sanctuary, which was the innermost part of the Temple, was a small raised room reserved exclusively for God. Only the High Priest could enter the holy of holies.

**Temple Mount, Jerusalem**
**Many scholars believe this to be the site of ancient temples.**

The sanctuary contained the ark of the covenant which was protected by two huge statues of angels called *cherubim*. In the Old Testament cherubim appeared as God's attendants. They served as symbols of God's presence in the sanctuary, where God was believed to reside invisibly in the ark of the covenant.

The nave of the Temple was a larger room in front of the sanctuary. It contained a small altar for burning incense. The altar had golden candle holders and other sacred objects. The altar was richly decorated with cedar paneling and gold ornaments. A flight of steps and a doorway with a curtain across it led from the nave to the sanctuary.

On three sides of the sanctuary and nave, Solomon built a series of smaller rooms. These were used for storage or were reserved for the priests who worked in the Temple.

In front of the Temple stood the Court of the Priests. It contained a great altar designed for the offering of sacrifices of various kinds. Other equipment included a great bronze bowl in which the priests were to wash themselves before and after offering sacrifices to God.

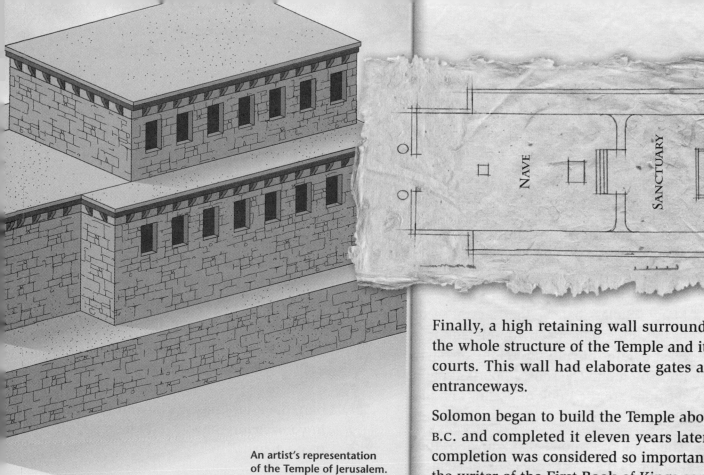

An artist's representation of the Temple of Jerusalem.

NAVE

SANCTUARY

Beyond the Court of the Priests, was a series of larger walled courts. These courts surrounded the entire Temple. One of them was reserved for male Israelites, one was designed for female Israelites, and one was for visitors who were not Israelites. Walls and columns separated each of these courts from one another.

Finally, a high retaining wall surrounded the whole structure of the Temple and its courts. This wall had elaborate gates and entranceways.

Solomon began to build the Temple about 968 B.C. and completed it eleven years later. Its completion was considered so important that the writer of the First Book of Kings compared it to the founding of the Israelite nation on Mount Sinai.

For the biblical writer the successful completion of the Temple symbolized God's permanent presence among his chosen people in the promised land. The building of the Temple in Jerusalem was Solomon's greatest achievement.

## WE RESPOND

Use the blueprint above to plan a sacred, or holy, space. Design this space in a way that people will feel God's presence there.

# The psalms teach us how to pray.

### WE GATHER

✝ *God, we will praise you all the days of our lives.*

How important is music in your life? What kinds of music do you like? Why?

### WE BELIEVE

Many scholars believe that several sections of the Bible have been completed, or at least begun, during the reigns of David and Solomon. The most important of these writings are the Book of Psalms and the Song of Songs.

The Book of Psalms, also known as the Psalter, is the great collection of Hebrew religious songs. A **psalm** is a poetic prayer designed to be sung or chanted to some kind of musical accompaniment. David is thought to have written many of the psalms. That would make sense because we know that David was a poet and a musician. Other psalms may have been composed by Solomon. And still others were written many centuries later.

As a Jew, Jesus prayed the psalms often. Today the psalms are still prayed by the Jewish people, and the psalms are also an important part of the liturgical life of all Christians. The psalms are intended for use in public worship. They help us to pray and to deepen our relationship with God.

The psalms are found in the Liturgy of the Hours, part of the official prayer of the Church, and in other prayer books. Psalms are found in the missals or song books that we use in church, and are prayed and sung during the celebration of Mass. The psalms are also a good guide to personal prayer. There are many kinds of psalms. They can be grouped most easily by content or mood. The most important groupings include:

- *Royal Psalms.* These psalms were composed to celebrate various occasions in the reign of a king—a coronation, a wedding, or a victory in battle. Examples include Psalms 2, 21, and 45.

"LORD, the king finds joy in your power;
in your victory how greatly he rejoices!"
(Psalm 21:2)

In Christian tradition the royal psalms are applied to Jesus because he was the Messiah, or Anointed One. For that reason we sometimes called them *messianic psalms.*

- *Hymns praising God and Zion.* These psalms seem to have been composed for use in public worship. They focus on God's power and mighty acts or on the glory of Zion. Zion is another name for the hill on which Jerusalem is built. Examples include Psalms 8, 47, and 84.

"God is king over all the earth;
sing hymns of praise." (Psalm 47:8)

**psalm** a poetic prayer designed to be sung or chanted to some kind of musical accompaniment

- *Laments*. This is the type of psalm that occurs most frequently in the Psalter. A lament is a poem or song expressing sorrow, mourning, or regret. Laments can come from individuals or whole communities. Examples include Psalms 13, 14, 67–71, 79, 106, 140–143.

"LORD, hear my prayer;
   in your faithfulness listen to my pleading;
   answer me in your justice." (Psalm 143:1)

- *Wisdom Poems*. These psalms are somewhat different in content and style from the other types of psalms. They are designed to teach rather than to encourage prayer. Examples include Psalms 1, 73, and 128.

"How good God is to the upright,
   the Lord, to those who are clean of heart!"
   (Psalm 73:1)

The Song of Songs is another important Old Testament book. It is traditionally said to have been composed by Solomon, but no one is exactly certain who wrote it. It is a collection of love poems. In the Song of Songs, the Lord is the one who loves, the Israelites are his beloved, and the covenant between them is described as their marriage. While the psalms contains some of the most beautiful religious songs ever written, the Song of Songs contains some of the most beautiful love poems ever written.

## WE RESPOND

### ♫ Psalm 122: Qué Alegría/ I Rejoiced

Refrain:
I rejoiced when I heard them say,
"Let us go to the house of the Lord.
Let us go to the house of the Lord."

I rejoiced when they said to me,
"We will go to the house of the Lord."
And now inside your gates we
   stand, Jerusalem,
we stand, Jerusalem. (Refrain)

Refrain:
Qué alegría cuando me dijeron:
"Vamos a la casa del Señor.
Vamos a la casa del Señor".

Qué alegría cuando me dijeron:
"Vamos a la casa del Señor".
Y ahora en tus portales
entramos ya, Jerusalén,
entramos ya, Jerusalén. (Refrain)

**Underline the correct answer.**

1. Under the rule of (**David/Solomon**) Israel achieved its greatest prosperity and peace in ancient times.

2. In a dream, Solomon asked God for (**glory/wisdom**) to help him rule the Israelites.

3. Solomon built (**a temple/a palace**) to show his love of God and desire to be faithful to the covenant.

4. The (**sanctuary/nave**) of the Temple contained the ark of the covenant.

**Choose a word(s) from the box to complete each sentence.**

| Hymns of God and Zion | Wisdom poems | Laments | Royal |

5. _____ Psalms were composed to celebrate various occasions in the reign of a king.

6. _____ are psalms designed to teach rather than to encourage prayer.

7. _____ are psalms that express sorrow, mourning, or regret.

8. _____ are psalms that focus on God's power or on the glory of Zion.

**Write a paragraph to answer this question.**

9–10. How does the story of Solomon help us to understand the importance of wisdom?

ASSESSMENT

Plan a presentation on King Solomon. Explain who Solomon was and the way he ruled Israel. Highlight important events and happenings during his reign. Describe what Israel, especially Jerusalem, was like during this time.

# We Respond in Faith

## Reflect & Pray

What are some times you praise God? When do you rely on God for help? When do you call out for his mercy?

Lord, help me to turn to you when

_____

_____

_____

## Remember

- Solomon's reign was a time of peace and prosperity.

- Solomon gained fame for his wisdom.

- The Temple was built in Jerusalem.

- The psalms teach us how to pray.

## OUR CATHOLIC LIFE

### House of Prayer

Every church, from the smallest parish to the largest cathedral, is a house of prayer and a holy place. We show our reverence for this sacred space in many ways. We appreciate the work of the architect who planned this church. We admire the work of artists and craftspeople who contributed to its beauty. We thank God for all the people who sacrificed in the past to build this house of prayer. We are grateful for those who take care of the interior of the church, the vestments, and altar vessels. We join with all those who celebrate together in this sacred place.

This week say a special prayer for all those who have prayed and worked together in your parish Church.

# SHARING FAITH
## with My Family

## Sharing What I Learned

Discuss the following with your family:

- Solomon
- peace and prosperity for Israel
- the Temple of Jerusalem
- types of psalms.

## Questions About Judaism

**Q:** What is a synagogue?

**A:** *Synagogue* is a Greek word meaning "a place of gathering for people." Modeled after the Temple of Jerusalem built by Solomon, a synagogue is the central institution of Jewish life in a community.

A synagogue is a Jewish house of prayer, a place of study, and a place for community gathering.

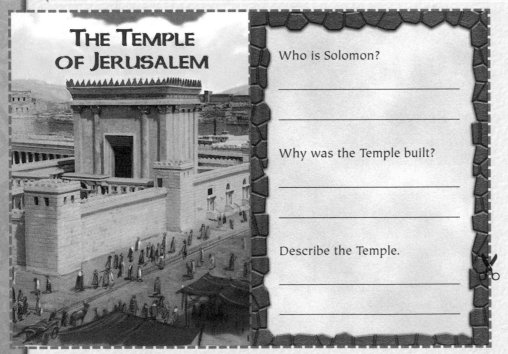

### THE TEMPLE OF JERUSALEM

Who is Solomon?

_____

_____

Why was the Temple built?

_____

_____

Describe the Temple.

_____

_____

## We Believe Trading Cards

Complete the facts on the back of the trading card. Then share with your family what you have learned about the Temple of Jerusalem.

Visit Sadlier's

**www.WeBelieveweb.com**

**Connect to the Catechism**
For adult background and reflection, see paragraphs 1831, 2580, and 2586.

# Advent

Advent | Christmas | Ordinary Time | Lent | Triduum | Easter | Ordinary Time

"Then the wolf shall be the guest of the lamb,
and the leopard shall lie down with the kid;
The calf and the young lion shall browse together,
with a little child to guide them."

Isaiah 11:6

155

# During Advent, the Church prepares for the celebration of Christmas.

## WE GATHER

✝ *Jesus, bring us peace as we prepare to celebrate your birth.*

What does the word *peace* mean to you? How would you describe peace in the world? in your neighborhood? in your school?

## WE BELIEVE

The season of Advent is a time of waiting and expectation. We are preparing, celebrating, and anticipating the coming of Christ into the world.

The word *Advent* means "coming," and the four weeks of Advent are a special time of joyous anticipation and preparation.

- We hope for Christ's coming in the future, and we prepare by being faithful to him and living in peace with one another.

- We celebrate Christ's presence in the world today. Jesus comes to us every day in the celebration of the Eucharist, in all the sacraments, and in the love we have for one another. His presence gives us hope and strengthens us to make the world a more just, peaceful place.

- We wait with joyful expectation to celebrate that the only Son of God first came into the world over two thousand years ago in the town of Bethlehem in Judea.

The color violet is a symbol of this waiting and joyful expectation. It also reminds us of the need for penance. During Advent the celebration of the sacrament of Reconciliation is an important way to prepare for the coming of Christ.

**The prophet Isaiah** The powerful voice of Isaiah the prophet rings out in many of our readings during the season of Advent. Isaiah expresses the longings of God's people as they wait for the savior God has promised to send. Isaiah assures them that the Messiah will come from among God's own people and that he will call the people to choose peace, not war. The Israelites believe that the Messiah will be a just king who will bring them freedom and peace.

During Advent and Christmas we hear the title Emmanuel. This, too, comes from the prophet Isaiah. In the Book of Isaiah we read of *Immanuel*, which is a Hebrew word meaning, "With us is God." Isaiah used this word as a name for the savior, and he described Immanuel this way:

"For a child is born to us, a son is given us;
    upon his shoulder dominion rests.
They name him Wonder-Counselor, God-Hero,
    Father-Forever, Prince of Peace" (Isaiah 9:5).

The Messiah Isaiah speaks of will have authority. He will be wise and prudent. He will act as a warrior and defender of the people, like God himself. And his Kingdom will be one of peace.

Christians believe that the savior, promised by God through his prophet Isaiah, has already come. We believe that Jesus Christ is the Messiah. He is our Emmanuel. He is the child and son born to us. Jesus Christ is God the Son who became one of us. He fulfills God's promises. He brings a message of love and respect for all of us, and he shows us how to do the same.

Isaiah used images to tell the people that the savior would come and call them to turn violence into peace. Some of those images are of a wolf as a guest of a lamb, a cow and a bear as neighbors, a lion eating hay like an ox, and a baby playing in safety by a cobra's den. In groups work to list some images that Isaiah might use today to get across this same message. Then illustrate one image.

**John the Baptist**   In the early weeks of Advent we hear the words of John the Baptist, often called a New Testament prophet. The writers of all four gospels describe John with words from the prophet Isaiah.

"A voice of one crying out in the desert:
　'Prepare the way of the Lord,
　　make straight his paths.'" (Mark 1:3)

John fulfills the words of Isaiah. He prepares the people for the coming of the Messiah. He preaches a message of repentance and conversion. He points out Jesus as the Messiah. John's greatest joy is proclaiming that Jesus is the Messiah, the hoped-for savior, "Behold, the Lamb of God, who takes away the sin of the world" (John 1:29).

We pray these words of John the Baptist at every Eucharist, before we receive the Body and Blood of Christ in Holy Communion. Jesus, the Savior of the world, is no longer a hope. He is truly "Emmanuel," truly God with us.

Isaiah the Prophet　　　　　Jesse Tree　　　　　John the Baptist

157

**The Jesse Tree** The Jesse Tree is a symbolic way of presenting the story of God's love and action in the lives of his people throughout the centuries. The name comes from Scripture:

> "But a shoot shall sprout from the
> stump of Jesse,
> and from his roots a bud shall
> blossom" (Isaiah 11:1).

The Jesse Tree is a way to connect the season of Advent to God's faithfulness to his people for over four thousand years. God promises Israel that the glory they had during King David's rule will be theirs again. There will be another king from David's family. Jesus was "of the house and family of David." The Jesse Tree is like a family tree that shows Jesus' ancestry.

Traditionally a different symbolic ornament is placed on the Jesse Tree for each of the days of Advent. There is also one for Christmas Day. The chart below lists some people and events that are part of the history of our salvation.

## THE JESSE TREE

|  | People | Theme / Event | Symbolic Ornament |
|---|---|---|---|
| **Week 1 of Advent** | Abraham | The promise | Field of stars |
| **Week 2 of Advent** | Moses | God's leadership | Burning bush |
|  | Israelites | Passover and Exodus | Lamb |
|  | Samuel | The beginning of the kingdom | Crown |
| **Week 3 of Advent** | David | A shepherd for the people | Shepherd's crook or harp |
|  | Isaiah | The call to holiness | Fire tongs with hot coal |
| **Week 4 of Advent** | John the Baptist | Repentance | Scallop shell |
|  | Mary | The hope of the future | White lily |
|  | Elizabeth (mother of John the Baptist) | Joy | Mother and child |
|  | Joseph | Trust | Carpenter's square or hammer |
|  | Magi | Worship | Star |
| **Christmas Eve** | Jesus | Birth of the Messiah | Manger |
| **Christmas** | Christ | The Son of God | Chi-Rho symbol |

## WE RESPOND

How does our preparation during Advent help us to remember the themes and events on the Jesse tree?

Research to find more people and events represented on the Jesse Tree.

# ✞ We Respond in Prayer

**Leader:** Our help is in the name of the Lord.

**All:** Who made heaven and earth.

**Leader:** In the short days and long nights of Advent, we realize how we are always waiting for deliverance from our God.

**Reader:** A reading from the Book of the Prophet Jeremiah

"The days are coming, says the LORD, when I will fulfill the promise I made to the house of Israel and Judah. In those days, in that time, I will raise up for David a just shoot; he shall do what is right and just in the land." (Jeremiah 33:14–15)

The word of the Lord.

**All:** Thanks be to God.

**Leader:** Lord our God,
we praise you for your Son, Jesus Christ:
he is Emmanuel, the hope of the peoples,
he is the wisdom that teaches and guides us,
he is the Savior of every nation.
Come, Lord Jesus.

**All:** Come quickly and do not delay.

### ♫ Prepare the Way

Echo each line

Prepare the way for the coming of God!
Make a straight path for the coming of God!
Ev'ry valley will be filled in,
all hills and mountains will be made low;
crooked roads will be straightened out,
all the rough land will be made smooth.
And all the people on the earth
shall see the saving pow'r of God.

ADVENT

# SHARING FAITH
## with My Family

## Sharing What I Learned

Discuss the following with your family:

- the season of Advent
- Isaiah and John the Baptist
- the Jesse Tree.

## Around the Table

Advent is a busy time for most families. Discuss these questions together: How can we find peace in the midst of all the things that keep us so busy? What are the important things we need to do every day to prepare for Jesus Christ?

## A Family Prayer

As a family, choose one way of praying or working for peace during Advent. Here are some suggestions:

- If your family keeps the tradition of an Advent wreath at home, add a short prayer like "Come Lord Jesus, bring us peace" to the lighting of the candles each week.

- Find out and list the Joyful Mysteries of the Rosary. Use your list to pray the rosary with your family during Advent.

- Find out ways your parish helps those in need. Decide how you will participate in these parish activities.

Visit Sadlier's

www.WeBelieveweb.com

**Connect to the Catechism**
For adult background and reflection, see paragraph 524.

# Christmas

WELCOME FRIENDS

"Come, you nations, and adore the Lord.
Today a great light has come upon the earth."
Introductory Rites, Monday after Second Sunday after Christmas

## WE GATHER

✝ *Lord, we thank you for your constant presence.*

How do you show others that you know they are present in your home? in your school? in your parish? in your life?

## WE BELIEVE

What we celebrate on Christmas Day, and during the entire Christmas season, is the wonderful gift of Emmanuel, God-with-us. We celebrate that God is with us today and always.

The season of Christmas is a time to rejoice in the Incarnation, the truth that the Son of God became man. We celebrate Christ's presence among us now as well as his first coming into the world over two thousand years ago. We recall that God so loved the world that he sent his only Son to be our Savior.

The Christmas season begins on December 25 and ends with the feast of the Baptism of the Lord. This feast is usually celebrated around the second week of January. During the Christmas season we have several feasts that help us to celebrate the Son of God's coming into the world and his presence with us today. Here are a few of them.

**Saint Stephen** On December 26 we remember Saint Stephen, the first martyr for the faith. We read about Stephen's life in the New Testament in the Acts of the Apostles. He spread the good news of Christ, the Son of God and Savior. Stephen preached in Jerusalem, and many people came to believe and were baptized. This angered the leaders in Jerusalem. They had Stephen taken out of the city and killed. He died praying for those who were about to take his life. Stephen's belief in Jesus, as well as his love for his enemies, is an example for all of us.

**Saint John** On December 27 we remember Saint John, one of Christ's apostles. John is credited with writing one of the four gospels. His gospel records the life and ministry of Jesus from his very personal view as Jesus' friend and disciple. John proclaimed that in the Son of God the Word became flesh for our salvation.

"And the Word became flesh
and made his dwelling among us,
and we saw his glory,
the glory as of the Father's only Son,
full of grace and truth."(John 1:14)

During the Christmas season we rejoice that the Word is among us, today and always. "The Word among us" and "the Word made flesh" are titles for Christ, but more importantly they are explanations for the Incarnation. In fact, the word *Incarnation* means "becoming flesh."

**Holy Innocents**   On December 28 we remember the children, called the Holy Innocents, who lost their lives near the time of Jesus' birth.

The wise men, or magi, from the East told King Herod about a newborn king of the Jews. Then they traveled on to find this child. They found the child Jesus, praised him, and offered him their gifts.

Herod, afraid that he would lose his power, wanted this newborn king killed. To be sure that this would happen Herod ordered his soldiers to kill all the baby boys in Bethlehem and the surrounding areas who were under two years of age. But the angel of the Lord had appeared to Joseph and told him to flee to Egypt with the newborn Jesus and Mary. So Jesus was saved.

**Feast of the Holy Family**   On the Sunday after Christmas, we honor Jesus, Mary, and Joseph, the Holy Family. We do not know much about Jesus' family life, but what we do know shows us that he grew up in a loving, faith-filled home. Mary, Joseph, and Jesus' relatives followed Jewish traditions, prayed, and celebrated the religious feasts of their time. Jesus was obedient to his parents, and as he grew older he continued to live by the covenant.

On Holy Family Sunday we pray for our own families, and hear readings at Mass that challenge us to be loving and obedient in our own family life. The Church teaches that our families should learn to be like the Holy Family and love and respect one another. All the members contribute to the holiness of the family by the way they live.

**Mary, Mother of God**   On January 1 we celebrate one of Mary's feasts. We say "Hail, holy Mother! The child to whom you gave birth is the King of heaven and earth for ever." We celebrate Mary's role in God's saving action in history. Jesus was truly human and truly divine. He is God the Son, the second Person of the Blessed Trinity who became man. So Mary is the Mother of God. Mary's love for her son extends to his Church. We honor Mary as the mother of the Church, too.

**Epiphany** On the Sunday between January 2 and January 8 we celebrate the feast of the Epiphany. We celebrate that God the Father revealed his Son to all nations. On this day we celebrate Jesus' epiphany, or the showing of Jesus, to the whole world. We hear in the Gospel of Matthew that when Jesus was born in Bethlehem, magi, or wise men, from the east traveled to find him. They arrived in Jerusalem asking, "Where is the newborn king of the Jews? We saw his star at its rising and have come to do him homage" (Matthew 2:2).

During the time of Jesus, many people believed that a new star appeared in the sky at the birth of a new ruler. The magi saw this star from lands far away and came in search of the new king. The magi themselves were not Jewish, but they still wanted to honor Jesus with gifts of gold, frankincense, and myrrh. On Epiphany Sunday we celebrate that Jesus' coming into the world was important to the whole world. The good news of Jesus Christ is meant for everyone.

**Baptism of the Lord** On the Sunday after Epiphany we celebrate Jesus' baptism by John the Baptist at the Jordan River. Even though Jesus is without sin, he asks John to baptize him. John knows that Jesus does not need this baptism with water. He knows that Jesus is the Messiah. Yet Jesus convinces John to baptize him. By his baptism Jesus identifies himself with all of those who struggle to follow God's law and live by the covenant. Jesus shows that he understands what it means to be human.

And it is after Jesus' baptism that his divinity is revealed. The Spirit of God descended on Jesus, "And a voice came from the heavens, saying, 'This is my beloved Son, with whom I am well pleased'" (Matthew 3:17).

The Christmas season begins with the birth of Jesus and ends with his baptism. During the Christmas season, birth and baptism are connected for us, too. We celebrate Jesus, our Savior, born to us on earth, and we celebrate his new life born in us through the sacrament of Baptism.

## WE RESPOND

In groups brainstorm some special ways that you can celebrate the feasts of the Christmas season. As a class share your ideas. Then make a database of the top five and find a way to share your ideas with other classes.

# ✝ We Respond in Prayer

**Leader:** Glory to the Father, and to the Son, and to the Holy Spirit:

**All:** as it was in the beginning, is now, and will be for ever. Amen.

**Reader:** A reading from the Acts of the Apostles

"In truth, I see that God shows no partiality. Rather, in every nation whoever fears him and acts uprightly is acceptable to him. You know the word [that] he sent to the Israelites as he proclaimed peace through Jesus Christ, who is Lord of all, what has happened all over Judea, beginning in Galilee after the baptism that John preached, how God anointed Jesus of Nazareth with the holy Spirit and power. He went about doing good and healing all those oppressed. . . for God was with him." (Acts of the Apostles 10:34–38)

The word of the Lord.

**All:** Thanks be to God.

**Side 1:** "Here is my servant whom I uphold,
my chosen one with whom I am pleased,

**Side 2:** Upon whom I have put my spirit;
he shall bring forth justice to the nations."
(Isaiah 42:1)

🎵 **Psalm 98: All the Ends of the Earth**

Refrain

All the ends of the earth have seen
the saving pow'r of God.
All the ends of the earth have seen
the saving power of God.

The Lord has made his salvation known:
in the sight of the nations
he has revealed his justice.
He has remembered his kindness
and his faithfulness
toward the house of Israel. (Refrain)

# SHARING FAITH
## with My Family

## Sharing What I Learned

Discuss the following with your family:

- the season of Christmas
- the Incarnation
- the Epiphany and the Baptism of the Lord.

## Around the Table

Talk about ways your family can celebrate Christmas throughout the entire Christmas season. Here are a few ideas:

- Celebrate the traditional "twelve days of Christmas" (from December 26 to January 6) by doing something kind for your family members each day.

- Bake a "King Cake" for the feast of the Epiphany. Decorate it with white, purple, and gold icing (kingly colors!). Insert candy inside before you frost the cake. The person who gets the piece of cake with the candy is king for the day.

## A Family Prayer

A family member may light a Christmas candle as you begin this table grace:

**Leader:** Glory to God in the highest.

**All:** And peace to his people on earth.

**Leader:** Lord Jesus,
in the peace of this season
our spirits rejoice:
With the beasts and angels,
the shepherds and stars,
with Mary and Joseph
we sing God's praise.

By your coming
may the hungry be filled
with good things,
and may our table and home
be blessed.
Glory to God in the highest.

**All:** And peace to his people on earth.

Visit Sadlier's

www.WeBelieveweb.com

**Connect to the Catechism**
For adult background and reflection, see paragraph 461.

**Underline the correct answer.**

1. The word *exodus* comes from the Greek word for **(departure/freedom)**.

2. As Christians, when we read about God saving his people by helping them pass safely through the waters of the Red Sea, we are reminded of our stewardship of **(creation/Baptism)**.

3. In the Book of Exodus we learn about the Israelites' years in Egypt and about God's carrying out his plan to bring his people to **(Canaan/Sinai)**.

4. As the Israelites journeyed through the wilderness, God fed them with a sweet tasting, bread-like food called **(manna/Nazirite)**.

5. To Christians, the twelve pillars of the altar that Moses set up in the wilderness are symbols not only of the twelve tribes of Israel but also of the **(gospels/apostles)**.

6. To thank God for the gift of a son, Hannah dedicated her son **(Saul/Samuel)** to God's service.

7. The great collection of Hebrew religious songs that Jesus prayed and that both Jews and Christians pray today is the **(Book of Psalms/Book of Joshua)**.

8. To show his love of God and his desire to be faithful to the covenant, Solomon built the **(ark of the covenant/Temple in Jerusalem)**.

**Write the letter of the phrase that best describes the person.**

9. _____ Deborah

10. _____ Joshua

11. _____ Samson

12. _____ David

13. _____ Saul

14. _____ Ruth

15. _____ Solomon

16. _____ Moses

**a.** the first king of Israel

**b.** the shepherd-king who conquered the Philistines

**c.** the person God chose to lead his people out of slavery in Egypt

**d.** the judge who, with God's help, guided Barak to victory over the Canaanites

**e.** the person who said, "your people shall be my people and your God my God"

**f.** the leader who brought God's people into the land God had promised them

**g.** the king of Israel who prayed for an understanding heart and to whom God granted wisdom

**Answer the questions.**

**17–18.** How was King Solomon's reign different from King David's? For what is each king remembered?

**19–20.** What is the importance of the special meal of remembrance that Jewish families eat at the Passover? Why is the Passover meal that Jesus ate with his followers on the night before he died so important to Christians?

# Redefining the Covenant People

## Coping with Crisis

At one time or another, most families will experience some type of crisis. Whether in the home, the school, or the community, families must do what they can to assist their children in coping with difficult situations. Here are some suggestions:

- Talk to children honestly; provide them with accurate information in understandable terms.

- Encourage children to express their thoughts and feelings. Let them know that you value what they are telling you.

- Children need to be assured that in time things will get better.

- Offer the children consolation and the hope of a brighter future.

- Children need to know that you are present and that you will see the family through the crisis and its aftermath.

- Watch for signs that suggest the need for professional help. These signs can include depression, extended periods of high emotion, a slip in academic performance, an inability to concentrate, or a sudden change in behavior.

## What Your Child Will Learn in Unit 3

In Unit 3, the history of the God's people continues. The children are introduced to the period of history where the people of Israel are redefined by geography, religion, and social problems. They learn about the division of Solomon's empire into two kingdoms. Life in the Northern Kingdom, now known as Israel, is first examined. Next, the children learn about life in the Southern Kingdom, known as Judah. They read about the prophets Isaiah, Micah, Zephaniah, and Habakkuk. The idea of vocation, a call to serve God, is discussed in the story of the prophet Jeremiah. Unit 3 continues with the history and struggles of the divided kingdom, and the eventual exile to Babylon. The children are introduced to the wisdom literature of the Bible; for example the Psalms and Proverbs. The children learn that the people prosper in exile and later begin a long journey back to Judah. Unit 3 presents the fulfillment of God's promise with the coming of the Messiah. The children read about the Annunciation, Mary and Joseph, and Elizabeth and Zechariah. They also learn that the Son of God became man. Finally the early life of Jesus, the preaching of John the Baptist, and John's baptism of Jesus are presented.

## Plan & Preview

▶ Scissors should be on hand to cut out the *We Believe* Trading Card (*Chapters 15–19*).

▶ Pieces of cardboard or stiff paper can be used for the trading cards. The front and back of the cards can be glued to the cardboard to form a sturdy trading card.

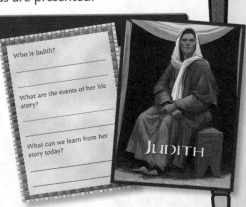

Who is Judith?

What are the events of her life story?

What can we learn from her story today?

JUDITH

# Our Old Testament Roots

**Judaism's Holy Shrine: The Western Wall**

Mount Moriah, in the heart of the Old City of Jerusalem, is known as the Temple Mount. From the day after the Temple of Jerusalem's final destruction by the Romans in 70 A.D., Jews have gathered to mourn its ruins. While nothing remains of the Second Temple itself, part of the retaining wall that raised up the Temple Mount has survived.

## From the Catechism

"The relationships within the family bring an affinity of feelings, affections, and interests, arising above all from the members' respect for one another."
*(Catechism of the Catholic Church, 2206)*

Today, the 18 meter long Western Wall—sometimes called the Wailing Wall because of the mournful prayers said there—is the only surviving relic of Judaism's most sacred shrine. It is considered the holiest Jewish site because of its proximity to the destroyed ancient Temples. Today, the area in front of the Wall is used as an outdoor temple.

## Bible Q & A

**Q:** My sixth grader is learning about the Old Testament. Where can I find stories about the women of the Old Testament that we can read together?

—*Oklahoma City, Oklahoma*

**A:** There are three Old Testament books that have women's names as their titles: Ruth, Judith, and Esther. You might also want to read current books that retell stories of great biblical women in language your child might more easily understand. An example is *Great Men and Women of the Bible* by Marlee Alex, Anne de Graaf, and Ben Alex. Check your library, bookstore or the Internet for other books about biblical women.

## ✝ We Gather in Prayer

**Leader:** The Lord speaks to us in many different ways and through many people. Here is the way he spoke to the prophet Elijah.

**Narrator:** The prophet Elijah challenged the king and the people to turn away from evil and keep their covenant with God. The queen then ordered the prophet to be killed. Elijah fled. He walked for forty days into the wilderness and took shelter in a cave. Then he heard,

**All:** "Why are you here, Elijah?"
(1 Kings 19:9)

**Narrator:** Elijah answered:

**Elijah:** The Israelites have disobeyed your covenant, "torn down your altars, and put your prophets to the sword. I alone am left, and they seek to take my life"
(1 Kings 19:10).

**Narrator:** "Then the LORD said,

**All:** 'Go outside and stand on the mountain before the LORD; the LORD will be passing by.'"
(1 Kings 19:11)

**Narrator:** A strong and heavy wind was beating at the mountains—

**All:** "but the LORD was not in the wind.

**Narrator:** After the wind there was an earthquake—

**All:** but the LORD was not in the earthquake.

**Narrator:** After the earthquake there was fire—

**All:** but the LORD was not in the fire.

**Narrator:** After the fire there was a tiny whispering sound. When he heard this, Elijah hid his face in his cloak"
(1 Kings 19:11–13).

**All:** For it was the voice of God.

**Leader:** Often God speaks to us in stillness. When we are quiet, we can hear God speaking to us in our hearts. Let us pause now in stillness and quiet, and invite the Lord to enter our hearts and minds.
(Silent pause)

God, help us to listen carefully to your voice in the "tiny whispering sound" within our hearts and minds.

**All:** Amen.

171

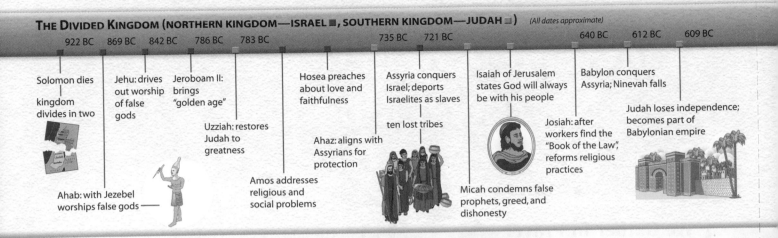

922 BC — Solomon dies; kingdom divides in two

869 BC — Jehu: drives out worship of false gods

842 BC — Ahab: with Jezebel worships false gods

786 BC — Jeroboam II: brings "golden age"; Uzziah: restores Judah to greatness

783 BC — Amos addresses religious and social problems

735 BC — Hosea preaches about love and faithfulness; Ahaz: aligns with Assyrians for protection

721 BC — Assyria conquers Israel; deports Israelites as slaves; ten lost tribes

Isaiah of Jerusalem states God will always be with his people; Micah condemns false prophets, greed, and dishonesty

640 BC — Josiah: after workers find the "Book of the Law", reforms religious practices

612 BC — Babylon conquers Assyria; Ninevah falls

609 BC — Judah loses independence; becomes part of Babylonian empire

# Solomon's kingdom was divided.

## WE GATHER

✝ *Lord, may we always do your will.*

What are some reasons why two friends might stop talking to each other?

How would this affect their other friends?

## WE BELIEVE

God loves us so much that he gives us the ability to love and care for one another. He also gives us the freedom to choose to love. God wants us to be happy and at peace. He wants what is best for us. However, our choices sometimes may lead us to live in ways that are not good for us.

It seems that this happened to King Solomon, too. Some of Solomon's choices greatly hurt his friendship with God, and this affected all of God's people.

King Solomon, the son of David, was a powerful man who ruled a united Israel. Many projects including the building of the Temple in Jerusalem were completed during his reign. However, Solomon made the people pay heavy taxes and forced them to work long hours on his many projects.

Solomon's heart was slowly turned away from God. He gradually forgot the covenant. He followed the ways of many false gods. He even built altars, burned incense, and offered sacrifices to these false gods.

Since Solomon had chosen to worship false gods and failed to keep the covenant, the kingdom would no longer be his to rule. God said, "I will not do this during your lifetime, however, for the sake of your father David; it is your son whom I will deprive. Nor will I take away the whole kingdom" (1 Kings 11:12–13).

By the time Solomon died in 922 B.C., the Israelites had grown discontent. Solomon's son Rehoboam became the next king. The people asked for lighter taxes and less of a workload. But Rehoboam announced even heavier burdens.

When the ten northern tribes heard this, they refused to accept Rehoboam as king. Instead they followed a man named Jeroboam. The words of the Lord to Solomon were fulfilled, and Solomon's empire was divided into two separate kingdoms. The kingdom made up of the ten northern tribes, with Jeroboam as king, was known as Israel. The kingdom made up of the two southern tribes, with Rehoboam as king, was known as Judah.

🏃 Highlight or underline reasons why Solomon's kingdom divided.

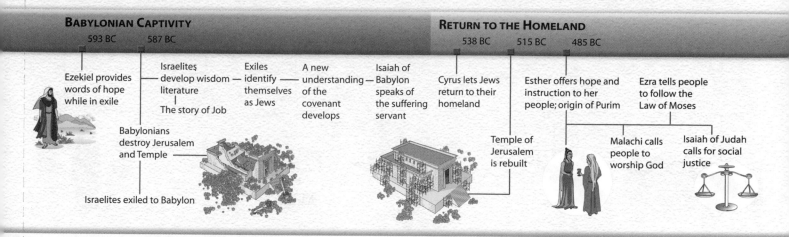

**BABYLONIAN CAPTIVITY**
593 BC    587 BC

Ezekiel provides words of hope while in exile

Israelites develop wisdom literature

The story of Job

Babylonians destroy Jerusalem and Temple

Israelites exiled to Babylon

Exiles identify themselves as Jews

A new understanding of the covenant develops

Isaiah of Babylon speaks of the suffering servant

**RETURN TO THE HOMELAND**
538 BC    515 BC    485 BC

Cyrus lets Jews return to their homeland

Temple of Jerusalem is rebuilt

Esther offers hope and instruction to her people; origin of Purim

Malachi calls people to worship God

Ezra tells people to follow the Law of Moses

Isaiah of Judah calls for social justice

**A People Divided** Jeroboam did not want his people going to Jerusalem, now in the southern kingdom, to offer sacrifices in the Temple. He feared that worshiping with the southern tribes might reunite the people. So he set up places for his people to worship. He provided each place with an altar and a great golden bull. The bulls were meant only to represent the legs of the throne of God, but many of the people worshiped them as gods. By his actions, Jeroboam led the people into idolatry. **Idolatry** means giving worship to a creature or thing instead of to God. Idolatry is forbidden by the first commandment.

Jeroboam was also appointing false priests. He "made priests from among the people who were not Levites" (1 Kings 12:31). God sent a prophet to warn Jeroboam about his evil ways, but Jeroboam did not listen. And though God had given Jeroboam rule over Israel, Jeroboam was not keeping God's commandments. He did not worship God with all his heart. He led Israel to forget their covenant with the one true God.

In Judah, Rehoboam, too, allowed the people to turn away from their covenant promise. "Judah did evil in the sight of the LORD, and by their sins angered him even more than their fathers had done." (1 Kings 14:22)

The first commandment calls us to love and honor God above all else. We honor God by our belief in him. We adore God through prayer and worship, by giving thanks and praise to him alone. The commandment also calls us to place our hope and trust in God. Even if we forget God's love and care for us, God's everlasting love for us remains. Unfortunately the kings did not remind their people of this.

Both Jeroboam and Rehoboam led the people away from God. Their northern and southern kingdoms constantly battled with each other, and the divided kingdom continued to decline.

How did the leaders of Israel and Judah fail their people?

**Key Word**

**idolatry** giving worship to a creature or thing instead of to God

**WE RESPOND**

Solomon's kingdom broke apart, and the people were divided. List some things that divide people today.

_____

_____

_____

In groups discuss ways people can work together to heal relationships and bring people back together. What can you and your classmates do to prevent divisions?

173

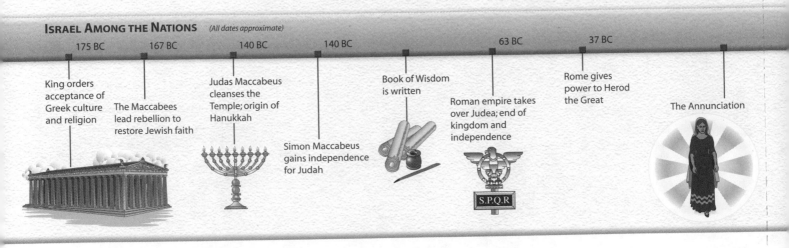

175 BC — King orders acceptance of Greek culture and religion

167 BC — The Maccabees lead rebellion to restore Jewish faith

140 BC — Judas Maccabeus cleanses the Temple; origin of Hanukkah

140 BC — Simon Maccabeus gains independence for Judah

Book of Wisdom is written

63 BC — Roman empire takes over Judea; end of kingdom and independence

37 BC — Rome gives power to Herod the Great

The Annunciation

# Elijah and Elisha proclaimed God's faithfulness.

## WE GATHER

✝ *God, help us keep our faith in you.*

Has anyone ever said something that made you stop and think and see things in a different way? In what ways were you, or the way you thought, changed?

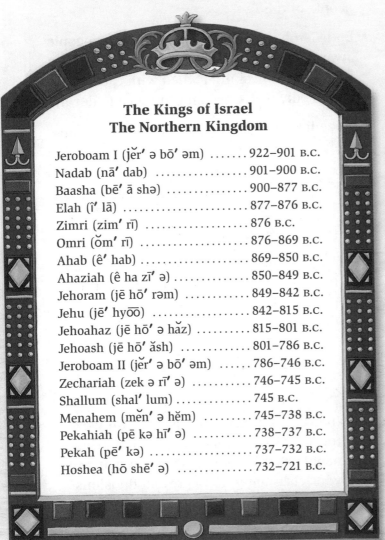

### The Kings of Israel
### The Northern Kingdom

Jeroboam I (jĕr′ ə bō′ əm) . . . . . . . 922–901 B.C.
Nadab (nā′ dab) . . . . . . . . . . . . . . 901–900 B.C.
Baasha (bē′ ā shə) . . . . . . . . . . . . . 900–877 B.C.
Elah (ĭ′ lā) . . . . . . . . . . . . . . . . . . . 877–876 B.C.
Zimri (zim′ rī) . . . . . . . . . . . . . . . . 876 B.C.
Omri (ŏm′ rī) . . . . . . . . . . . . . . . . . 876–869 B.C.
Ahab (ê′ hab) . . . . . . . . . . . . . . . . . 869–850 B.C.
Ahaziah (ê ha zī′ ə) . . . . . . . . . . . . 850–849 B.C.
Jehoram (jē hō′ rəm) . . . . . . . . . . . 849–842 B.C.
Jehu (jē′ hyōō) . . . . . . . . . . . . . . . . 842–815 B.C.
Jehoahaz (jē hō′ ə hăz) . . . . . . . . . 815–801 B.C.
Jehoash (jē hō′ ăsh) . . . . . . . . . . . . 801–786 B.C.
Jeroboam II (jĕr′ ə bō′ əm) . . . . . . 786–746 B.C.
Zechariah (zek ə rī′ ə) . . . . . . . . . . 746–745 B.C.
Shallum (shal′ lum) . . . . . . . . . . . . 745 B.C.
Menahem (mĕn′ ə hĕm) . . . . . . . . 745–738 B.C.
Pekahiah (pē kə hī′ ə) . . . . . . . . . . 738–737 B.C.
Pekah (pē′ kə) . . . . . . . . . . . . . . . . 737–732 B.C.
Hoshea (hō shē′ ə) . . . . . . . . . . . . . 732–721 B.C.

## WE BELIEVE

As the kings ignored their responsibilities to the covenant, some of God's people challenged them. The prophets tried to convince the kings and God's people to live justly. But after Jeroboam died, the northern kingdom continued to practice the idolatry which he had introduced. Many of the kings that followed him were not interested in leading the people back to God. They were weak and greedy, and they did not live by the covenant. We find out about these kings in the First Book of Kings and the Second Book of Chronicles.

One of the worst northern kings was Ahab. He did "evil in the sight of the LORD more than any of his predecessors" (1 Kings 16:30). Early in his reign Ahab married a foreign princess named Jezebel. She worshiped a false god named Baal, and King Ahab began to worship Baal, too. Ahab built a temple to Baal in Samaria, the capital city of the northern kingdom. Ahab also used false priests and prophets as advisors.

**Broken idol of the false god, Baal.**

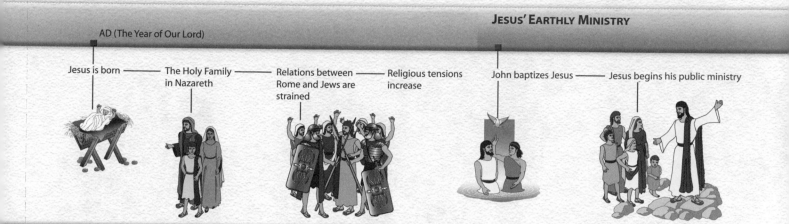

AD (The Year of Our Lord)

Jesus is born — The Holy Family in Nazareth — Relations between Rome and Jews are strained — Religious tensions increase — John baptizes Jesus — Jesus begins his public ministry

Jezebel tried to plant her beliefs in the heart of the people of the northern kingdom. She set up statues of her gods everywhere. Eventually Ahab even allowed Jezebel to kill hundreds of people who believed in the one true God.

**Prophets Speak for God** God tried to help the people of the kingdom of Israel to stay close to him. He sent prophets to guide the people in his ways. Because they experienced God's love and presence in their own lives, the prophets clearly saw the wrongs that were taking place in their communities. The prophets told the people to stop and think about the way they were living. They called the people to be faithful to God just as God was faithful to them.

The first prophet whom God sent to the northern kingdom was Elijah. Elijah lived during the reign of King Ahab. The name Elijah means "Yahweh is my God." Elijah's message called the people to faith in the one true God.

Elijah eventually anointed Elisha to do God's work, too. Elijah threw his cloak over Elisha as a sign that he was called to the mission of a prophet. So Elisha had the spirit of God upon him, just as Elijah did. These two prophets spoke God's words to many and urged the people to live in justice and faithfulness.

The deeds of Elijah and Elisha are recorded in the First and Second Book of Kings. All of their works show that the power of a prophet comes from the one true God. Their words and actions show that God is loving and faithful to his people, even when they are not faithful to him.

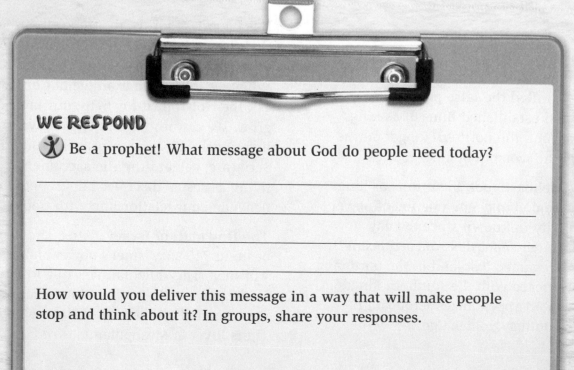

## WE RESPOND

Be a prophet! What message about God do people need today?

_____

_____

_____

_____

How would you deliver this message in a way that will make people stop and think about it? In groups, share your responses.

# The Assyrians destroyed the northern kingdom.

## WE GATHER

✝ *Lord, help us to be strong in our faith.*

What are some ways that one person can influence another? How can people resist bad influences?

## WE BELIEVE

In 850 B.C. King Ahab died in battle. He had not been a good influence on God's people. He had led them away from their covenant with God. Ahab was first succeeded by one of his sons and then by another. These young leaders tried to get Israel, the northern kingdom, to worship the one true God. However, they had very little success because their mother, Jezebel, was still too powerful.

In 842 B.C., Jezebel and most of Ahab's family were killed by Jehu, a general. Jehu also destroyed the places where false gods were worshiped, killed the false priests and officials, and established himself as king. Because of Jehu the northern kingdom was freed from the worship of false gods.

In 801 B.C. Jehoash took the throne as king. His reign seemed to begin a period of power and prosperity unknown since the days of Solomon. Under Jehoash's son, Jeroboam II, Israel even regained lost land in the north and established peace with the southern kingdom of Judah. To all appearances Jeroboam II's reign was another "golden age."

**Problems in Israel**  Unfortunately, what seemed to be a time of success and prosperity was not one for all the people. While some people in Israel were wealthy, many others were poor. Most Israelites lived a hard life, and the government did little or nothing to make life easier. Economic differences, which had not previously existed, now became a problem. Many people of all economic levels grew greedier and acted in evil ways.

Along with these social injustices, there were also religious problems. Though the great religious centers were filled with worshipers, the faith of the people was still influenced by the worship of false gods. The real meaning of the covenant was forgotten. Many people no longer fulfilled their promises to God. In fact, the faith of the Israelite people was almost completely lost.

It is important for us, too, to keep our faith in God strong. Because faith is a gift from God, we need to turn to God to strengthen our faith. When we follow the example of Christ, and ask the Holy Spirit for help, our faith can grow. We can respond to God's love in our lives. Spending time in prayer, studying Scripture, celebrating the sacraments, and living as Jesus' disciples all strengthen our belief and our relationship with God.

**The Downfall of Israel**  After Jeroboam II's death in 746 B.C., Israel's power and prosperity vanished. This downfall was due to the rise of a new power—the nation of Assyria. Assyria was centered on the city of Nineveh on the Tigris River in Mesopotamia.

Assyria had slowly been building its empire and was getting ready to make Israel a part of this empire.

In 724 B.C. the king of Assyria attacked Israel and took over the countryside. He took the king of Israel prisoner and occupied all the land except for Samaria, the capital city. Then in 721 B.C. Samaria finally fell to Assyria. Great numbers of Israelites were sent away, or deported, to Mesopotamia and other places to live as slaves. The Assyrians filled the northern kingdom with people from other lands, and Israel became a province of the Assyrian empire. The Israelites who were deported—over twenty-seven thousand in all—were never heard from again. They became known as the ten lost tribes of Israel. Thus, the northern kingdom of Israel became just another part of the Assyrian empire.

The experience of God's people shows us that sinfulness does not lead to life. Faithfulness to God and to one another is necessary for living as God calls us to live.

## WE RESPOND

List some ways that your parish shows faithfulness to God and one another.

_____

_____

_____

As a class discuss ways that people your age can participate in these parish activities.

# Other prophets brought God's message to Israel.

## WE GATHER

✝ *God, help us hear your voice.*

Sometimes even helpful, or constructive, criticism is difficult to accept. Think of a situation where you might have to give someone constructive criticism.

## WE BELIEVE

In encouraging the people to change their lives, prophets often had to point out the ways God's people failed to show him love. This was not always easy for the people to accept.

Elijah and Elisha were prophets who tried to help the people of the northern kingdom to turn back to God. Though Elijah and Elisha left no written records of their own, a number of other northern prophets did. Amos was a prophet who left such records. His message can be found in the Book of Amos, one of the prophetic books of the Old Testament.

Amos was a shepherd who lived during the middle of the reign of Jeroboam II. Though Amos was from the southern kingdom of Judah, God called him to preach in the northern kingdom. As we have seen, the reign of Jeroboam II seemed like a time of prosperity. In reality, however, many social and religious problems existed. Amos addressed these problems fearlessly.

The message Amos delivered to Israel was difficult yet necessary for the people to hear. Amos told them that they were heartless, greedy, and dishonest. He accused them of turning their backs on God. He pointed out that they had forgotten those who were poor and orphaned, unjustly taxed widows and farmers, and committed crimes and other social injustices. Amos challenged people who claimed they served God, while in their hearts they worshiped the gods of luxury, wealth, and idleness.

### The Call to Justice

Amos told the people that God was not impressed by their religious practices when he saw that they were not living justly. Amos warned that if people were going to make offerings to God,

"then let justice surge like water,
   and goodness like an unfailing stream"
(Amos 5:24).

Amos insisted that Israel's only hope of salvation was to act justly. He called the people of Israel to remember that their actions must show what was in their hearts. He proclaimed,

"Seek good and not evil,
   that you may live;
Then truly will the LORD, the God of hosts,
   be with you as you claim!" (Amos 5:14).

Just like God's people thousands of years ago, we are called to act justly and stand up for what is fair and right. We all share in the work of social justice. The Church calls each of us to follow Christ's example of faith in God the Father and outreach to those who are oppressed, neglected, or in need in any way. We cannot separate love for God and love for neighbor.

Unfortunately many people ignored Amos' message and refused to act justly. Amos saw no clear sign that the people of Israel would change their ways. For that reason Amos declared that Israel would be punished, and he predicted the kingdom's final destruction. His words later proved true when Assyria took over Israel.

What was Amos' message to God's people?

**The Message of Hosea**   Another northern prophet, Hosea, lived around the time of Amos. His message is preserved in the Book of Hosea, another Old Testament prophetic book.

Hosea's story was about his love for and marriage to a woman named Gomer. Gomer was not faithful to him, just as Israel was not faithful to God. Though Hosea was horrified by Gomer's unfaithfulness, Hosea loved her so much that he could not give her up. Hosea told the people that God felt the same way about Israel: God refused to abandon Israel even though its people had been unfaithful to him.

For Hosea, Israel's lack of faith showed up in their idolatry and in their injustices against the poor. He told them that their promise of faithfulness to God was empty unless they could show their love by the way they lived.

How can we follow Hosea's message today?

## As Catholics...

We need prophets today in our Church and in our world. Through their words and actions, prophets offer us constructive criticism about the ways we are following the gospel. They remind us that justice, peace, and love of neighbor—especially those who are poor and oppressed—must be part of our Christian way of life. Such people in our modern times include Mother Teresa, Pope John Paul II, Dorothy Day, César Chavez, Dr. Martin Luther King, Jr., and Sister Thea Bowman.

Choose one of these people to research. Discover why we call that person a prophet for today.

**WE RESPOND**

Plan a short commercial that encourages people to stay faithful to God.

**Write the name of the prophet described.**

| Jezebel | Elisha | Hosea | Elijiah | Amos |

1. _____ preached a message about the people of Israel being unfaithful to God.

2. _____ preached a message to address the social and religious problems that existed in the northern kingdom.

3. _____ was the first prophet God sent to the northern kingdom to call the people to have faith in the one true God.

4. _____ was anointed and had a cloak thrown over him to show that he was called by God to the mission of a prophet.

**Write True or False for the following sentences.**
**Then change the false sentences to make them true.**

5. _____ God sent Israel prophets to keep them close to him and to guide them.

_____

6. _____ Judah was the kingdom of the ten northern tribes where Jeroboam was king.

_____

7. _____ Assyria was the kingdom of the two southern tribes where Rehoboam was king.

_____

8. _____ God refused to abandon Israel even though its people were unfaithful to him.

_____

**Write a paragraph to answer these questions.**

**9–10.** What is idolatry? Why is it forbidden by the first commandment?

ASSESSMENT

Write a short essay or make a large poster explaining the role of God's prophets in the northern kingdom. Then include someone you think is a modern-day prophet in the Church or society.

# We Respond in Faith

## Reflect & Pray

When I see injustice, I will try to

_____

_____

Dear Jesus, teach us to share the goods of this world with one another.
Amen.

**Key Word**

idolatry (p. 173)

## Remember

- Solomon's kingdom was divided.
- Elijah and Elisha proclaimed God's faithfulness.
- The Assyrians destroyed the northern kingdom.
- Other prophets brought God's message to Israel.

## OUR CATHOLIC LIFE

### Catholic Relief Services

In 1943, the bishops of the United States founded Catholic Relief Services (CRS) to assist people outside of the United States who are poor or in need in any way. CRS follows the teaching and example of Jesus Christ by trying to stop human suffering and poverty, by working for the development of people all over the world, and by encouraging peace and justice in the world. CRS aids those who are in need of food, health care, homes, and education. It operates in eighty countries and territories around the world and honors the dignity of all people. CRS helps people to make their communities safer and to find better places to live. CRS also educates Catholics in the United States about the responsibilities of caring for all members of the human family, no matter what their religion, race, or geographical location might be.

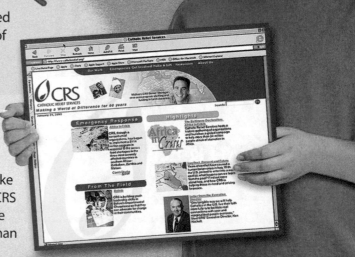

# SHARING FAITH
## with My Family

## Sharing What I Learned

Discuss the following with your family:

- the division of Solomon's kingdom
- the prophets Elijah and Elisha
- life in Israel
- the prophets Amos and Hosea.

## Share a Prayer

This Jewish prayer is said before going to sleep at night.

Write a prayer that you can pray before going to sleep at night. Share your prayer with your family.

"May the Lord bless you and keep you. May the Lord make His glory shine upon you and be kindly toward you. May the Lord turn His glory unto You and grant you peace."

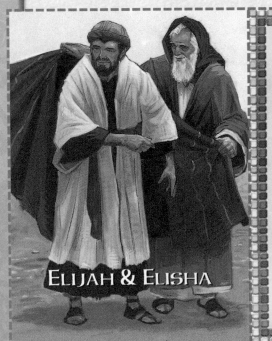

ELIJAH & ELISHA

What is the mission of God's prophets?

_____

_____

Who are Elijah and Elisha?

_____

_____

What do their messages tell us about God?

_____

_____

## We Believe Trading Cards

Complete the facts on the back of the trading card. Then share with your family what you have learned about the prophets Elijah and Elisha.

Visit Sadlier's

www.WeBelieveweb.com

**Connect to the Catechism**
For adult background and reflection, see paragraphs 709, 2583, and 2584.

# A Divided People: Judah, the Southern Kingdom

## ✝ We Gather in Prayer

**Leader:** As God's people, we are called to faith in the one true God who is ever faithful.

**Side 1:** "Praise the LORD, all you nations! Give glory, all you peoples!

**Side 2:** The LORD's love for us is strong; the LORD is faithful forever."

(Psalm 117:1–2)

**Side 1:** Glory to the Father, and to the Son, and to the Holy Spirit:

**Side 2:** as it was in the beginning, is now, and will be for ever. Amen.

🎵 **Though the Mountains May Fall**

Though the mountains may fall
and the hills turn to dust,
yet the love of the Lord will stand
as a shelter for all who will call on his name.
Sing the praise and the glory of God.

# Judah struggled to remain faithful to God.

## WE GATHER

✝ *Holy Spirit, guide us to be faithful.*

Name someone you know or have heard of who has made a difference in the lives of other people. Explain your choice.

## WE BELIEVE

Each person who ruled the people of God had the responsibility to help them stay close to God. Some took this responsibility very seriously, and others did not. Rehoboam, the king of Judah, and his successor Abijah, permitted the worship of false gods and practices against God's law. This greatly affected the attitude of God's people in Judah.

However, Asa, the next king, was different. During Asa's reign only followers of the one true God were allowed to be officials in the government. Asa also worked to free Judah from practices against the one true God. In the words of the writer of the Second Book of Chronicles, Asa ordered the people of Judah "to seek the LORD, the God of their fathers, and to observe the law and its commands" (2 Chronicles 14:3). Asa's son Jehoshaphat also firmly believed in God and acted to bring the people back to faithfulness to God.

Unfortunately, through the wife of the next king, the worship of the false god Baal was introduced into Jerusalem. Yet despite all that took place during each king's reign, the people's faith in God never completely failed.

When Uzziah became king, he restored Judah to a greatness unknown since the days of Solomon. Both the northern and southern kingdoms experienced revivals of power and prosperity. However, only the southern kingdom, Judah, remained faithful to God.

**Threats to Prosperity** About 735 B.C., the king of Israel and the king of Syria invited the king of Judah to join their alliance against the

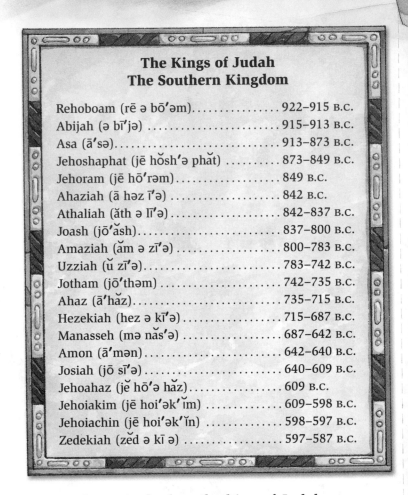

### The Kings of Judah
### The Southern Kingdom

| | |
|---|---|
| Rehoboam (rē ə bō′əm) | 922–915 B.C. |
| Abijah (ə bī′jə) | 915–913 B.C. |
| Asa (ā′sə) | 913–873 B.C. |
| Jehoshaphat (jē hŏsh′ə phăt) | 873–849 B.C. |
| Jehoram (jē hō′rəm) | 849 B.C. |
| Ahaziah (ā həz ī′ə) | 842 B.C. |
| Athaliah (ăth ə lī′ə) | 842–837 B.C. |
| Joash (jō′ăsh) | 837–800 B.C. |
| Amaziah (ăm ə zī′ə) | 800–783 B.C. |
| Uzziah (ŭ zī′ə) | 783–742 B.C. |
| Jotham (jō′thəm) | 742–735 B.C. |
| Ahaz (ā′hăz) | 735–715 B.C. |
| Hezekiah (hez ə kī′ə) | 715–687 B.C. |
| Manasseh (mə năs′ə) | 687–642 B.C. |
| Amon (ā′mən) | 642–640 B.C. |
| Josiah (jō sī′ə) | 640–609 B.C. |
| Jehoahaz (jĕ hō′ə hăz) | 609 B.C. |
| Jehoiakim (jē hoi′ək′ĭm) | 609–598 B.C. |
| Jehoiachin (jē hoi′ək′ĭn) | 598–597 B.C. |
| Zedekiah (zĕd ə kī ə) | 597–587 B.C. |

Assyrians. And when the king of Judah refused, there was a real threat of war with Israel and Syria.

When the next king, Ahaz, began his reign, he feared an invasion from Syria and Israel. In order to protect Judah from this, Ahaz asked the Assyrians for help. The king of Assyria agreed to protect Judah, and soon the Assyrian armies conquered Israel and Syria. However, to get Assyria's help Ahaz had to pay a price. Judah had to give up its independence and pledge loyalty to Assyria.

**The Prophet Isaiah**   Mistreated by the Assyrians, the people of Judah questioned God's power and doubted him. God wanted his people to stay close to him, so he sent a great prophet to reassure them. We call this prophet Isaiah of Jerusalem. Like Amos before him, Isaiah spoke out against all forms of idolatry and injustice. His message is recorded in Chapters 1—39 of the Book of Isaiah. This was the first of three different messages that were recorded in this prophetic book of the Old Testament.

Isaiah reminded the king and the people of God's love for them. He told them how to be faithful to God. Isaiah was one of King Ahaz's advisors. Isaiah did not think the king should rely on Assyria, and he warned the king that the people would suffer because of the Assyrians. He preached that Judah and Israel would lose their freedom. King Ahaz refused to listen to the prophet.

The Assyrians forced the people of Judah to recognize Assyria's false gods. Ahaz felt that he had no choice but to obey Assyria. The Assyrians even set up a huge altar in the Temple in Jerusalem. And as a result, the people practiced idolatry once again. The Assyrians also made the people of Judah pay heavy taxes. Poverty, suffering, and injustice began to spread in Judah just as they had in the northern kingdom of Israel.

Despite the prophet's words, Ahaz and the people turned away from God and from their covenant with him, and "the LORD had brought Judah low because of Ahaz, . . . who let Judah go its own way and proved utterly faithless to the LORD" (2 Chronicles 28:19). Yet, Isaiah insisted that God's punishment was not meant to destroy Judah, but to make it pure and faithful again. Isaiah's message was one of hope and comfort to the people of Judah.

## WE RESPOND

Talk about why it is important for world leaders to make just decisions for their people and to treat neighboring countries with respect.

In this space, write a prayer for world leaders.

_____

_____

_____

_____

185

# Prophets brought Judah hope and comfort.

## WE GATHER

✝ *O God, we place our hope in you.*

Think of times when someone's just actions might cause people to dislike him or her. Discuss in small groups.

## WE BELIEVE

The actions of the prophet Isaiah were not always easy to accept. He called kings to act justly on behalf of God's people. King Ahaz did not listen to Isaiah. However, King Hezekiah, his successor, did. He stopped practices against the one true God, removed foreign idols from the Temple, and closed local shrines where the false gods and goddesses were worshiped.

Hezekiah also tried to help the poor and those who were suffering because of the many injustices in Judah. Twice Hezekiah tried to free Judah from the Assyrians. Although he failed both times, he still prevented the Assyrians from completely destroying Judah. More importantly, Hezekiah managed to keep the people of Judah faithful to the worship of the one true God. "This Hezekiah did in all Judah. He did what was good, upright and faithful before the LORD, his God. Everything that he undertook, for the service of the house of God or for the law and commandments, was to do the will of his God. He did this wholeheartedly, and he prospered."
(2 Chronicles 31:20–21)

Hezekiah knew that God wanted all people to live in justice and peace. In small groups list some ways your class can make your school a more just and peaceful place.

_____

_____

_____

**Isaiah's Message**   Isaiah told Hezekiah that Jerusalem would not be taken nor Judah destroyed. God would use foreign nations to make Judah pure and once again faithful to his commands. However, the power of these nations would be subject to God's will. Out of his great love for his people, God would not allow these nations to destroy them.

Isaiah pointed out that even if events went against his people, God, who always kept his promises, would be with them. God would bring new life out of death and destruction.

"God indeed is my savior;
  I am confident and unafraid.

My strength and my courage is the LORD,
  and he has been my savior."   (Isaiah 12:2)

For Isaiah, faith was complete trust in God's plan and wisdom. Isaiah brought hope and comfort to the people of Judah. He told them that in his mercy God would spare a remnant of the people. A *remnant* is a small piece left over from something larger. This remnant, or small group of God's people, would survive and live just and holy lives as God's faithful community.

**Micah the Prophet**   Micah was another prophet who preached in Judah. Micah had a deep understanding of people and their relationship with God. His messages are recorded in the Old Testament in a prophetic book that bears his name—the Book of Micah.

Micah began his work around the time of Isaiah of Jerusalem. Micah spoke out against false prophets. False prophets tried to become popular by telling their listeners only what they wanted to hear. Unfortunately, Micah's message was difficult for people to accept, so they often ignored or rejected his words.

Micah was angered by the sinful actions of God's people. He had particularly harsh words for the greed, dishonesty, and corruption of those around him. Micah preached that goodness lies in the practice of social justice and in faithfulness to the one true God. It was not enough, he said, to perform elaborate religious ceremonies without faith or to say one thing and believe another. God was not interested in such false worship. Micah told the people that God required them,

"Only to do the right and to love goodness,
    and to walk humbly with your God"
(Micah 6:8).

The prophet Micah saw the terrible effects of sin at work in both the northern and southern kingdoms. For that reason he warned of the eventual destruction of both kingdoms. But Micah assured the people that God would not abandon his chosen people nor allow them to be destroyed. God would welcome his people back and forgive their sins. He would restore them through the work of a new David.

As Christians we believe that this promise of a new David has been fulfilled in Jesus Christ. Jesus Christ, the Son of God, did what was right, loved goodness, and was humble before God his Father. He spoke out against injustices and, in a way no one else could, brought the people back to God.

## WE RESPOND

If Micah or Isaiah were living today, what issues and concerns would they be preaching about? As followers of Jesus Christ, how can we address their issues and concerns? Write your answers on the chart below.

| The Prophet's Message Today | Our Response as Followers of Jesus Christ |
| --- | --- |
| _____ | _____ |
| _____ | _____ |
| _____ | _____ |
| _____ | _____ |
| _____ | _____ |
| _____ | _____ |

# The kingdom of Judah came to an end.

## WE GATHER

✝ *Jesus, help us never to turn away from you.*

🧑 The verb *reform* can mean to improve something by correcting an error. It can also mean to get rid of abuses or wrong practices. As a noun the word *reform* often means a change for the better or a correction of abuses. In groups discuss ways you may have heard the word *reform* being used or situations in which it could be used.

## WE BELIEVE

When Josiah became king of Judah in 640 B.C., the Assyrian empire was falling apart. Josiah helped Judah to slowly regain its independence. However, Josiah was remembered for something much more important. While some of his workers were repairing the Temple, they found a copy of "the book of the law." This was probably an early version of the Book of Deuteronomy.

When Josiah read the book, he was surprised to discover how different the worship of his day was from that of the time of Moses. Thus, Josiah began a reform of religious practices in Judah. Josiah banned all false practices. Even local places of worship to the one true God were closed, and their priests were brought to the Temple.

The prophet Zephaniah appeared early in Josiah's reign. His message is in the Book of Zephaniah. Like Isaiah before him, Zephaniah condemned the worship of false gods. He welcomed Josiah's reforms. The prophet urged the people to change their ways and to return to the faith of Moses. Zephaniah said that God, in his great love, would allow a faithful remnant to at last enjoy the peace, prosperity, and justice that the covenant promised.

Why was Josiah's rule important to Judah?

**Babylon Conquers Judah** In 609 B.C., Josiah died in a battle against the king of Egypt. Judah once again lost its independence and now had to pledge loyalty to Egypt. This did not last for long, however.

We can read in the Book of Nahum that Assyria was eventually conquered. The king of Babylon destroyed Nineveh, the capital of Assyria. He also attacked and defeated Egypt. So Judah now became a part of the Babylonian empire. As a result, the king of Judah, had to pledge loyalty to Babylon. The king did not remain faithful to God. He encouraged idolatry. Violence and social injustice flourished and many people turned their backs on God.

When the king of Judah was disloyal to the king of Babylon, revenge was taken on Judah. Babylon invaded Judah in 598 B.C. The king of Babylon ruined the crop and pasture lands, and captured Jerusalem in 597 B.C. He forced the new king of Judah, the royal family, the court officials, and many other people to leave Judah and go to Babylon. This was the first step of the exile, or forced removal, of God's people from their own land.

The king of Babylon also carried off as much of Judah's wealth as he could. He left Zedekiah in charge of Judah. Later Zedekiah rebelled against the king. In 594 B.C. the king of Babylon invaded Judah a second time. Once again he ruined farm lands, deported more of the people to Babylon, and carried off more of Judah's wealth. Despite these losses, Zedekiah continued to resist the king of Babylon. But in 587 B.C. the king of Babylon invaded Judah a third time. He destroyed Jerusalem, including the Temple, and deported even more people to Babylon. The people of Judah were in exile. This was the end of Judah, the southern kingdom, and its proud line of kings descended from David.

## WE RESPOND

Think about the messages of Isaiah, Micah, and Zephaniah. Then pretend you are a prophet calling the people of Judah to turn back to God. What is your message to them? Write some notes here.

_____

_____

_____

In small groups deliver your speeches to one another.

# Prophets called the people to faithfulness.

## WE GATHER

✝ *God, help us to show your love to others.*

How do you serve God and your parish community now? How do you think God will call you to serve in the future?

## WE BELIEVE

Prophets served God by constantly calling the people to change their ways and to rely on God, especially during the difficult times. One of these prophets was Habakkuk, who appeared between 605 and 597 B.C. His message can still be read in the Book of Habakkuk. The prophet questioned God's ways saying,

"Why do you let me see ruin;
    why must I look at misery?"
(Habakkuk 1:3).

In reply, God told him that Babylon was an instrument for purifying Judah of its sins. However, God added that those who were faithful to him and just to their neighbors would continue to remain in his love.

God calls each of us to be cleansed of our sins and strengthened to be faithful to him. It is in the sacrament of Baptism that we are first freed from sin. We sometimes fail to follow God's laws and then it is in the sacrament of Reconciliation that we are forgiven our sins. Our promise to perform a penance shows that we are sorry for turning away from God and not loving others. We try to focus on loving God and the things that are important in our lives as Christians. Part of reconciliation is our firm purpose to rely on God and not to sin again.

**The Prophet Jeremiah**   Another prophet named Jeremiah lived from around 650 B.C. until just after 583 B.C. These were very troubled times. They affected Jeremiah deeply and caused him to struggle with his vocation. A **vocation** is God's call to serve him. In Jeremiah's case, it was a call to be God's prophet.

God is with each of us too, as we work to serve God and others.

Jeremiah resisted God's call at first, saying,
    "I know not how to speak; I am too
        young."
But God replied,
"Have no fear . . .
because I am with you . . ."
Then God touched Jeremiah's mouth and said,
"See, I place my words in your mouth!"
(Jeremiah 1:6, 8, 9). Thereafter, Jeremiah was dedicated to God's service.

In 627 B.C. after "the book of the law" had been found, King Josiah called the people to follow their covenant relationship with God. Jeremiah supported the king, but Jeremiah soon had doubts about these reforms. He saw people openly perform religious ceremonies, but they did not have an inner understanding of the covenant and how it called them to live justly. The people simply did not have their hearts in God's service. Jeremiah wept at this unfaithfulness.

Jeremiah warned the people of awful consequences for failing to live by the covenant. He told the people of Judah that nothing would remain, not even a remnant, *unless* they started to live according to the covenant. "Only if you thoroughly reform your ways and your deeds; if each of you deals justly with his neighbor . . . will I remain with you in this place, in the land which I gave your fathers long ago and forever" (Jeremiah 7:5, 7).

When the people heard Jeremiah's threatening prediction, they accused him of blasphemy. **Blasphemy** is a thought, word, or act that refers to God without respect or reverence. Jeremiah was rejected, attacked, and imprisoned. Still, Jeremiah continued to speak out against the sins of the nation. He begged God to let him abandon his vocation. But God told Jeremiah to remain faithful, for God would be with him.

In 587 B.C., just before the final destruction of Jerusalem, Jeremiah advised the people not to resist the Babylonian invaders. He said, "Serve the king of Babylon that you may live; else this city will become a heap of ruins" (Jeremiah 27:17). Jeremiah urged the people to do this so that Jerusalem and its Temple might be spared from complete destruction. The people were very angry and did not accept that the Babylonians were part of God's plan. Thus, the people did not listen to Jeremiah. They did not realize what was about to happen to Jerusalem and to the Temple.

How is the message of Jeremiah similar to that of other prophets?

**Baruch Assures the People** The prophetic writing in the Book of Baruch was similar to that of Jeremiah. It was written to bring comfort to people who had lost their homeland. It stressed belief in the one true God, faithfulness to the Law of Moses, repentance, and hope.

**Key Words**

**vocation** God's call to serve him in a special way

**blasphemy** a thought, word, or act that refers to God without respect or reverence

## As Catholics...

A vocation is God's call to serve him, and it is a way of living our faith. As baptized Christians we all share a common vocation. We are called to grow in holiness and to become more like Jesus Christ. We are called to bring the good news of Jesus to others so that they, too, will love and follow him.

God also calls each of us to serve him in a particular way. We can follow our vocation in the single life, married life, religious life, or priesthood.

Like Jeremiah, we may be unsure of God's call. But the Holy Spirit will guide us as we pray and find out more about the different vocations. Family, friends, and teachers also help us to discover how God is calling us to serve him.

In groups identify the vocations of different people in your lives.

## WE RESPOND

Jeremiah asks that each of us treat our "neighbors" justly. Who are our neighbors? With a partner list some ways that we can work for justice for all people.

_____

_____

_____

Act out some of your ideas for the class. Have the members of your class try to guess your works of justice.

**Circle the letter of the correct answer.**

1. _____ began a reform of religious practices in Judah, banning all false practices.

   **a.** Ahaz     **b.** Manasseh     **c.** Josiah

2. The life of the prophet _____ was tragic and his message was not often accepted, but he never lost hope. He knew that God was always with his people.

   **a.** Jeremiah     **b.** Jehoiakim     **c.** Josiah

3. _____ is a thought, word, or act that refers to God without respect or reverence.

   **a.** Blasphemy     **b.** Vocation     **c.** Remnant

4. God sent the prophet _____ to keep the people of Judah close to him. His message was one of hope and comfort to the people.

   **a.** Ahaz     **b.** Isaiah     **c.** Hezekiah

**Short Answers**

5. What was Jeremiah's vocation?

   _____

6. What was stressed in the prophetic writing in the Book of Baruch?

   _____

7. What happened to Judah after it became part of the Babylonian empire?

   _____

8. What did Micah say about goodness?

   _____

**Write a paragraph to answer this question.**

**9–10.** What did Isaiah say about a remnant of God's people?

ASSESSMENT

Make a time line of key events that took place in Judah from the time Solomon's empire divided to the time that the Babylonians took over. Present your time line to the class.

# We Respond in Faith

## Reflect & Pray

All of us are called to be God's prophets to those around us. With God's help I will carry out this mission by

_____

_____

_____

Dear God, help us always to remember that you are the center of our lives. Amen.

**Key Words**

**vocation** (p. 191)
**blasphemy** (p. 191)

## Remember

- Judah struggled to remain faithful to God.
- Prophets brought Judah hope and comfort.
- The kingdom of Judah came to an end.
- Prophets called the people to faithfulness.

## OUR CATHOLIC LIFE

### Encyclicals

One of the ways that the Church has carried on the mission of the prophets has been through encyclicals. Encyclicals are teachings that the popes have sent in letter form to the whole Church. Encyclicals are first addressed to the bishops of the Church, then to all people of good will.

Encyclicals help us to understand what is happening in the world, and how we can help society by living out the gospel. In 1963, Pope John XXIII wrote an encyclical about the right of all people to live in peace and freedom. In 1995, Pope John Paul II wrote an encyclical on the value of human life.

Like the writings of the prophets, these letters from the popes give us words of wisdom for our times. They call us to live as faithful followers of Jesus Christ.

# SHARING FAITH
## with My Family

## Sharing What I Learned

Discuss the following with your family:

- life in Judah
- the prophets Isaiah and Micah
- vocation
- the prophet Jeremiah.

## Share a Prayer

This Jewish prayer is said after eating a meal.

Write a prayer that you can pray after eating a meal. Share your prayer with your family.

"Blessed are You, O Lord our God, King of all the world, Who created so many living things, all with their own needs, and also created the means of giving each his food and life."

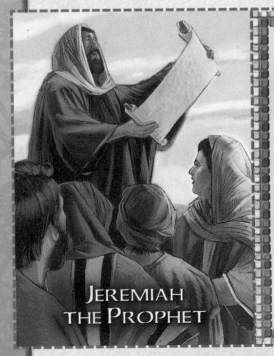

JEREMIAH THE PROPHET

Who is Jeremiah?

_____

_____

What was his vocation?

_____

_____

How is his message still important today?

_____

_____

## We Believe Trading Cards

Complete the facts on the back of the trading card. Then share with your family what you have learned about the prophet Jeremiah.

Visit Sadlier's
www.WEBELIEVEweb.com

**Connect to the Catechism**
For adult background and reflection, see paragraphs 716, 710, and 873.

## ✚ We Gather in Prayer

**Leader:** There are many people in our world who live in exile, who have been sent away from their home or country. Let us pray for them.

**Reader 1:** For those who are homeless in our towns and cities, let us pray.

**All:** Lord, help us to help them.

**Reader 2:** For those in prison, especially for those who are unjustly accused, and for their families, let us pray.

**All:** Lord, help us to help them.

**Reader 3:** For refugees from war, famine, and oppression, let us pray.

**All:** Lord, help us to help them.

**Reader 4:** For all children without homes, let us pray.

**All:** Lord, help us to help them.

**Reader 5:** For all those in hospitals, let us pray.

**All:** Lord, help us to help them.

**Reader 6:** For those who are dying, that they may reach their heavenly home in peace, let us pray.

**All:** Lord, help us to help them.

**Leader:** Let us pray.
Lord, we remember all who are in exile today,
all who are kept from their homes by war, poverty, and illness.
May we find ways to help them in prayer and action.
We ask this in your name, Lord Jesus.

**All:** Amen.

# Prophets continued to share God's message.

## WE GATHER

✝ *God, save your people and grant us your salvation.*

What are some different ways that people show their sorrow? Think of a time when you felt sorrow and shared it with someone.

## WE BELIEVE

The destruction of Jerusalem was a frightening and sorrowful experience for God's people. They mourned for their nation, their Temple, and the people who had been lost. The Book of Lamentations expresses what the people were feeling during this time. A **lamentation** is a sorrow that is expressed in the form of a poem.

The Book of Lamentations contains five such poems. These poems describe in detail the destruction of Judah and the suffering and grief of the people. The biblical writer of Lamentations, most likely the prophet Jeremiah, knew that only firm faith in God's love could comfort the people.

The prophet Ezekiel had a message very similar to Jeremiah's. Ezekiel was a priest and almost certainly was one of the Israelites exiled to Babylon in 597 B.C. Called to be God's prophet in 593 B.C., he carried out his twenty-year ministry among the Israelites exiled in far-off Babylon. His message is found in the Book of Ezekiel.

Ezekiel called the people back to God and condemned all forms of social injustice, idolatry, and superstition. **Superstition** is the false belief that living creatures or things possess powers that in fact they do not have.

Superstitions take away from the honor we owe the all-knowing and all-powerful God. What are some superstitions that you have seen on television shows or in movies?

We, too, are called to trust in God and his desire for our well being. We are called to follow Christ's example of complete confidence in God the Father's blessings for us.

**The Message of Ezekiel** In powerful language Ezekiel described a vision that he had. In this vision the glory of God abandoned Jerusalem. The glory of God first left the holy of holies, then the Temple itself, and finally the city of Jerusalem. Ezekiel declared that, by their actions, the people had rejected God. Now as Ezekiel's vision showed, God rejected Jerusalem and the Temple as his dwelling place.

**lamentation** a sorrow that is expressed in the form of a poem

**superstition** the false belief that living creatures or things possess powers that in fact they do not have

Ezekiel's message went further than Jeremiah's by declaring that the people had been unfaithful to God from the very beginning. Ezekiel delivered these stinging words of God to the people. "Can your heart remain firm, will your hands be strong, in the days when I deal with you? I, the LORD, have spoken, and I will act. I will disperse you among the nations and scatter you over foreign lands, so that I may purge your uncleanness." (Ezekiel 22:14–15) These words of Ezekiel came true after the final destruction of Jerusalem in 587 B.C.

During the time of the exile, Ezekiel began to offer words of hope and comfort to the people. He told them that God had said, "I will give you a new heart and place a new spirit within you" (Ezekiel 36:26).

Ezekiel described a new exodus and desert experience. Ezekiel said that God would purify those who remained true to him. He would shepherd them triumphantly back to their homes in the promised land. There Israel would live forever in peace. Prosperity and justice would prevail under the guidance of the one true God. God would again choose Jerusalem as his dwelling place. He would give the city a new name meaning "The LORD is here" (Ezekiel 48:35).

## WE RESPOND

How do you think the people in exile received Ezekiel's message of hope and comfort?

Imagine that Ezekiel had not spoken this message, but had painted a picture or made a sculpture to symbolize the return to the promised land. What might this look like? Design your own work to assure others that God brings comfort and hope.

Babylonian ruins in the Middle East.

## God's people in exile were given hope.

### WE GATHER

✝ *God, my God, in you we hope.*

How did you first learn about God's unfailing love? Has your understanding of it changed as you have grown older? How has your faith grown?

### WE BELIEVE

As exiles in Babylon, God's people were afraid and confused, but this experience also helped them to grow. The way they understood themselves and their relationship with God changed. For the first time the exiles identified themselves as Jews and called their religion *Judaism*. More importantly, they began to realize just how unfaithful they had been to God.

The Jewish people asked themselves what their covenant with God involved. They began to see that it was not birth in the promised land or citizenship in an independent Judah that made a person one of God's people. Rather, being one of God's people meant truly following his will, having absolute faith in him, and making a personal commitment to follow the covenant. For the Jews this was a new understanding of their relationship with God. This understanding of faith still influences Jewish faith and practices today.

The Babylonians treated the exiles quite well, and the Jews were able to remain a community. The Babylonians gave them fertile land on which to live and allowed the exiles to go freely about their lives. As a result, many of the exiles became quite wealthy, and some were even appointed to important positions at the royal court. In these ways God continued to protect his people and to set in place his plan for their future.

**Isaiah in Babylon**   Late in the exile another prophet appeared in Babylon. He was known as Isaiah of Babylon, and his clear message of hope to the people of Israel can be read in the Book of Isaiah. It is found in Chapters 40—55. His message is the second prophetic message in the Book of Isaiah.

Like faith, hope is a gift from God. **Hope** enables us to trust in God's promise to be with us always. Hope enables us to be confident in God's love and care for us.

Isaiah called the people to be faithful to God and to have hope. He reminded them that God remained as faithful and loving as he was to his people when they were in Egypt. He proclaimed that God was about to save them in an even greater way than he had when their ancestors crossed to freedom at the Red Sea.

But Isaiah said that salvation would come only through the suffering of a servant of the Lord. This servant would be without sin.

"Through his suffering, my servant shall
   justify many,
  and their guilt he shall bear . . .
And he shall take away the sins of many,
  and win pardon for their offenses."
(Isaiah 53:11, 12)

The writers of the New Testament understand these passages to be fulfilled in Jesus Christ. He is the sinless servant who "did not come to be served but to serve and to give his life as a ransom for many" (Matthew 20:28).

As Christians we believe that God showed us his great love by sending his only Son to us. In Jesus Christ God's love is made present to us, so our hope is in Christ. Hope helps us to rely not on our own strength, but on the strength of God the Holy Spirit—sent to us by the Father and the Son.

**Key Word**

**hope** a gift from God that enables us to trust in God's promise to be with us always; it enables us to be confident in God's love and care for us

## As Catholics...

We believe that Jesus Christ is the suffering servant about whom Isaiah spoke. Christ is the Messiah, or Anointed One for whom the people waited and yearned. At Jesus' baptism, the Father made it known that Jesus was his Son. The Holy Spirit came upon him, anointing him as priest, prophet, and king.

We call Jesus a priest because he offered the perfect sacrifice that no one else could. Jesus offered himself to save us. Jesus was a prophet because he delivered God's message of love and forgiveness. He spoke out for truth and justice. Jesus showed himself to be a king by the care he gave to all his people. Jesus lived among the people as one of them. He came to serve, not to be served. Jesus' reign, or rule, makes God's love present and active in the lives of his people.

As baptized members of the Church, we share in Jesus' role as priest, prophet, and king. How can we serve others by what we say and do?

## WE RESPOND

 Pretend that you are in Babylon listening to Isaiah preach. With a group role-play the situation. Have one person be Isaiah and deliver God's message. Have others ask Isaiah questions about this message and about the way God would save them.

199

# God's people searched for wisdom.

## WE GATHER

✝ *God, grant us wisdom.*

Think about communities in your neighborhood, city, or state. How do the customs of many countries influence the people in these communities?

## WE BELIEVE

During the years of the Babylonian captivity, and throughout their long history, the Jews met people who had different beliefs and customs. Jewish people became particularly attracted to the tradition of writing about wisdom.

The Jewish people went on to write a body of wisdom literature of their own. Some of this material is contained in the wisdom books of the Old Testament. The wisdom books give practical guidance on how to live. Some of these books use proverbs to teach. A **proverb** is a brief saying that gives wise advice. It makes a clear point that can be easily remembered.

## The Wisdom Literature of the Old Testament

| | |
|---|---|
| **Book of Job** | This book reminds us that suffering is a part of life for all people. Those who are innocent and faithful to God suffer, too, and are brought to a deeper trust in God. |
| **Book of Psalms** | This book is a collection of poetic prayers and songs known as psalms. These psalms help us to give worship to God. They are an important part of the Church's liturgy. |
| **Book of Proverbs** | This book gives advice on how to live. It covers a wide range of topics, from the simplest everyday concerns to the most complicated thoughts about God and our faith. |
| **Book of Ecclesiastes** | This book teaches us that riches, pleasure, and even wisdom, only bring happiness for a while. God alone can provide lasting happiness. |
| **Song of Songs** | This book is a collection of love poems that use symbolic language to help us understand God's love for us and our covenant relationship with him. |
| **Book of Wisdom** | This book is designed to urge people to live a good and holy life. For that reason it argues *against* greed, selfishness, and idolatry, and *for* faith in the one true God. |
| **Book of Sirach (or Ecclesiasticus)** | This book deals with growing in faith and teaches that we can grow in faith by living a good and holy life. |

**The Book of Job** One of the most famous examples of wisdom literature is the Book of Job. It tells the story of what happened to Job, a wealthy and powerful man.

Job had a wonderful wife, a large family, many relatives and servants, and a great number of possessions. He was also a good and just man of God. Suddenly, everything went wrong for Job. He lost his children and his possessions. Worse yet, a dreadful disease took hold of his body, and he began to feel desperate. Throughout his unexplainable suffering he remained faithful to God and said "We accept good things from God; and should we not accept evil?" (Job 2:10).

When Job cried out to God during his sufferings, God reminded Job that human beings did not always understand God's purposes. Suffering, the Lord explained, also came to those who were faithful to God. Job accepted this explanation, and he was suddenly filled with a deeper trust in God. Eventually the Lord rewarded his faithful follower and everything that Job had lost was given back to him in a double measure.

What does the story of Job teach us? Do you know people who suffer yet remain faithful to God?

**WE RESPOND**

 As a class start a book of proverbs that is a how-to-manual for living a good and just life. What will you call your book of wisdom?

**Key Word**

**proverb** a brief saying that gives wise advice

# The long return to Judah happened in three stages.

## WE GATHER

✝ *Jesus, be our guide.*

Think about a project that you have completed. What were the different stages that you went through before the project was finally accomplished?

## WE BELIEVE

Throughout history God shows that his love is everlasting. We see God's constant love for his people, Israel, as he planned the stages of their return to the land that he had promised them.

In 539 B.C. the Persians came down from the mountains of what is now Iran and Afghanistan and took over the Babylonian empire. A year later, the Jews in exile received unbelievable news. Cyrus, the Persian king, had decided to let them return to their homeland. They would be free to rebuild the Temple and practice their faith in peace. Though Judah would still belong to Persia and have a Persian governor, the Jews would be allowed to govern themselves in local and religious matters. This news was greeted with joyous celebrations, and Cyrus became an instant hero.

**First Stage of the Return to Judah** Returning to Judah and rebuilding the nation would

not be an easy task. It would have to be accomplished in stages. In 538 B.C. Cyrus appointed a prominent descendant of David to lead a group of Jews back to Judah. This group began the rebuilding of the Jewish nation.

Then Cyrus unexpectedly died in battle. And the rebuilding project was delayed and work on the Temple was stopped. Still, the exile was over and Jews were in their homeland again.

Around 520 B.C. the voices of two new prophets, Haggai and Zechariah, were heard. They cried out to those who had returned to stop concentrating only on their own interest and to rebuild the Temple. They wanted the unfinished work to be completed. We can still read their stirring arguments in the Book of Haggai and in the Book of Zechariah, Chapters 1—8.

By this time a strong new ruler was reorganizing the Persian empire. He appointed two prominent Jews to lead a large Jewish expedition back to Judah. With the help of the rousing calls of Haggai and Zechariah, this group succeeded in rebuilding the Temple and resettling a large part of the land. The incomplete Temple was dedicated in 520 B.C., and the Temple was finally finished around 515 B.C. In this manner God completed the first stage of his plan to reestablish the exiled Jews in their homeland: Jews occupied the land, and the Temple was restored.

## Second Stage of the Return to Judah

About seventy years after the Temple was rebuilt, Judah was again in danger. Foreign people were trying to take Jewish land in the south and southeast. Nehemiah was sent to protect the city from these attacks by rebuilding the walls of Jerusalem. His work moved God's plan for his people forward. God completed the second stage of the return: Judah was freed from foreign attack. This part of the history of Judah can be read about in the Book of Nehemiah.

## Third Stage of the Return to Judah

Nehemiah's mission had been a military one, but another Jew, Ezra, wanted to reform the religious and social practices in Judah. Ezra obtained Persian permission to lead a group of Jewish exiles back to Judah. The Book of Ezra records what happened. To carry out his task, Ezra brought along a copy of the law that was transcribed in Babylon about 560 B.C. He ordered it to be read publicly in Jerusalem. At first the people were very enthusiastic. Then Ezra told them that they should be following the Law of Moses or the Torah, and that they had failed in doing so too many times. The **Torah** is the Hebrew name for the first five books of the Old Testament.

In a dramatic scene in the Temple Ezra wept publicly and recalled the people's sins against God. The people were so moved that they repented and agreed to follow God's law. In this way God accomplished the last stage of the return to Judah: The people submitted fully to God's law.

Though Judah remained a Persian province until 331 B.C., the people were serving God, not the Persian king.

**Key Word**

**Torah** the Hebrew name for the first five books of the Old Testament

## WE RESPOND

We, too, are called to follow God's law. We do this when we live by the teachings of Jesus Christ.

With a partner brainstorm different ways that we, as members of the Church, can say and do the things that Jesus Christ taught us to do.

_____

_____

_____

Choose one thing that you will do this week to show that you follow Jesus' teaching.

**Write the letter that best defines each term.**

1. _____ hope

2. _____ lamentation

3. _____ proverb

4. _____ superstition

**a.** false belief that living creatures or things possess powers that in fact they do not have

**b.** the Hebrew name for the first five books of the Old Testament

**c.** a gift from God that enables us to trust in God's promise to be with us always

**d.** a sorrow expressed in the form of a poem

**e.** a brief saying that gives wise advice

**Short Answers**

5. How are the messages of the prophets Ezekiel and Jeremiah similar?

_____

6. Name some important changes that took place while God's people were exiled in Babylon.

_____

7. What was the outcome of each of the three stages in God's plan for the return of the exiled people to Judah?

_____

8. Name three wisdom books of the Old Testament that give practical guidance on how to live.

_____

**Write a paragraph to answer this question.**

9–10. According to Isaiah of Babylon, how will God save his people?

ASSESSMENT

God's people in exile were given hope. God protected his people and set plans in place for their future. Make a photo or caption collage that illustrates, in modern day terms, how God gave his exiled people hope and protection.

# We Respond in Faith

## Reflect & Pray

The Church has a special Mass for Refugees and Exiles at which we pray:

Lord,
no one is a stranger to you
and no one is ever far from your
    loving care.
Amen.

I will keep the refugees of the world in my prayers this week by

_____

**Key Words**

lamentation (p. 196)
superstition (p. 196)
hope (p. 199)
proverb (p. 200)
Torah (p. 203)

## Remember

- Prophets continued to share God's message.

- God's people in exile were given hope.

- God's people searched for wisdom.

- The long return to Judah happened in three stages.

## OUR CATHOLIC LIFE

### Saint Bonaventure

Saint Bonaventure was born in 1221 in Tuscany, Italy. At a young age he joined the Franciscan order, a religious community that had recently been founded by Saint Francis of Assisi. Bonaventure moved from Italy to Paris, France, where he studied at the university. He became a wonderful scholar and writer. He wrote about God and became known for his great love of God. He kept a large crucifix of Jesus on his desk, and he said that all the beautiful things he wrote about God came from Jesus, his only teacher. Bonaventure wrote a biography on the life of Saint Francis of Assisi. Bonaventure's books made him famous, but he remained humble.

In 1273 Bonaventure was named a cardinal, and his knowledge and wisdom were of great help to the pope and bishops. He died in 1274. His feast day is July 15.

# SHARING FAITH
## with My Family

### Sharing What I Learned

Discuss the following with your family:

- living in exile
- the prophets Ezekiel and Isaiah
- the wisdom books
- the return to Judah.

### Share a Prayer

This Jewish blessing is prayed at first sight of an ocean or sea.

Write a prayer that you can pray when you look at God's creation. Share your prayer with your family.

"Blessed are You,
O Lord our God,
King of all the world,
Who made the great sea."

JOB

Who is Job?

_____

_____

What is his story?

_____

_____

What can we learn from his story today?

_____

_____

### We Believe Trading Cards

Complete the facts on the back of the trading card. Then share with your family what you have learned about the story of Job.

Visit Sadlier's

**www.WeBelieveweb.com**

**Connect to the Catechism**
For adult background and reflection, see paragraphs 711, 713, and 1831.

# A Strong People

## ✠ We Gather in Prayer

**Leader:** The wise walk in the ways of the Lord. They listen to the messages that God sends them.

Let us listen to these words of wisdom from Scripture.

**Reader 1:** "He who walks honestly walks securely, but he whose ways are crooked will fare badly."
(Proverbs 10:9)

**All:** Lord, give us wisdom to speak and act with honesty.

**Reader 2:** "Hatred stirs up disputes, but love covers all offenses."
(Proverbs 10:12)

**All:** Lord, give us wisdom to grow in love for all people.

**Reader 3:** "Better a little with virtue, than a large income with injustice."
(Proverbs 16:8)

**All:** Lord, give us wisdom to act justly and with compassion.

**Reader 4:** "He sins who despises the hungry; but happy is he who is kind to the poor!"
(Proverbs 14:21)

**All:** Lord, give us wisdom to find and serve you in all our brothers and sisters.

**Reader 5:** "A faithful friend is a sturdy shelter; he who finds one finds a treasure."
(Sirach 6:14)

**All:** Lord, give us wisdom to be faithful and true friends to others.

**Reader 6:** "A cheerful glance brings joy to the heart; good news invigorates the bones."
(Proverbs 15:30)

**All:** Lord, give us wisdom to understand the good news that you send to us. Let it fill us with joy!

**Leader:** Lord, teach us your ways. Help us grow in grace and truth. Let us pray:

**All:** Give us the peace of mind to accept what cannot be changed. Give us the courage to change what can be changed. And give us the wisdom to know the one from the other. Amen.

# The Jews lived and worshiped together.

## WE GATHER

✝ *We will go up to the house of the Lord.*

Think of a book, television show, or movie that contains an important message for people.
What is the message?
How is the message communicated?

## WE BELIEVE

As we have seen, each of the prophets had a message for God's people. Through the prophets, God showed the people love and concern. Ezra was a priest who also helped God's people. He called them back to faithfulness to God's laws.

The prophets supported Ezra's reforms. One of these prophets was known as Isaiah of Judah. His message, the third prophetic message in the Book of Isaiah, can still be read in Chapters 56—66 of that book.

Like Ezra, Isaiah focused on true worship. However, Isaiah made a connection between worship and the fair and just treatment of others. Isaiah linked praising God and social justice. Isaiah called the people to care for the needs of all those who suffered. Worship, he said, must lead people to act with justice or it is meaningless. Isaiah told the people that since they had been faithful to God during their exile in Babylon, God would restore them to their former glory, and they would be a light to all nations. Isaiah said,
"Rise up in splendor! Your light has come,
 the glory of the Lord shines upon you."
(Isaiah 60:1)

**Other Biblical Writings** The Book of Malachi is a short prophetic book, and is the message of a person who goes by the title Malachi, meaning "my messenger." He called the people to worship God and to be just. He foresaw a day when God would come to judge his people. He mentioned a messenger who would prepare the way for repentance and true worship. We read about such a messenger in the Gospel of Matthew when John the Baptist appears in Judea:

"A voice of one crying out in the desert,
'Prepare the way of the Lord,
 make straight his paths.'" (Matthew 3:3)

The Book of Obadiah reminds us that God is just. This book was written at a time when the Jewish people were having problems with the Edomites. Edom was a small area to the southeast of Judah. The people living in Edom worshiped false gods. During the Jewish return from Babylon, the Edomites started to settle in southern Judah and this caused God's people many problems. The Book of Obadiah presents the hope for the survival of the Jewish people and the return of the kingdom begun by David.

The Book of Joel uses images to show the people the need for true repentance.
"Rend your hearts, not your garments,
 and return to the LORD, your God" (Joel 2:13),
the prophet insists. He tells the people that only in this way will Israel be restored to God's favor.

The Book of Daniel gives insight into the long years of Babylonian exile and Persian domination. Stories about Daniel and his companions convey a religious message. These stories express hope and tell of the importance of behavior that is acceptable to the Lord. They show that God's people are able to be faithful to their religious traditions even in a foreign land. They also demonstrate that God is always at work protecting his people, whatever happens to them.

The Book of Esther, like the Book of Daniel, is a kind of historical romance. It is a mixture of fact and fiction designed to offer hope and instruction to a defeated people.

Esther appeals to the king of Persia. A page from the Megillat—The Book of Esther, 18th century.

Mordecai wrote a letter to Jews everywhere telling them of these events. He asked them to mark this day when God delivered the Jews from destruction. This day would be celebrated by a new festival—the feast of Purim. Jews today continue to celebrate this feast recalling that through God's help Esther saved God's people.

## WE RESPOND

Throughout history God has worked through his people. What are some ways that God works through people

in your family?

_____

_____

in your parish?

_____

_____

in your city or town?

_____

_____

in your state or country?

_____

_____

in the world?

_____

_____

Esther was a virtuous Jewish girl. She was also married to the king of Persia. The king appointed Esther's guardian, Mordecai, to a high office. When Mordecai displeased Haman, a Persian nobleman, Haman plotted to destroy Mordecai and all the other Jews in the Persian empire. Haman convinced the king that the Jews were traitors because they lived apart and worshiped the one true God. The king agreed that the Jews should be killed and the day of this terrible event would be decided by casting lots, or in Hebrew, *purim*.

Mordecai begged Esther for help. Esther prayed and fasted and, then at great risk to herself, appealed to the king to save the Jews. God heard Esther's prayer. The king spared the Jews.

# God continued to work through his people.

## WE GATHER

✝ *God, help us to see your work in our lives.*

What are some favorite stories from your childhood? Are they about people you know and things that happened, or are they from books that you have read?

Why did you enjoy these stories?

## WE BELIEVE

Storytelling is an important way that the biblical writers help people to understand their relationship with God. The stories in the Bible are sometimes a part of historical or prophetic books. Other times the story is recorded in a specific book of the Bible—often bearing the name of a character in the story. Either way the stories contain symbolic, interesting characters who deal with the issue of God's providence. Providence is God's constant care for and protection of his people.

**The Story of Tobit** Tobit was a wealthy Jew living in Nineveh, Assyria. His story is recorded in the Book of Tobit. When Tobit had financial losses and then became blind, he prayed that God would let him die because he was so miserable. Tobit sent his son Tobiah to Media, a Persian province, to collect a large sum of money that was owed to him.

Meanwhile, a young woman named Sarah lived in Media. She too was very sad. Every one of the seven husbands that she had married had died. God decided to send the angel Raphael in disguise to help Tobit, Tobiah, and Sarah.

Raphael helped Tobiah recover his father's money and arranged for Tobiah to marry Sarah. Then Tobiah, Sarah, and Raphael returned to Nineveh. There Raphael showed Tobiah how to cure his father's blindness. Finally Raphael revealed his true identity and returned to heaven. Tobit then sang a beautiful hymn. His song began,
"Blessed be God who lives forever,
    because his kingdom lasts for all ages"
(Tobit 13:1).
Tobit's hymn praised God for his providence.

In what ways is God present in our lives? In what ways do we praise God for his care and concern for us?

Detail of *Judith*, by Giorgione (1476–1510)

**The Story of Judith** Providence is also the principal theme of the Book of Judith. As her story opens, the Jews had refused to help Assyria fight against its enemies. Thus, the king of Assyria had sent his commander-in-chief to punish the Jewish people. The Jews fought for thirty-four days protecting themselves, but eventually were ready to surrender.

In the story Judith quickly offered to rescue the Jews from danger. Her offer was accepted. After fasting and praying for God's help, Judith went to the Assyrian camp. There Judith was the last to leave a banquet at which the Assyrian commander had had too much to drink.

The story goes on to portray Judith as a great heroine whose brave actions rescued the Jews. So through Judith's courage, God saved his people from their enemies.

**The Story of Jonah**   One of the most interesting writings of the time is the short story that makes up the Book of Jonah. The story of Jonah is also known as a parable. A **parable** is a short story that has a message. A parable is usually about something familiar, but it is told to make a point about something else.

In the story, Jonah was called to be one of God's prophets. But he flatly refused to carry God's message of doom to the sinful city of Nineveh. Instead Jonah sailed off on a ship because he did not believe that the people of Nineveh would listen to him. While he was at sea, there was a great storm. Thinking he was bad luck, the crew threw Jonah overboard and he was swallowed by a huge fish. After three days, the fish coughed up Jonah safe and sound onto dry land. Then God sent him back to Nineveh to complete his mission.

Jonah's story is very symbolic. As Christians, it reminds us of the Resurrection. Just as God wanted Jonah to deliver a message, God sent Jesus Christ to bring his life and love to all people. And just as Jonah spent three days in the belly of the fish, Jesus Christ rose from the dead after three days in the tomb.

The people of Nineveh listened to Jonah's message and repented and God spared the city. This unexpected turn of events made Jonah angry. He complained that God should have punished the wicked people of Nineveh. God reminded Jonah that these people were also God's creation.

This story conveys a message: God extends his mercy to all who truly repent. It reminds us not to be narrow-minded but to have a tolerant attitude toward all people.

## As Catholics...

Jesus often used parables in his teaching. His parables compare one thing to another or identify one thing by an example of another. For instance, Jesus used examples from nature, farming, feasts, and everyday work to describe the Kingdom of God— the power of God's love coming into the world and into our lives. Jesus also told parables to help his disciples understand God's mercy and God's justice.

With your family select one parable from Chapter 13 of the Gospel of Matthew and discuss what you think it means.

**WE RESPOND**

Make a mural that illustrates the meaning of one of the stories from the Books of Tobit, Judith, and Jonah. Write a caption to explain the importance of the story today.

**parable** short story that has a message

# The Maccabees defended the Jewish faith.

### WE GATHER

✝ *Jesus, our faith is in you.*

🯊 Throughout history, territories and even countries, passed from one group of people to another. Often national holidays were set up to remember these events. Make a list of these kinds of holidays. Which one is your favorite?

### WE BELIEVE

The rule of Judah changed hands several times. At various times, Judah was part of different kingdoms. In 323 B.C. Judah, which was part of Palestine, came under Syrian-Mesopotamian rule. However, none of Judah's traditional political and religious arrangements changed. The Jews continued to live as they had under the Persians.

In 175 B.C., the king of Syria-Mesopotamia was warned about the Roman empire trying to take over his land. So he decided that his kingdom should be more united. He required that everyone accept the Greek culture and practice the Greek religion.

This policy split the Jewish community in Palestine. Some Jews favored the introduction of Greek culture; they were called Hellenists, or the Greek party. Others disagreed; they were the Hasidim, or the Pious party. When the king saw that his policy was being resisted, he began to persecute the Hasidim. He also captured Jerusalem, removed the high priest, and damaged the Temple.

This caused a rebellion in 167 B.C. It was led by a man called Mattathias. The events of this rebellion were recorded in the First and Second Books of Maccabees. In 166 B.C. Judas Maccabeus took charge of the revolt. The Hasidim joined Judas in rebellion against the Syrian armies and won many battles. Judas and his followers recaptured Jerusalem.

In 164 B.C. Judas cleansed the Temple and rededicated it to the worship of God. The Temple menorah, or lamp stand, was lit once again. Judas asked the people to remember this event with a festival. The festival was called the "the feast of lights" because a one-day's supply of oil in the menorah lasted for eight days. This was the origin of the festival of Hanukkah, which Jews still celebrate today. They celebrate the deeds of the people of God who refused to give up their faith.

When Judas died in battle in 160 B.C., his brother Jonathan led the people. For seventeen years they were successful in their struggle against Syria, which had been weakened by a civil war. Then Jonathan died, and his brother Simon took his place as the leader of the rebellion against the Syrian armies.

Simon took advantage of the Syrian weakness and negotiated independence for Judah. He became the country's first Jewish king since 587 B.C. Simon was also the high priest. Judah was strengthened because Simon had both civil and religious authority.

The writers of the books of Maccabees have shown us that God's providence again saved his people. The heroism and diplomacy of many men and women helped God's people survive. They could again live their faith and their covenant with God.

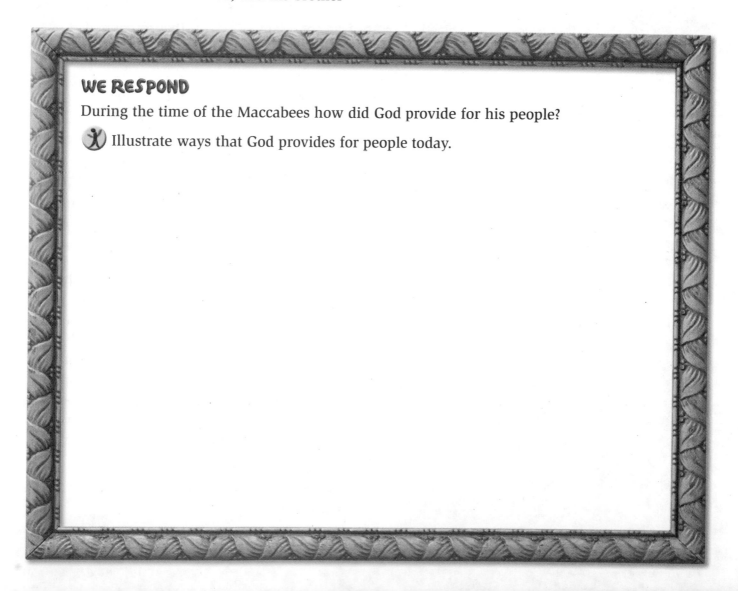

## WE RESPOND

During the time of the Maccabees how did God provide for his people?

Illustrate ways that God provides for people today.

# Judea lost its independence to Roman rule.

## WE GATHER

✝ *Holy Spirit, enlighten all leaders.*

Which countries today are ruled by kings or queens? What kind of decisions do these kings and queens make for the people in their countries?

## WE BELIEVE

In 134 B.C. Simon Maccabeus was killed and his son, John Hyrcanus, became king. John acquired a great deal of land in the south.

Because he was also the high priest, he insisted that the people living there worship the one true God and give up their false religious practices.

During John's reign there was disunity and fighting among the Pious party, the Hasidim. They questioned whether John had the right to the office of high priest. So different groups within the Hasidim formed. However, most Jews continued to worship at the Temple and did not join any of these groups.

| Groups within the Hasidim | | |
|---|---|---|
| • They refused to have anything to do with John, and were persecuted by John. | • They rejected most of John's policies. John distanced himself from this group. | • They worked closely with John to achieve his goals, and were supported by him. |
| • They no longer worshiped in Jerusalem, where John was high priest. | • They did not accept John's right to the office of high priest. | • They recognized John's title as high priest. |
| • They were believed to have set up a community at Qumran on the Dead Sea. | • They continued to worship at the Temple in Jerusalem. | • They continued to worship at the Temple in Jerusalem. |
| • They became known as the **Essenes**. | • They became known as the **Pharisees**. | • They became known as the **Sadducees**. |

When John died, his younger son, Alexander Jannaeus, became king. Like his father, he expanded his kingdom. He acquired Galilee in the east and Samaria in the north. Alexander insisted that everyone under his leadership worship only the one true God. He began to persecute the Pharisees, because they opposed his policies. Still, when he died, he left behind him a much stronger Judea. Judea was a translation for Judah, the land where the Jews had resettled.

Describe how the people reacted to the reign of John Hyrcanus.

### Rome Casts Its Long Shadow Over Judea

When Alexander Jannaeus died his wife, Alexandra, took over the leadership of Judea, and his oldest son became the high priest. This displeased his younger son, who selfishly wanted to be both king and high priest himself. When Alexandra died, a civil war broke out between the two brothers. Rome sensed the trouble in Judea and decided to get involved.

In 63 B.C. the Senate, the governing body in Rome, decided to send its most able general, Pompey the Great, to settle matters in the East. By this time Syria-Mesopotamia had fallen apart, and Rome had extended its territory into Asia Minor and elsewhere. Pompey made what remained of Syria-Mesopotamia a Roman province. He filled it with Roman troops. He also tried to end the civil war in Judea. Pompey invaded Judea, captured Jerusalem, and brought the kingdom of Judea under Roman rule. This marked the end of the kingdom, as well as the end of Jewish independence for over two thousand years.

The next thirty-three years or so saw a confused struggle for power, not only in Judea but also in Rome. During these conflicts, many Jews and many Romans, including Pompey himself, were killed.

**Herod Rules in Judea**   When peace returned in 30 B.C., Judea found itself under Roman rule. Rome gave power in Judea to a complete outsider, a man known to history as Herod the Great. Herod was a descendant of one of the families from the southern lands that had been forced by John Hyrcanus to accept the one true God. For that reason many Jews doubted whether Herod was a Jew at all.

Herod's main concern, however, was not to convince the Jews about his faithfulness to God, but to survive in a dangerous world. So Herod tried to please the all-powerful Rome, now governed by the emperor Caesar Augustus. To do this Herod stopped all local attempts to free Judea from Rome's control. He changed the office of the high priesthood from one of inheritance to one of appointment. He encouraged Greek and Roman culture in all parts of his territory. Herod also put to death all who challenged his authority, even members of his own family. The Romans were so happy with the way Herod was ruling that they made him king of Judea.

In order to have the money for his programs and to pay the huge amounts of money demanded by Rome, Herod also imposed heavy taxes on the people of Judea. Thus he was hated by many Jews and admired by most Romans.

Why was Herod hated by the Jews and admired by the Romans?

### WE RESPOND

What can leaders do to show respect for the religious beliefs of their citizens? How can we show that we respect the religious beliefs of others?

**Underline the correct answer.**

1. The prophet (**Isaiah/Malachi**) foresaw a day when God would come to judge his people, and mentioned a messenger who would prepare the way for repentance and true worship.

2. The book of (**Obadiah/Daniel**) contains stories that express hope and tell of the importance of behavior that is acceptable to the Lord.

3. The book of (**Tobit/Judith**) describes how on one occasion God rescued the Jews from their enemies through one person's courage.

4. The writers of the books of the (**Maccabees/Romans**) show us that God's providence saved his people, and allowed them to again follow their faith.

**Short Answers**

5. What does the Jewish feast of Purim celebrate?

   _____

6. What is God's providence?

   _____

7. Why is the story of Jonah considered to be symbolic of the Resurrection?

   _____

8. What does the Jewish feast of Hanukkah celebrate?

   _____

**Write a paragraph to answer this question.**

9–10. How did Judea lose its independence to Roman rule?

ASSESSMENT

God works through his people in many ways. Think about two of the people that you have learned about in this chapter. How did God work through them? Write a dialogue between these two people in which they share their experiences with one another.

# We Respond in Faith

## Reflect & Pray

God raised up great prophets to guide the people in times of trouble and distress. They reminded the people that they needed to be faithful to God.

This week I will demonstrate my faithfulness to God by

_____

God, help me _____

_____

**Key Word**

**parable** (p. 211)

## Remember

- The Jews lived and worshiped together.
- God continued to work through his people.
- The Maccabees defended the Jewish faith.
- Judea lost its independence to Roman rule.

## OUR CATHOLIC LIFE

### Saint Genevieve

Genevieve was born in the fifth century in a small village not far from Paris. When she was fifteen she dedicated her life to God. After the death of her parents, she lived with her godmother in Paris. There she prayed every day, and she worked very hard to care for those in need. She grew closer to Jesus and wanted to share his goodness with others. Legend has it that once when the people of Paris were starving she successfully led an expedition in search of food.

She became well-known for her courage, her faith, and her just ways. Once she convinced the people of Paris to trust in God and remain in the city when an enemy attack was feared. She had them pray and fast to show their faith. Paris was spared!

Saint Genevieve's feast day is January 3. She is the patron saint of Paris.

# SHARING FAITH
## with My Family

## Sharing What I Learned

Discuss the following with your family:

- the prophets Isaiah and Malachi
- the stories of Daniel, Tobit, Judith, and Jonah
- the Jewish feasts of Purim and Hanukkah
- Judea under Roman rule.

## Share a Prayer

This Jewish blessing is prayed when looking at a rainbow in the sky.

Write a prayer that you can pray when you see a rainbow in the sky. Share your prayer with your family.

"Blessed are You, O Lord our God, King of all the world, Who always remembers the promise made when Noah saw the rainbow, and will always keep that promise."

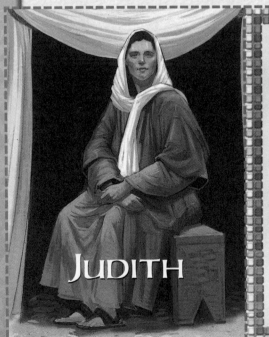

JUDITH

Who is Judith?

_____

_____

What are the events of her life story?

_____

_____

What can we learn from her story today?

_____

_____

## We Believe Trading Cards

Complete the facts on the back of the trading card. Then share with your family what you have learned about the story of Judith.

Visit Sadlier's

www.WEBELIEVEweb.com

**Connect to the Catechism**
For adult background and reflection, see paragraphs 715, 584, and 423.

# God Fulfills His Promise

## ✝ We Gather in Prayer

### 🎵 Christ, Be Our Light

Refrain:
Christ, be our light!
Shine in our hearts.
Shine through the darkness.
Christ, be our light!
Shine in your church gathered today.

Longing for light, we wait in darkness.
Longing for truth, we turn to you.
Make us your own, your holy people,
light for the world to see. (Refrain)

**Reader:** The words of Isaiah the prophet are repeated as Saint Mark writes about the mission of John the Baptist.

A reading from the holy Gospel according to Mark

**All:** Glory to you, Lord.

**Reader:** "Behold, I am sending my messenger ahead of you;
he will prepare your way.
A voice of one crying out in the desert:
'Prepare the way of the Lord,
make straight his paths.'"

(Mark 1:2–3)

The Gospel of the Lord.

**All:** Praise to you, Lord Jesus Christ.

Refrain:
Christ, be our light!
Shine in our hearts.
Shine through the darkness.
Christ, be our light!
Shine in your church gathered today.

Longing for peace, our world is troubled.
Longing for hope, many despair.
Your word alone has pow'r to save us.
Make us your living voice. (Refrain)

A painting from the *Annuciation Series*, by Maria Pia Marrella, 1995.

# Mary is blessed by God.

## WE GATHER

✝ *Hail Mary, full of grace, pray for us.*

What is the most important thing that has happened to you?

What do you consider the most important event in history? Why?

## WE BELIEVE

During the last year or two of King Herod's reign over Judea, the most important event in the history of salvation took place. The world was changed when an angel of God was sent to the town of Nazareth in Galilee. The angel gave a message to a young girl named Mary, who was engaged to Joseph. Joseph was a descendant of King David. Joseph's ancestry could be traced back through the generations to Abraham, the father of God's chosen people.

The angel said to Mary, "Hail, favored one! The Lord is with you" (Luke 1:28). When the angel saw that Mary was frightened, he continued, "Do not be afraid, Mary, for you have found favor with God. Behold, you will conceive in your womb and bear a son, and you shall name him Jesus. He will be great and will be called Son of the Most High, and the Lord God will give him the throne of David his father, and he will rule over the house of Jacob forever, and of his kingdom there will be no end" (Luke 1:30–33).

Mary did not understand how all of this would happen to her. She was not even married yet. But the angel explained, "The holy Spirit will come upon you, and the power of the Most High will overshadow you. Therefore the child to be born will be called holy, the Son of God" (Luke 1:35).

Take a moment to imagine how Mary must have felt.

The angel also told Mary that her relative Elizabeth would conceive a child. Elizabeth had never been able to have a child, and she was now very old. But the angel said that nothing was impossible with God.

Mary spoke to the angel saying, "Behold, I am the handmaid of the Lord. May it be done to me according to your word" (Luke 1:38). Mary's words showed her complete faith in God and her choice to accept and follow God's plan. The fulfillment of all that God had promised through the prophets had now begun. The long-awaited Messiah, the Savior of all people, would soon come into the world.

**Joseph and Mary** Mary was blessed by God. The child that she had conceived was the Son of God. Through Mary, God the Son, the second Person of the Blessed Trinity, would become one of us. Joseph was unaware that this was part of God's plan. So Joseph was going to leave Mary quietly. Then an angel of the Lord came to Joseph in a dream. The angel said, "Joseph, son of David, do not be afraid to take Mary your wife into your home. For it is through the holy Spirit that this child has been conceived in her. She will bear a son and you are to name him Jesus, because he will save his people from their sins" (Matthew 1:20–21).

When Joseph woke up he realized what had been revealed to him. Like Mary, Joseph did what the Lord asked of him. He welcomed Mary into his home. He protected her and cared for her and for the son that she was now carrying within her.

What did the angel tell Joseph? How did Joseph respond? How do you think he felt?

### WE RESPOND

Imagine that you have been asked to announce the coming of God's Son. Design a television news alert, a press release, or an Internet banner advertisement to share the good news. Share your design with a partner, then discuss how you think people would react to the news.

# Mary and Elizabeth had special roles in God's plan.

## WE GATHER

✝ *We proclaim the greatness of the Lord.*

Talk about some ways that your family shares good news.

## WE BELIEVE

Throughout the history of the Jewish people, God had called many women to help his people to grow strong and faithful. Now he called Mary and Elizabeth. God had special work for these two women. They had important roles in God's plan to save his people.

After the angel's visit to her, Mary began her journey to see her relatives Elizabeth and Zechariah. Zechariah had been visited by an angel, too. The angel told Zechariah that his wife, Elizabeth, would have a child and the child should be named John. Because Zechariah did not believe that this could happen, he lost his ability to speak. The angel told him that he would not speak again until his son was born.

When Mary arrived at Zechariah's house she greeted Elizabeth. The child that Elizabeth was carrying moved within her in the presence of Mary and her unborn child. Filled with the Holy Spirit and recognizing the presence of God, Elizabeth said, "Most blessed are you among women, and blessed is the fruit of your womb. And how does this happen to me, that the mother of my Lord should come to me? For at the moment the sound of your greeting reached my ears, the infant in my womb leaped for joy. Blessed are you who believed that what was spoken to you by the Lord would be fulfilled" (Luke 1:42–45).

What do Elizabeth's words tell us about Mary?

*The Visitation,* Franco-Flemish school, 15th century

Mary responded to Elizabeth's joyful words. As a servant of the Lord, Mary praised God in a song. Like Miriam and Hannah before her, Mary showed her joy and wonder at the fact that God had chosen her to bring about the fulfillment of his promises. Here is part of Mary's song of praise to God, or her canticle. The whole song, known as the Magnificat, can be found on page 326.

"My soul proclaims the greatness of the Lord;
   my spirit rejoices in God my savior.
For he has looked upon his handmaid's
      lowliness;
   behold, from now on will all ages call me
   blessed.
The Mighty One has done great things for
   me, and holy is his name." (Luke 1:46–49)

Mary stayed with Elizabeth and Zechariah for about three months. Then she traveled home again.

**John's Birth**   When Elizabeth gave birth to a son, she, Zechariah, and all their relatives and friends rejoiced. When it was time to name the child, everyone thought that he would be called Zechariah. But his father wrote on a tablet "John is his name" (Luke 1:63). It was then that Zechariah was able to speak again. All his relatives and neighbors wondered "'What, then, will this child be?' For surely the hand of the Lord was with him" (Luke 1:66).

Then Zechariah, filled with the Holy Spirit, spoke. Here is part of his prophesy.

"Blessed be the Lord, the God of Israel,
   for he has visited and brought redemption
      to his people . . .
And you, child, will be called prophet of the
   Most High,
   for you will go before the Lord to prepare
   his ways,

to give his people knowledge of salvation
   through the forgiveness of their sins . . .
   to guide our feet into the path of peace."
(Luke 1:68 76–77, 79)

Zechariah's prophesy is called The Canticle of Zechariah and can be found on page 328.

Elizabeth and Zechariah's child, John, only a baby now, would grow strong in body and spirit. John, too, would have an important part in the fulfillment of God's promise to his people. Like the prophets before him, John would prepare the way for the coming of the Messiah.

**WE RESPOND**

Sing together this contemporary version of the canticles of Mary and Zechariah.

🎵 **Luke 1: Magnificat/Benedictus**

With joyful heart I sing God's praise,
and love my Savior all my days.
God chooses me in lowliness
to be the one forever blessed.
God raised me up for all to see,
and holy is God's name to me.

To God of Israel be praise,
who saves us all from sinful ways.
From David's house and family
a Savior comes to set us free.
Our enemies we need not fear,
the prophets said, "The Lord is near!"

# God the Son became man.

✝ *Jesus, save us.*

What are important things that parents can pass on to their children?

## WE BELIEVE

Mary and Joseph began their life together in Nazareth, a town in Galilee. There they waited for the child to be born. They prepared for his birth and for the life that they would share with him.

God had spoken to each of them about this child. The event that was about to take place was beyond Mary and Joseph's understanding. The child who was about to be born of Mary was the Son of God.

At this time in Judea, a census, or count of the people, was being taken. Joseph and Mary went up to Bethlehem of Judea, the city of King David's birth. Joseph and Mary went there because all men had to enroll their families in the city of their ancestors, and Joseph was a descendant of David. Mary, too, was of the house of David.

It was in Bethlehem that Mary gave birth to her son. Thus, the words of the prophet Micah were fulfilled. Bethlehem is the birthplace of the "one who is to be ruler in Israel" (Micah 5:1).

Following the instructions of the angel in Joseph's dream, Mary and Joseph named the child Jesus. This name means "God saves." God the Son became one of us. "And the Word became flesh
   and made his dwelling among us."
(John 1:14)

This mystery is called the Incarnation. The **Incarnation** is the truth that the Son of God, the second Person of the Blessed Trinity, became man.

This child of Mary, conceived by the power of the Holy Spirit, came to save people from all that would keep them from the love of God. Jesus is the Savior sent to fulfill God's promise. Jesus is true God and true man, and so he shares God's life and love with all people.

**The Presentation in the Temple**  Mary and Joseph followed the laws of their Jewish faith, and so they traveled to Jerusalem to present Jesus in the Temple. There they met a holy man named Simeon. "It had been revealed to him by the holy Spirit that he should not see death before he had seen the Messiah of the Lord." (Luke 2:26) When Simeon saw Jesus, he took the baby in his arms and said,

"Now, Master, you may let your servant go
   in peace, according to your word,
for my eyes have seen your salvation,
   which you prepared in sight of all the
      peoples,
a light for revelation to the Gentiles,
   and glory for your people Israel"
(Luke 2:29–32).

A prophetess named Anna witnessed all of this and gave thanks to God. She spoke about this child to all who were waiting for the fulfillment of God's promise of salvation.

Mary, Joseph, and Jesus settled in Nazareth, and Jesus grew up there with his relatives and friends. There he played, studied, and learned much from his mother and foster father. Jesus heard about his Jewish ancestors, their faith, and the ways to live out God's covenant. With his family and friends he celebrated the Jewish feasts. And on certain feasts his family traveled to the Temple in Jerusalem.

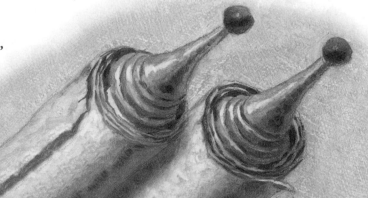

**Key Word**

**Incarnation** the truth that the Son of God, the second Person of the Blessed Trinity, became man

📖 Luke 2:41–52

**The Finding in the Temple**   Each year Mary and Joseph went to Jerusalem to celebrate the feast of Passover. When Jesus was twelve years old, he went up to Jerusalem with them. As they were returning home to Nazareth, Jesus remained behind in Jerusalem. But Mary and Joseph did not know this. They thought he was among their relatives and acquaintances. When they could not find him, they went back to Jerusalem to look for him.

They found him three days later, listening and questioning the teachers. People were astounded by his knowledge and understanding. His parents were astounded, too, but they were very anxious. Jesus said that they should have known that he was in his Father's house. "But they did not understand what he said to them. He went down with them and came to Nazareth, and was obedient to them; and his mother kept all these things in her heart. And Jesus advanced [in] wisdom and age and favor before God and man" (Luke 2:50–52).

This is one of the few accounts we have of Jesus' early years. We learn from it that Jesus was a faithful, obedient Jewish child. We also see that he had deep understanding and knowledge of God. In his Father's house, meaning the house of God, Jesus did his Father's work. This would be a theme throughout Jesus' life.

How do you think Mary and Joseph felt when they could not find Jesus? Why?

**WE RESPOND**

🏃 Role-play the story of Mary, Joseph, and Jesus during their visit to Jerusalem to celebrate Passover as found in Luke 2:41–52. Characters will include: a narrator, Mary, Joseph, Jesus (12 years old), friends and relatives, and teachers in the temple.

Write your own script and present your play.

# John prepared the way for Jesus.

## WE GATHER

✝ *Glory to the Father, and to the Son, and to the Holy Spirit.*

What are some reasons that groups of people do not get along? What can happen because of these conflicts?

## WE BELIEVE

From the gospels we do not learn much about Jesus' life until he was about thirty years old. During these "hidden" years, as they are called, things changed in Judea.

When Herod the Great, king of Judea, died his relatives could not agree on his successor. So Caesar Augustus in Rome was called upon to settle the argument. He used this opportunity to weaken Judea by dividing Herod's territories among his sons Archelaus, Philip, and Herod Antipas. None of Herod's children were pleased with this division of their father's territory.

When Archelaus turned out to be a terrible leader, Augustus removed him and decided that Rome would rule this part of Herod's old kingdom. Caesar Augustus set up a procurator, a kind of deputy governor. For about forty years, Philip and Herod Antipas continued to lead their territories. But Rome was slowly taking over complete control of Judea, which the Romans called Palestine.

Judea was a divided country. In Judea the Jews were only a part of the population now. Some regions were ruled directly by Rome, and others were governed by Jewish princes who were reporting to the Romans. Therefore, relations between Rome and the Jews were very strained. In fact, many of the Jews came to distrust and dislike the Romans. Rome worried about the possibility of new revolts by the Jews.

Religious tensions were also a problem in Judea at this time. The Jews were fearful that they would not be allowed to keep the Law of Moses. They feared that the Romans would interfere with their worship and observance of the covenant with God. Religious divisions, problems between the rich and the poor, and many other social injustices were widespread. It was in these troubled times that " . . . the word of God came to John the son of Zechariah in the desert" (Luke 3:2).

John, the cousin of Jesus, began to preach and to prophesy throughout the land. He urged the people to repent and to ask God for forgiveness. He encouraged them to change their lives and to get ready for the coming of the Messiah, the Anointed One, the one foretold by the prophets. Since people came to be baptized by him in the Jordan River, he was known as John the Baptist.

Jesus' Baptism from the TV mini series, *Jesus of Nazareth* (1977).

This baptism by John showed people's willingness to change their lives. "And the crowds asked him, 'What then should we do?' He said to them in reply, 'Whoever has two cloaks should share with the person who has none. And whoever has food should do likewise.' Even tax collectors came to be baptized and they said to him, 'Teacher, what should we do?' He answered them, 'Stop collecting more than what is prescribed.' Soldiers also asked him, 'And what is it that we should do?' He told them, 'Do not practice extortion, do not falsely accuse anyone, and be satisfied with your wages.'" (Luke 3:10–14)

John told the people, "I am baptizing you with water, but one mightier than I is coming . . . He will baptize you with the holy Spirit and fire" (Luke 3:16).

It was about this time that Jesus left Nazareth and went to the Jordan River to hear John preach and to be baptized by him. "After all the people had been baptized and Jesus also had been baptized and was praying, heaven was opened and the holy Spirit descended upon him in bodily form like a dove. And a voice came from heaven, 'You are my beloved Son; with you I am well pleased.'" (Luke 3:21–22)

Truly, Jesus is the one who is beloved by God. He is the one who offers us himself and who shows us how to love. Like John, we can prepare the way for people to welcome Jesus, too. By Baptism, each of us is called to live as one of Jesus' disciples. When we do what is right and treat others fairly and with justice, we are showing what it is to be a follower of Jesus.

## WE RESPOND

Can you prepare the way for Jesus today? What will you say? What will you do? Write some ways here. Role-play one of them.

_____

_____

_____

_____

_____

**Circle the letter of the correct answer.**

1. _____ told Mary that her cousin Elizabeth was with child.

   **a.** Anna   **b.** An angel   **c.** Zechariah

2. _____ was born to prepare the people for the Messiah.

   **a.** Elijah   **b.** Zechariah   **c.** John

3. Zechariah lost his ability to speak because he was _____.

   **a.** old   **b.** sick   **c.** unbelieving

4. _____ was a descendant of King David.

   **a.** Joseph   **b.** Simeon   **c.** Zechariah

**Short Answers**

5. What role did angels play in the coming of the Messiah?

   _____

6. Why was Jesus born in Bethlehem?

   _____

7. What is the Incarnation?

   _____

8. Why is the story of the finding of Jesus in the Temple important?

   _____

**Write a paragraph to answer this question.**

**9–10.** How was Mary blessed by God?

**ASSESSMENT**

The families of John and Jesus were faithful to God's call and helped their children to learn and practice their faith. Through a video, photo album, poster, poem, or song show how these families practiced their faith. Present your completed project to your class or family.

# We Respond in Faith

 Key Word
**Incarnation** (p. 225)

## Reflect & Pray

Hail Mary, full of grace,
the Lord is with you!

Holy Mary, pray for us.
Help me to

_____

## Remember

- Mary is blessed by God.
- Mary and Elizabeth had special roles in God's plan.
- God the Son became man.
- John prepared the way for Jesus.

## OUR CATHOLIC LIFE

### Liturgy of the Hours

Every day, the people of God, the Church, pray the Liturgy of the Hours. The Liturgy of the Hours is part of the official public prayer of the Church. The Liturgy of the Hours helps us to praise God throughout the entire day. These prayers remind us that God is always active and present in our lives. The Liturgy of the Hours is celebrated at various times during the day, and is made up of psalms, readings from Scripture and Church teachings, prayers, and hymns. Morning Prayer and Evening Prayer are the two most important prayers of the Liturgy of the Hours.

At Morning Prayer, the Canticle of Zechariah is always prayed. In this canticle, the Savior, Jesus, is referred to as "the daybreak from on high." At Evening Prayer, the Canticle of Mary is always prayed. This prayer is known as the *Magnificat*, the Latin translation for its first words. In this prayer we, along with Mary, praise God for all he has done for us.

# SHARING FAITH
## with My Family

## Sharing What I Learned

Discuss the following with your family:

- the roles of Mary and Joseph in God's plan
- the story of Elizabeth and Zechariah
- the birth and early life of Jesus
- John prepares the way for Jesus.

## Share a Prayer

This Jewish prayer, known as the Shema, is prayed to show faith in the one true God.

Write a prayer that you can pray to show your faith in God. Share your prayer with your family.

"Hear, O Israel! The LORD is our God, the LORD alone! Therefore, you shall love the LORD, your God, with all your heart, and with all your soul, and with all your strength."

(Deuteronomy 6:4–5)

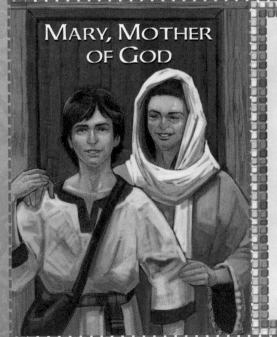

MARY, MOTHER OF GOD

Who is Mary?

_____

_____

What are some events in Mary's life?

_____

_____

How is Mary a model of discipleship for us today?

_____

_____

## We Believe Trading Cards

Complete the facts on the back of the trading card. Then share with your family what you have learned about Mary.

Visit Sadlier's

www.WeBelieveweb.com

**Connect to the Catechism**
For adult background and reflection, see paragraphs 484, 495, 534, and 535.

# Lent

Our hope is the God
of mercy and forgiveness.

# The season of Lent is a period of preparation for Easter.

## WE GATHER

✝ *Jesus, help us to follow in your way.*

Have you ever been on a trip away from home? Where did you go? Was this a vacation trip or was it taken for another reason? What did you learn from your travels?

## WE BELIEVE

The entire season of Lent is like a pilgrimage. A pilgrimage is a trip taken to a shrine or sacred place. As Christians, a pilgrimage is a prayer journey that helps us follow Christ more closely. During Lent we focus on following Christ and thinking about the relationship that we began with him at Baptism. In Baptism we are united to Christ and to all others who are baptized. Through the waters of Baptism we die with Christ only to rise to new life with him.

Lent is a journey during which we prepare to celebrate at Easter Christ's dying and rising to new life. The entire Church takes part in this preparation through our worship and by the way we live. This season is the final time of preparation for those who will celebrate the sacraments of Christian initiation at Easter. These three sacraments—Baptism, Confirmation, and the Eucharist—are called the Easter sacraments. Those who receive them will share in Jesus' death and Resurrection and have new life in Christ. We pray for them, support them, and welcome them into our parish.

On Ash Wednesday Catholics and other Christians can receive ashes, a sign of both sorrow and hope.

The season of Lent begins on Ash Wednesday and ends many weeks later on Holy Thursday evening. Absence and simplicity describe the season of Lent. There are signs of this absence in our churches and in our liturgy. Water is usually removed from the holy water and baptismal fonts as preparation for the Easter sacraments. During the liturgy, alleluia is not said or sung nor are bells rung. Dark purple is the color used in worship, and green plants and flowers may be removed from the churches. All of these changes remind us of our need to recommit ourselves to Christ and to the Church.

They help us to prepare to renew our baptismal promises at Easter and to celebrate the new life Christ has won for us by his cross and Resurrection.

The way we live during this season is also a sign of absence and simplicity. We are called to follow the Lenten practices of prayer, fasting, and almsgiving, or practicing works of compassion. The word *alms* comes from a Greek word meaning "compassion." Almsgiving can be the giving of time, money, or goods to those in need. Prayer, fasting, and almsgiving are always part of Christian living. However, during Lent they take on special meaning as we prepare to renew our Baptism.

### Prayer

During Lent we focus on God's mercy and forgiveness. We call out to God to remember us and strengthen us to live by his laws. Lent is a good time to spend extra time in conversation with God. We may devote more time to personal prayer and to prayer with our parish community.

The Church prays especially for those who are preparing to receive the sacraments of Christian initiation. Many parishes gather for the stations of the cross and have special celebrations of the sacrament of Reconciliation.

### Fasting

Fasting is a way to cleanse our bodies of harmful things and our hearts and minds of things that keep us from loving God and others. Fasting is also a form of penance. Doing penance helps us to turn to God and to focus on the things that are important in our lives as Christians. Doing penance is a way to show that we are sorry for our sins.

One way to fast is to give up things we enjoy, like a favorite food or activity. Catholics of a certain age are called to fast from food on Ash Wednesday and Good Friday. They are also called to give up meat on these days and on all the Fridays during Lent.

### Almsgiving

During Lent we also show special concern for those in need. We follow Jesus' example of providing for the hungry and caring for the sick. We try to help other people to get the things they need and make sure that people have what is rightfully theirs.

Many parishes have food and clothing drives during this time of year. Families may participate in these drives and also volunteer at soup kitchens, visit those who are sick, and practice other works of mercy.

**Stations of the Cross** In Lent, as always, we are traveling toward the happiness of living forever with God. We have many opportunities to follow in the footsteps of Jesus. One of the most famous places to follow Jesus is the land where he once walked, or the Holy Land. Through the centuries, Christians have made pilgrimages to the Holy Land. They have walked in the footsteps of Jesus along the way of the cross. Since most people could not travel to the Holy Land, stations of the cross began to be placed in parish churches. In this way, everyone could follow Jesus on his path from death to Resurrection. Everyone could be a pilgrim.

Following the stations of the cross became a devotion that takes place often during the season of Lent. The word *station* comes from a Latin word meaning "stopping point." In a parish the stations are usually fourteen statues, pictures, or crosses placed along the walls of the church. At each station we stop, we remember, and we pray.

At each station we usually pray this way:

We adore you, O Christ,
   and we bless you.
Because by your holy cross,
   you have redeemed the world.

## WE RESPOND

Break into pairs or small groups and choose one station. Using various art materials design your station and write a meditation or prayer about that station. Use this space to brainstorm your ideas.

### Stations of the Cross

1. Jesus is condemned to die.
2. Jesus takes up his cross.
3. Jesus falls the first time.
4. Jesus meets his mother.
5. Simon helps Jesus carry his cross.
6. Veronica wipes the face of Jesus.
7. Jesus falls the second time.
8. Jesus meets the women of Jerusalem.
9. Jesus falls the third time.
10. Jesus is stripped of his garments.
11. Jesus is nailed to the cross.
12. Jesus dies on the cross.
13. Jesus is taken down from the cross.
14. Jesus is laid in the tomb.

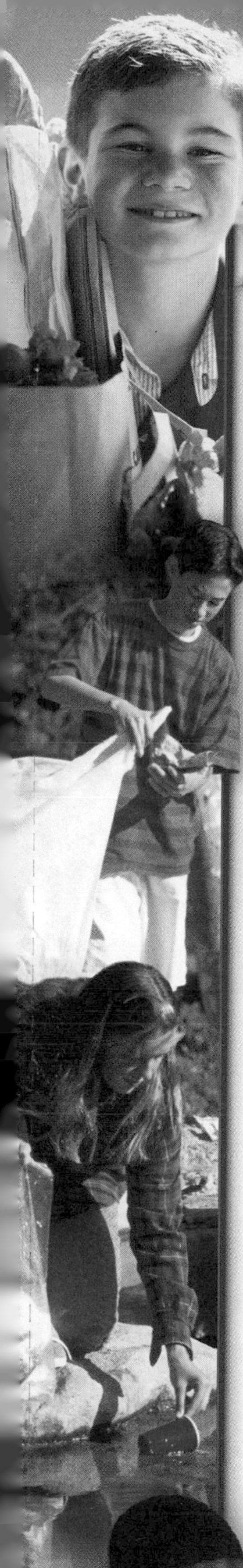

# ✝ We Respond in Prayer

**Leader:** Blessed are you, Lord, God of all creation:
**All:** you make us hunger and thirst for holiness.

**Leader:** Blessed are you, Lord, God of all creation:
**All:** you call us to true fasting:

**Leader:** to set free the oppressed,
to share our bread with the hungry,
to shelter the homeless and to clothe the naked.

**All:** Blessed be God for ever.

**Reader:** A reading from the Letter of Saint Paul to the Philippians

"Whatever is true, whatever is honorable, whatever is just,
whatever is pure, whatever is lovely, whatever is gracious,
if there is any excellence and if there is anything worthy
of praise, think about these things." (Philippians 4:8)

The word of the Lord.

**All:** Thanks be to God.

**Leader:** Let us now ask forgiveness of one another and of God.

**All:** I confess to almighty God,
and to you, my brothers and sisters,
that I have sinned through my own fault
in my thoughts and in my words,
in what I have done,
and in what I have failed to do;
and I ask blessed Mary, ever virgin,
all the angels and saints,
and you, my brothers and sisters,
to pray for me to the Lord our God.

### 🎵 My God, My God

My God, my God,
have mercy on me,
for all my hope is in you,
my God, all my hope is in you.

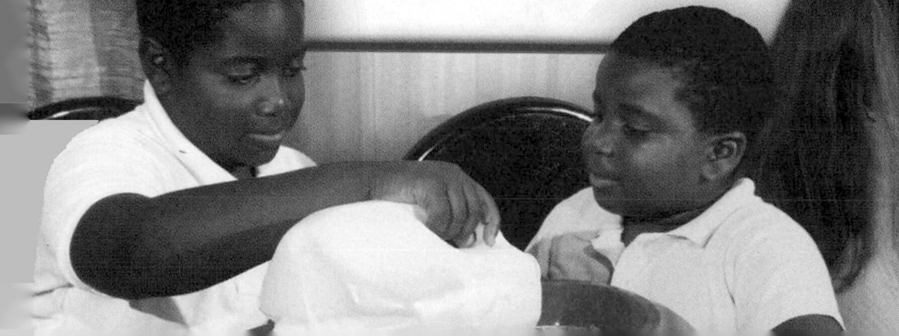

LENT

235

# SHARING FAITH
## with My Family

## Sharing What I Learned

Discuss the following with your family:

- the season of Lent

- Lenten practices as preparation for Easter

- pilgrimages and stations of the cross.

## Around the Table

Here are three Lenten practices. Use the questions to talk about them with your family.

### Prayer

How can we be more aware of God's goodness during Lent? What special Lenten prayers can we pray with our parish?

### Fasting

What can help us to remember to eat only what we need during this Lent? How can our fasting show our love for God and others? What else can we "fast" from besides food?

### Almsgiving

How can we give to those in need this Lent? How can we properly give of our time, our money, or our goods?

## A Family Prayer

During the season of Lent, we try to grow closer to Christ through prayer and acts of love. Pray these prayers with your family.

May God put our faith into action, to work in love, to persevere in hope, through our Lord Jesus Christ.

May God fully supply all our needs according to his generosity, with magnificence, in Christ Jesus! To God be glory for ever and ever!

**Connect to the Catechism**
For adult background and reflection, see paragraph 1429.

"Rejoice, O earth, in shining splendor,
radiant in the brightness of your King!
Christ has conquered! Glory fills you!
Darkness vanishes for ever!"

The Exsultet, the Easter Vigil

# The Easter Triduum is also known as the Christian Passover.

## WE GATHER

✝ *Jesus, take us with you into new life.*

Think about times when people count on a map to guide them in getting someplace. What would their experience be like without a map?

## WE BELIEVE

The Easter Triduum guides us on a journey. We journey with Jesus Christ from death to new life. When we celebrate the Easter Triduum, we are celebrating the most important three days of the year for Christians. These three days extend from the evening of Holy Thursday to the evening of Easter Sunday. They are counted as our Jewish ancestors in faith count their days—from sundown to sundown.

The liturgical celebrations of these three days are seen as one connected liturgy in which we celebrate Christ's passing from death to new life. These days focus on the whole Paschal Mystery of Christ—his passion, death, Resurrection, and Ascension. Paschal comes from the word *pasch* which means "Passover." So the Paschal Mystery is the mystery of Christ's sacrifice of himself and of his passing over from death to life.

**Holy Thursday** The Evening Mass of the Lord's Supper is not simply a reenactment of the events of the Last Supper when Jesus gathered to celebrate Passover with his disciples. It is a celebration of the new Passover, Christ's Body and Blood that he shared then and still shares with us today in the Eucharist. It is a celebration of the love and service Christ calls us to everyday.

During this Mass a ceremony of the washing of the feet takes place. This action commits us to follow the example of Jesus' love and service. He washed his disciples' feet as a sign of his love for them.

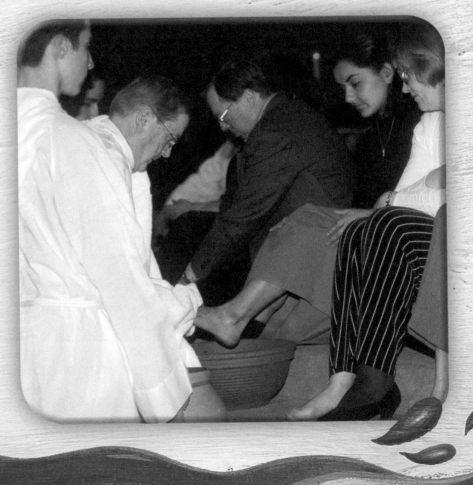

On Holy Thursday one way that we show our love and service for others is by contributing to a special collection for those who are in need.

**Good Friday** On this day we recall Jesus' suffering and death. The celebration often takes place in the afternoon around three o'clock P.M.

We hear the passion of Christ read from the Gospel of John, and we offer ten general intercessions that include prayers for the whole world. We also show reverence to the cross, for upon it hung the Savior of the world. The cross is the sign of Christ's death and of the victory he wins for us by his death. The cross is a symbol of the salvation Jesus Christ offers to the world.

Because the Liturgy of the Eucharist is not celebrated on Good Friday, a short communion service takes place and then all depart in silence.

**Holy Saturday** During the day we spend time thinking and praying. We remember that Jesus died to save all people and we thank God for this gift. We pray especially for those who will celebrate the Easter sacraments. On Sundays and very important feast days, the Church begins the liturgical celebration on the night before with a vigil.

On Holy Saturday evening we gather with our parish for the celebration of the Easter Vigil.

The Easter Vigil is the most important vigil of the year and it is the highpoint of the Triduum. It begins after sundown on the Saturday before Easter Sunday. It is a time of watchful waiting. Two beautiful symbols of our faith are a central part of this night: light and water.

Throughout the history of salvation, fire has been a symbol of the presence of God. On the night of the Easter Vigil, a fire is made outdoors or in the back of the Church. The priest prepares the paschal candle by marking the year on it. Then the paschal candle is lit from this new fire and the priest says, "May the light of Christ, rising in glory, dispel the darkness of our hearts and minds." The fire represents the fire of the burning bush, and the paschal candle reminds us of the pillar of fire that accompanied the Israelites on their journey out of Egypt. The paschal candle is more, though. It is a symbol of the risen Christ among us. It is a reminder of our own passing with Christ from death to life, from darkness to light.

The paschal candle is carried into the dark church with great reverence. The deacon or priest sings "Christ our light" three times. The assembly responds "Thanks be to God" each time. Often those assembled light small candles from the paschal candle, and the light of Christ spreads throughout the whole assembly.

Then the deacon or a parish member chants the Exsultet, or Easter Proclamation. To *exult* means to "rejoice with great joy and triumph." The Exsultet is a proclamation of our Easter faith. It is like a map of the celebration of Easter. The Exsultet proclaims God's plan, and notes that we are part of that plan.

"This is our passover feast,"
we hear. We also hear,
"This is the night when first you
        saved our fathers:
you freed the people of Israel
        from their slavery."

The waters of the Red Sea remind us of the waters of Baptism. Most importantly, we hear,

"This is the night when
        Jesus Christ
        broke the chains of death
        and rose triumphant
        from the grave."

This is the most beautiful and exciting night of the year! It is fitting that on this night new members of the Church are baptized, confirmed, and receive the Eucharist for the first time.

Water is another symbol that is very important to the Easter Vigil. It is important to the newly baptized and to all of us who renew our baptismal promises and are sprinkled with water. It is a symbol of our new Easter life. We, too, are risen with Christ.

**Easter Sunday**   Our joy continues at the Easter Sunday Eucharist as we pray:

"May the risen Lord
breathe on our minds
        and open our eyes
that we may know him in the
        breaking of bread,
and follow him in his risen life."

## WE RESPOND

What can you do to help others to believe and experience the new life that comes from Christ?

How can you spread the light of Christ in your home? your school? your parish? the world?

# ✝ We Respond in Prayer

**Leader:** Let us rejoice in the Resurrection of Jesus.

 **Resucitó/He Is Risen**

Refrain

> Resucitó, resucitó, resucitó, alleluya.
> Alleluya, alleluya, alleluya, resucitó.
> *(He is risen, alleluia.)*

**Leader:** Let us pray the great Easter Proclamation.

**Group 1:** "Rejoice, heavenly powers! Sing, choirs of angels!
    Exult, all creation around God's throne!
    Jesus Christ, our King, is risen!
    Sound the trumpet of salvation!"

**All:** *(Sing Refrain.)*

**Group 2:** "Rejoice, O earth, in shining splendor,
    radiant in the brightness of your King!
    Christ has conquered! Glory fills you!
    Darkness vanishes for ever!"

**All:** *(Sing Refrain.)*

**Group 3:** "Rejoice, O Mother Church! Exult in glory!
    The risen Savior shines upon you!
    Let this place resound with joy,
    echoing the mighty song of all God's people!"

**All:** *(Sing Refrain.)*

**Group 4:** "Most blessed of all nights, chosen by
    God to see Christ rising from the dead!

    Of this night scripture says:
        'The night will be as clear as day:
        it will become my light, my joy.'"

**All:** *(Sing Refrain.)*

TRIDUUM

241

# SHARING FAITH
## with My Family

## Sharing What I Learned

Discuss the following with your family:

- the Evening Mass of the Lord's Supper
- the celebration of the Lord's Passion
- the Easter Vigil.

## Around the Table

Talk with your family about ways to celebrate the Triduum, both at home and with your parish. Here are some suggestions.

- On Holy Thursday, participate in the Evening Mass of the Lord's Supper.

- On Good Friday, establish a silent atmosphere at home and prepare simple meals, like soup or sandwiches. Participate in the Good Friday liturgy at church.

- On Holy Saturday, help to prepare your home for Easter. Participate in the Easter Vigil and the Easter Sunday Eucharist. Rejoice! Jesus is risen! Alleluia!

### A Family Prayer

Pray this prayer with your family before and after your evening meals on the three days of the Triduum.

For our sake Christ was obedient,
  accepting even death, death on a cross.
Therefore God raised him on high
  and gave him the name above all
  other names.

Visit Sadlier's

**www.WeBelieveweb.com**

 **Connect to the Catechism**
For adult background and reflection, see paragraph 1096.

# Assessment

**Choose a word from the box that best completes each sentence.**

| | | | | |
|---|---|---|---|---|
| Amos | Ecclesiastes | Ezekiel | Herod | Isaiah |
| John | Josiah | Malachi | Micah | Purium |

1. Jesus' birth in the town of Bethlehem in Judea fulfilled the words of the prophet _____.

2. The great prophet _____ told King Hezekiah that God would not allow foreign nations to destroy Judah; he would always be with the people of Judah.

3. _____, the son of Elizabeth and Zechariah, was sent by God like the prophets before him to prepare the way for the coming of the Messiah.

4. God called the prophet _____ from the southern kingdom of Judah to go to the northern kingdom of Israel and tell the people there to live justly or their kingdom would be destroyed.

5. King _____ began a reform of religious practice in Judah, banned pagan practices, and returned true worship to the Temple in Jerusalem.

6. The prophet-priest _____ told the people that God would purify those who remained true to him and would shepherd them back from exile to the promised land.

7. In the Book of _____ we are reminded that God alone can provide lasting happiness.

8. When Jews celebrate the festival of _____, they recall that through God's help Esther saved God's people.

**Underline the correct answer.**

9. In the Book of (**Judith/Job**) we read about God's rescue of his people through the brave actions of a remarkable woman.

10. God sent the prophet (**Jonah/Elijah**) to the northern kingdom of Israel to show the people that the gods worshiped by King Ahab were false gods.

11. The prophet (**Hezekiah/Jeremiah**) was accused of blasphemy, rejected, and imprisoned, but he never lost hope because he knew that God is always with his people.

12. The prophet Elijah anointed a man named (**Elisha/Isaiah**) to carry on his work among God's people.

13. In the second of two attacks the city of Jerusalem, including the Temple, was destroyed and the people of Judah carried off to exile in (**Babylon/Assyria**).

14. The Book of (**Wisdom/Lamentations**) contains five poems describing the destruction of the kingdom of Judah and the sufferings of the people.

15. When Judas (**Maccabeus/Malachi**) rededicated the Temple, he asked the people to remember the event with a "feast of lights" that Jews celebrate today as the festival of Hanukkah.

16. During (**King Haman's/Herod's**) reign over Judea, an angel of God was sent to Mary to tell her she would be the mother of the Son of God.

**Answer the questions.**

17–18. In the Book of Jonah we read of a prophet who is swallowed by a huge fish. What symbolic meaning does the story of Jonah have for us as Christians?

19–20. The prophet Isaiah, preaching to God's people in exile in Babylon, said that salvation would come only through the suffering of a servant of the Lord—a servant without sin. How are these words of Isaiah's important to Christians?

# The Covenant Fulfilled in Jesus

# SHARING FAITH as a Family

## Kids Online

The world of cyberspace contains fascinating resources and information. Families who monitor their children's use of the Internet open up this world with care and attentiveness. As young people are given more freedom to surf the web, they can be asked to do so in a responsible way. Here are just a few pointers you may want to give your children:

• Do not give out personal information without permission from an adult family member. This includes names, addresses, phone numbers, e-mail addresses, locations of schools and workplaces.

• Never respond to a message that makes you feel uncomfortable. Instead, log off right away and tell a parent or another trusted adult about it.

• Insulting or rude messages are inappropriate—both on- and offline!

• Be careful about what you read on the Internet. Not all of its content is reliable. Check out additional sources of information so that you get the correct information, or ask an adult family member, teacher, or librarian.

Going online can be a fun, exciting, and an educational venture, especially when parents and children agree upon a healthy and responsible plan.

## What Your Child Will Learn in Unit 4

The focus of Unit 4 is the life of Jesus Christ and the origins of the Church. The life of Jesus is examined through the books of the New Testament. The unit begins with the stories of Jesus as a teacher and healer. The children will read about Jesus and his disciples, the Sermon on Mount, the Beatitudes, the apostles, and Jesus' miracles. The children will come to a fuller understanding of Jesus' teachings about the Kingdom of God. They will discover the origin of the Our Father, the prayer that Jesus taught us. The story of Jesus continues with the events leading up to his death and Resurrection: the Last Supper, the agony in the garden of Gethsemane, the crucifixion, the Resurrection. Then children read about the appearances of the risen Christ to his disciples and apostles, and about Jesus' Ascension. Unit 4 concludes with a history of the early Church, an overview of the Church described as one, holy, catholic, and apostolic, and the ways the Church relates to the world today.

## Plan & Preview

▶ Pieces of cardboard or stiff paper can be used for the trading cards. The front and back of the cards can be glued to the cardboard to form a sturdy trading card.

## A Story in Faith

### Father Mychal Judge

On September 11th, 2001, Father Mychal Judge, was crushed by falling debris as he was praying over a fallen firefighter. The photo of his lifeless body being carried out of the fiery furnace that had been called the Twin Towers in New York City would become famous all over the world.

"He was my idea of what a priest should be and above all, he was a

### From the Catechism

"Parents must regard their children as *children of God* and respect them as *human persons*." (*Catechism of the Catholic Church,* 2222)

living example of Jesus Christ." Those words were spoken by Steven MacDonald, a police officer who had become a close friend of Father Mike. No one was left out of his ministry whether they were homeless, alcoholics, women in need, or people with AIDS—all were welcomed. Father Mike had a special devotion to the New York City Fire Department, being one of its chaplains since 1992. Wherever there were firefighters who needed his prayers, Father Mike was there.

Every day on the Hudson River, commuter ferry boats travel back and forth from New Jersey to Manhattan. One of these boats—packed with commuters, students, and tourists— the "Father Mychal Judge," is named for Father Mike. As the laughter and talk and life leave the boat for the excitement of the city, it sails on as a fitting tribute to Father Mike, a "living example of Jesus Christ."

**Father Mychal Judge**

## ✝ We Gather in Prayer

**Reader:** A reading from the holy Gospel according to Matthew

"As he was walking by the Sea of Galilee, he saw two brothers, Simon who is called Peter, and his brother Andrew, casting a net into the sea; they were fishermen. He said to them, 'Come after me, and I will make you fishers of men.' At once they left their nets and followed him. He walked along from there and saw two other brothers, James, the son of Zebedee, and his brother John. They were in a boat, with their father Zebedee, mending their nets. He called them, and immediately they left their boat and their father and followed him." (Matthew 4:18–22)

The Gospel of the Lord.

**All:** Praise to you, Lord Jesus Christ.

**Leader:** We want to follow Jesus—but what must we leave behind?

**Reader 1:** May we leave behind selfishness, and follow Jesus in the spirit of gratitude and generosity.

**All:** Jesus, we want to follow you.
(Response to all five petitions.)

**Reader 2:** May we leave behind injustice, and follow Jesus with hope and help for those who suffer.

**Reader 3:** May we leave behind fear and self-consciousness, and follow Jesus by using our talents and abilities to help others.

**Reader 4:** May we leave behind pride and arrogance, and follow Jesus by showing mercy and forgiveness.

**Reader 5:** May we leave behind anger and desires for revenge, and follow Jesus by seeking ways to live in peace with all.

## 🎵 Pescador de Hombres/ Lord, You Have Come

Tú has venido a la orilla, no has buscado ni a sabios ni a ricos; tan sólo quieres que yo te siga.

Lord, you have come to the seashore, neither searching for the rich nor the wise, desiring only that I should follow.

Refrain:

Señor, me has mirado a los ojos, sonriendo has dicho mi nombre, en la arena he dejado mi barca, junto a ti buscaré otro mar.

O Lord, with your eyes set upon me, gently smiling, you have spoken my name; all I longed for I have found by the water, at your side, I will seek other shores.

The wedding at Cana — Jesus brings God's love to all people — Many become disciples — Sermon on the Mount, the Beatitudes — Jesus works many signs and miracles — At Last Supper, Jesus gives a new covenant — Jesus prays at Garden of Gethsemane — Judas betrays Jesus

# God makes himself known in his Son.

## WE GATHER

✝ *Jesus, open our hearts to your presence among us now and always.*

Why do you prepare for an important event? What are some ways that you get ready for it?

## WE BELIEVE

After Jesus' baptism at the Jordan River, the Holy Spirit led him into the desert. Jesus stayed there for forty days and forty nights. He prayed to his Father and fasted as a sign of his obedience. Jesus was preparing for his public life among the people.

Jesus returned to Galilee after his time in the desert and began to preach this message: "This is the time of fulfillment. The kingdom of God is at hand. Repent, and believe in the gospel" (Mark 1:15). The gospel is the good news about God at work in Jesus Christ. Jesus showed that the **Kingdom of God** is the power of God's love coming into the world and into our lives. The Kingdom came into the world with the coming of God the Son.

The Jewish people had been waiting for this fulfillment of God's promises. They were waiting for God's Kingdom. They expected God's Kingdom to be one of justice and fair rule.

Many hoped for Israel to be restored to its place of power. They were familiar with the idea of God as king. In the Old Testament God was considered the King of the universe and King of Israel. For this very reason the prophet Samuel did not want to appoint a human king to rule over God's people.

However, the Kingdom Jesus announced was not political. It was the power of God's love coming into the world and changing it. It was the power of God's love active in the lives of the people.

When Jesus said that the Kingdom, or reign, of God was near, he was saying that:

- God's presence and rule can be found in him and in the things he said and did

- freedom from sin and the gift of God's life of grace are offered to everyone

- by living in God's presence and for the kingdom, people can begin to live in God's life, the very life that we believe is life with God forever.

**Key Word**

**Kingdom of God**
the power of God's love coming into the world and into our lives

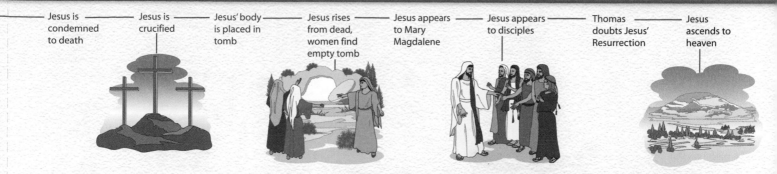

Jesus is condemned to death — Jesus is crucified — Jesus' body is placed in tomb — Jesus rises from dead, women find empty tomb — Jesus appears to Mary Magdalene — Jesus appears to disciples — Thomas doubts Jesus' Resurrection — Jesus ascends to heaven

**Jesus' Ministry** Jesus' mission was to share the life of God his Father with all people and to reconcile all people to God. Jesus brought God's love to all people and began to change the world. "The people were astonished at his teaching, for he taught them as one having authority." (Mark 1:22) He taught about the love of God his Father and encouraged all people to turn to God.

Jesus accepted and welcomed all people into his life. He showed concern for the hungry, and he often sat at table and ate with people who were ignored or neglected by the rest of society. Jesus treated others in ways that showed how loving and caring he was. Jesus' life was also a sign of God the Father's love and care. The Holy Spirit was truly active in Jesus.

During his ministry Jesus also forgave the sins of those who sought God's forgiveness and healed those who were suffering from many different kinds of illnesses. These actions of healing and forgiving were special signs that Jesus was not only human, but also divine.

The things that Jesus said and did are the greatest Revelation of who God is and of how God loves us. And the ways we speak and act and live our faith show our belief in God's own Son, Jesus Christ.

## As Catholics...

God revealed his Kingdom to us in the words of Christ, in the works of Christ, and in the very presence of Christ among us. After Christ's Resurrection the Church was planted like a seed in the world. Our mission is to bring forth the fruits of the Kingdom of God. What are these fruits? They are many, "but the greatest of these is love" (1 Corinthians 13:13).

What are some of the other fruits, or signs, of the Kingdom of God?

## WE RESPOND

Think about the Kingdom of God. Work together to list some signs that God's love is active in our lives. Using these signs as captions, make a poster entitled "The kingdom of God is at hand" (Mark 1:15).

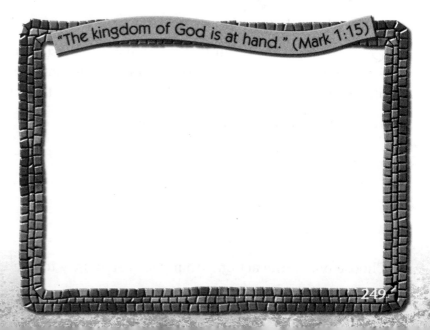

"The kingdom of God is at hand." (Mark 1:15)

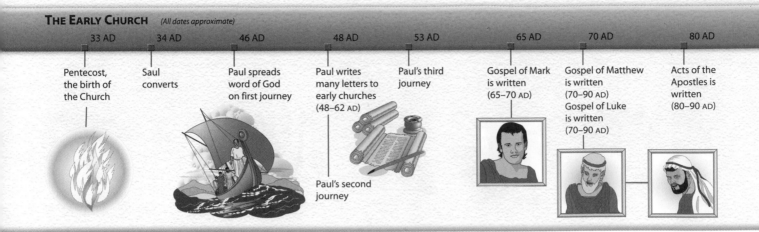

| 33 AD | 34 AD | 46 AD | 48 AD | 53 AD | 65 AD | 70 AD | 80 AD |
|---|---|---|---|---|---|---|---|

Pentecost, the birth of the Church

Saul converts

Paul spreads word of God on first journey

Paul writes many letters to early churches (48–62 AD)

Paul's second journey

Paul's third journey

Gospel of Mark is written (65–70 AD)

Gospel of Matthew is written (70–90 AD)
Gospel of Luke is written (70–90 AD)

Acts of the Apostles is written (80–90 AD)

# Many people heard Jesus' message and became his disciples.

## WE GATHER

✝ *Holy Spirit, give us the strength to live as disciples of Jesus Christ.*

Who do you spend time with? share with? To whom do you listen? From whom do you learn?

## WE BELIEVE

Jesus' message gave people hope. Many people wanted to get to know Jesus better. They wanted to learn more about God's love for them. They wanted to experience the peace and comfort that Jesus offered people. So they began to follow him.

Jesus invited all different kinds of people to follow him and live by his teachings. These women and men became his disciples. One day a large crowd followed Jesus to the mountains.

The message that Jesus gave to the people that day has become known as the *Sermon on the Mount*. Jesus told the people how to live as his disciples.

In the first part of the Sermon on the Mount, Jesus taught the people about the meaning of true happiness and the way to achieve that happiness. Jesus said that people would be happy only if they trusted in God and lived as he did.

We call these teachings that describe the way to live as Jesus' disciples the **Beatitudes**. In the Beatitudes *blessed* means "happy." As disciples of Jesus, we too are called to follow the Beatitudes. As Christians, we trust that the Holy Spirit helps us and the whole Church to do this.

Jesus' message of hope for all those who live the Beatitudes is: "Rejoice and be glad, for your reward will be great in heaven"(Matthew 5:12).

## WE RESPOND

🏃 Read about the Beatitudes on page 251. As Jesus' disciples we, too, can find true happiness by living out each Beatitude. List practical ways that can show others that we are living out each of the eight Beatitudes.

**Jesus' disciples can live the Beatitudes by:**

1. _____
2. _____
3. _____
4. _____

5. _____
6. _____
7. _____
8. _____

Choose one of the actions from your list and try to live it this week.

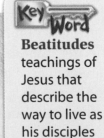

**Key Word**

**Beatitudes** teachings of Jesus that describe the way to live as his disciples

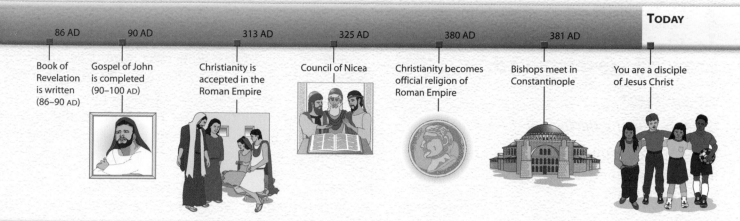

86 AD — Book of Revelation is written (86–90 AD)

90 AD — Gospel of John is completed (90–100 AD)

313 AD — Christianity is accepted in the Roman Empire

325 AD — Council of Nicea

380 AD — Christianity becomes official religion of Roman Empire

381 AD — Bishops meet in Constantinople

TODAY — You are a disciple of Jesus Christ

## The Beatitudes

Matthew 5:3–10

| | |
|---|---|
| "Blessed are the poor in spirit, for theirs is the kingdom of heaven." (Matthew 5:3) | This Beatitude tells us about our attitude toward the things we have; we should not be overly attached to possessions. Our confidence should be in God. We are called to share whatever we have with others. |
| "Blessed are they who mourn, for they will be comforted." (Matthew 5:4) | We are to be signs of hope despite the sadness, evil, and injustice we see in the world. As Jesus' disciples we are to comfort those who suffer injustice and loss. |
| "Blessed are the meek, for they will inherit the land." (Matthew 5:5) | The meek are the humble—that is, those who realize that their talents and abilities come from God. We are to use our God-given talents and abilities to do what is good, showing love for God and others. |
| "Blessed are they who hunger and thirst for righteousness, for they will be satisfied." (Matthew 5:6) | The greatest desire of those who hunger and thirst after righteousness is for God's power and presence to be at work in the world. As Jesus' disciples we try to do God's will. We put our trust in God and carry out Christ's work of justice. |
| "Blessed are the merciful for they will be shown mercy." (Matthew 5:7) | Those who show love and forgive others will themselves receive love and forgiveness in God's Kingdom. We are to show compassion to all people. |
| "Blessed are the clean of heart, for they will see God." (Matthew 5:8) | The clean of heart are those who are open to God and God's law. They are sincere in everything they do. We are to be faithful Christians and find Christ in others. |
| "Blessed are the peacemakers, for they will be called children of God." (Matthew 5:9) | God wants all people to love one another and to have the peace that comes from loving him and trusting in his will. We are called to be reconcilers in our homes, communities, and world. We are to bring people together. |
| "Blessed are they who are persecuted for the sake of righteousness, for theirs is the kingdom of heaven." (Matthew 5:10) | Prophets were often persecuted when they brought people God's message. We are to live out our Christian faith even when others do not understand our beliefs. |

## Jesus taught about living and growing closer to God.

### WE GATHER

✝ *Jesus, you are the light of the world.*

What are some things that are essential, or necessary, in life? Did you ever have to try to live without them?

### WE BELIEVE

In the Sermon on the Mount, Jesus went on to speak to his disciples about two items from everyday life: salt and light. He said, "You are the salt of the earth. But if salt loses its taste, with what can it be seasoned? . . . You are the light of the world. . . . your light must shine before others, that they may see your good deeds and glorify your heavenly Father" (Matthew 5:13, 14, 16).

When Jesus called his disciples to be like "salt" and "light" for each other and for all people, he was telling them that just as salt and light were important and necessary, so were they. Jesus wanted his disciples to show the way to him and to the Father. Jesus wanted his disciples to take an active part in their communities and to serve the Kingdom of God by sharing God's love and life with others.

List some benefits of salt and light in our lives.

_____

_____

_____

How can we be like salt and light in our communities? How can we help others to live and grow in God's love?

_____

_____

_____

Jesus told his disciples, "Love your enemies, and pray for those who persecute you" (Matthew 5:44). Jesus wanted his followers to be identified by their love for one another and for all people. By acting out of love, they could bring others to believe in Christ and to give glory and praise to the Father.

As disciples of Jesus, we too can be salt and light for others. We can help people to live and grow in love for God.

**About Prayer** During his Sermon on the Mount, Jesus also taught his disciples about prayer. Through prayer, they could stay close to God. They could speak to God and listen to God speaking to them.

Jesus himself often prayed in silence and alone. He went into the mountains or desert to put himself in the presence of God, his Father. However, Jesus also prayed with others. He studied the Scriptures in the synagogue, and observed the Sabbath. With his friends and family he participated in the great Jewish feasts.

While preaching the Sermon on the Mount, Jesus gave his disciples advice on the ways to pray. He told them that God the Father knows what we need before we ask. Jesus instructed them to pray to God our Father. So he taught them a very special prayer—the Lord's Prayer.

The Lord's Prayer is one of the most important prayers in the gospels and of the Church. This prayer is also called the Our Father. As followers of Jesus Christ, we pray the Lord's Prayer during Mass and at many other times in our lives.

The Lord's Prayer sums up Jesus' whole message of trust in and love for the Father. Each time we pray this prayer, we ask God to act in our lives and in the world. We ask the Holy Spirit to help us make the kingdom come alive in people's hearts and lives. We hope for the Lord's return at the end of time.

Catholic cathedral carved in salt mines near Kracow, Poland.

| We pray: | Our words mean: |
|---|---|
| Our Father, who art in heaven hallowed be thy name; thy kingdom come; thy will be done on earth as it is in heaven. | God is present to all who love him. We have become God's people and he is our God. We look forward to being with him forever. |
| | We ask God to unite us with the work of Christ and pray for God to bring about his kingdom. We pray to God for the ability to do his will. |
| Give us this day our daily bread; and forgive us our trespasses as we forgive those who trespass against us; | We ask God for everything we need for ourselves and for the world. We use his gifts to work toward his plan of salvation. We ask God to heal us and we ask for forgiveness from others when needed. We follow the example of Christ and forgive those who have hurt us. |
| and lead us not into temptation, but deliver us from evil. Amen. | We pray that God will protect us from all that could draw us away from his love. We ask him to guide us to choose good in our lives, and we ask him for the strength to follow his law. |

## WE RESPOND

How can prayer help you to show that the Kingdom of God has begun?

Work in a group and list different ways that prayer can be part of our lives.

Pray the Lord's Prayer together.

# Jesus worked signs and wonders among the people.

### WE GATHER

✝ *Mary, Mother of God, help us to be close to your son.*

Sometimes people say it is a miracle when a team wins a game. Talk about the many things that people today think of as miracles. Do you think these events and happenings are miracles? How do you define a miracle?

### WE BELIEVE

Jesus traveled through all of Galilee, "teaching in their synagogues, proclaiming the gospel of the kingdom, and curing every disease and illness among the people" (Matthew 4:23). Jesus worked many miracles. A miracle is an extraordinary event that is beyond human power and brought about by God. It is an action beyond the ordinary laws of nature. Jesus' miracles were all signs that he was the Son of God and that the Kingdom of God had arrived in him.

According to the Gospel of John, Jesus performed his first sign or miracle at a wedding feast in Cana of Galilee.

📖 John 2:1–12

One day Jesus and his mother, Mary, and some of Jesus' other disciples went to a wedding in the village of Cana. Cana was a few miles from Nazareth. At the wedding, however, the wine ran out in the middle of the banquet. Mary went to Jesus and told him that there was no more wine. Then Mary told the servants, "Do whatever he tells you" (John 2:5).

Jesus listened to his mother Mary. She knew the wedding party needed his help. Jesus pointed to some jars and told the servants, "Fill the jars with water." After they filled them to the top, Jesus said, "Draw some out now and take it to the headwaiter" (John 2:7, 8).

The servants did as he said. But Jesus had changed the water into wine. When the headwaiter tasted it, he was amazed that the wine was so good. He called the bridegroom and said to him, "Everyone serves good wine first, and then when people have drunk freely, an inferior one; but you have kept the good wine until now" (John 2:10).

Through this miracle, Jesus revealed not only that he was human, but also that he was divine. Through signs and his deep compassion and concern for others, the Kingdom of God continued to be made known. And his followers began to see who Jesus was and to believe in him and praise God.

**Jesus' Miracles** Everywhere Jesus went, to villages, towns, or farms, people brought those who were in need to him. Jesus did not work miracles as a show or to make himself popular. Jesus helped those who expressed faith in him.

We know from other accounts in the gospels that Jesus worked many miracles during his public ministry. Some of these miracles involved nature or everyday needs, such as calming a storm or feeding a multitude of people. From the Gospel of Matthew we learn that as Jesus' disciples were crossing the river in a boat, a great storm frightened them. Jesus "rebuked the winds and the sea, and there was great calm" (Matthew 8:26).

Another time Jesus was worried about a crowd of thousands of people who had been listening to him preach and had had nothing to eat. Among all the people there were only seven loaves of bread and a few fish. Jesus gave thanks and broke the loaves and gave them to his disciples to give to the people. "They all ate and were satisfied. They picked up the fragments left over—seven baskets full." (Matthew 15:37)

Other miracles that Jesus worked involved people. For example, Jesus healed people who were lame and others who were sick. They were cured and could then walk and be well. Most often these healings were brought about by a simple word, and sometimes by a touch. Once two blind men followed Jesus asking him for help. When Jesus approached them, he asked if they believed he could help them. They said yes, and Jesus touched their eyes saying, "Let it be done for you according to your faith" (Matthew 9:29). Immediately their eyes were opened, and they could see.

Jesus worked miracles because he loved people, especially those suffering and in need. He wanted them to have his Father's comfort and peace in their lives. He also wanted to strengthen their belief in the power of God's love and forgiveness. And many that Jesus healed left their own towns and followed him.

## WE RESPOND

How can you show that you are Jesus' disciple?

**Underline the correct answer.**

1. An extraordinary event that is beyond human power and brought about by God is a **(Beatitude/miracle)**.

2. The **(Torah/gospel)** is the good news about God at work in Jesus Christ.

3. The **(Beatitudes/apostles)** are the teachings of Jesus that describe the way to live as his disciples.

4. The **(Kingdom of God/Lord's Prayer)** is the power of God's love coming into the world and our lives.

**Short Answers**

5. What message did Jesus give to the people at the Sermon on the Mount?

_____

6. What are we asking God when we pray the words of the Lord's Prayer?

_____

7. What did Jesus tell his followers about the Kingdom of God?

_____

8. Why did Jesus work miracles?

_____

**Write a paragraph to answer this question.**

**9–10.** What did Jesus do to show God's love to people?

ASSESSMENT

You have been asked to write a biographical profile describing Jesus' life as a teacher and healer. This profile will be featured on a television program. What would you tell others about Jesus, especially those who do not know him? Prepare and deliver the profile.

# We Respond in Faith

## Reflect & Pray

Jesus, help me to be salt to others by

_____

Jesus, help me to be light to others by

_____

**Kingdom of God** (p. 248)
**Beatitudes** (p. 250)

## Remember

- God makes himself known in his Son.

- Many people heard Jesus' message and became his disciples.

- Jesus taught about living and growing closer to God.

- Jesus worked signs and wonders among the people.

## OUR CATHOLIC LIFE

### Sisters of the Good Shepherd

The women of this religious community imitate the compassion of Jesus, the Good Shepherd. They provide support to women and their families through counseling and by helping those in prison and those trying to start their lives again. The sisters offer spiritual guidance. They staff social services offices, and work to change unjust laws. Like Jesus the Good Shepherd, they seek to help those who may be lost or overlooked by society. Their motto is: "One person is more precious than the whole world."

# SHARING FAITH
## with My Family

## Sharing What I Learned

Discuss the following with your family:

- the gospel
- the Kingdom of God
- the Sermon on the Mount
- Jesus' miracles.

## A Family of Saints

**Saint Angela de Merici 1474–1540**

Saint Angela de Merici was concerned with the lack of education that was available for girls. She is the founder of the Company of Saint Ursula, known as the Ursulines. The Ursulines were the first group of women religious to work outside the cloister and the first teaching order of women. We celebrate the feast day of Saint Angela de Merici on January 27.

What ways can your family help educate children throughout the world?

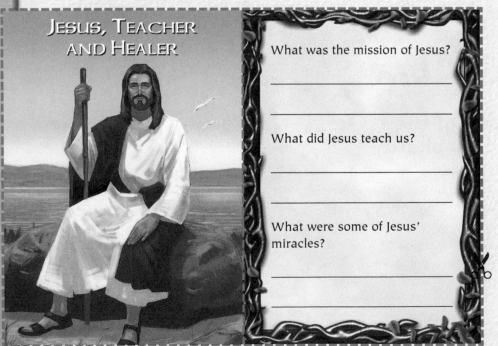

### JESUS, TEACHER AND HEALER

What was the mission of Jesus?

_____

_____

What did Jesus teach us?

_____

_____

What were some of Jesus' miracles?

_____

_____

## We Believe Trading Cards

Complete the facts on the back of the trading card. Then share with your family what you have learned about Jesus, Teacher and Healer.

Visit Sadlier's
**www.WeBelieveweb.com**

**Connect to the Catechism**
For adult background and reflection, see paragraphs 516, 1723, 2764, and 548.

# Jesus, Redeemer and Savior

## 23

## ✝ We Gather in Prayer

**Leader:** Lord Jesus, you are the Savior and Redeemer of the world. Blessed be your name.

**All:** Blessed be your name for ever.

**Leader:** Our passage from death to new life can only be made in our dying and rising with Christ. Listen as Saint Paul reminds his friends of the Paschal Mystery.

**Reader 1:** "You were buried with him in baptism, in which you were also raised with him through faith in the power of God, who raised him from the dead."(Colossians 2:12)

**All:** Lord Jesus, you are the Savior and Redeemer of the world.

**Reader 2:** "And whatever you do, in word or in deed, do everything in the name of the Lord Jesus, giving thanks to God the Father through him." (Colossians 3:17)

**All:** Lord Jesus, you are the Savior and Redeemer of the world.

**Leader:** It is Christ's perfect sacrifice of love and obedience that saved us from sin and grants us salvation. All praise and honor be yours, now and for ever.

**All:** Amen.

# Jesus gave us a new covenant.

## WE GATHER

✝ *Jesus, thank you for your presence in the Eucharist.*

Think of some leaders in different countries or cities. Are they popular with everyone? Why or why not?

## WE BELIEVE

During the time that Jesus was with his disciples and preaching among the people, many people said that he was the Messiah. This worried some of the authorities in Jerusalem. They feared that someone as popular as Jesus might lead a revolt against the Roman government.

Despite the political tension Jesus and the disciples went to Jerusalem as the feast of Passover approached. They were a family to one another. So like every other family, they prepared the Passover meal. At sundown they gathered for the meal, and as was the custom, they reclined on couches arranged around a low table.

Everything about the meal—the unleavened bread, the wine, the lamb, the bitter herbs—had a special meaning. The foods were symbols that reminded Jewish families of the great events of the Exodus from Egypt under the leadership of Moses. The Passover meal also reminded them of their covenant with God. It has the same meaning for Jews today.

Jesus, however, gave the Passover meal a new meaning. During the meal Jesus took some bread, prayed over it, broke it, and gave it to the disciples saying, "This is my body, which will be given for you" (Luke 22:19). Then he took a cup of wine, prayed over it, and gave it to them saying, "This cup is the new covenant in my blood, which will be shed for you" (Luke 22:20). Like God had done before, Jesus was giving his followers a new covenant and a new covenant meal. The Passover celebration now had a new meaning. As the priest of the new covenant, Jesus was offering himself as the paschal lamb. Jesus told his disciples to "do this in memory of me" (Luke 22:19). We call the Passover meal that Jesus shared with his disciples on the night before he died the **Last Supper**.

Jesus' disciples continued to share this meal as a memorial to Jesus. Jesus was with them as they broke the bread and drank from the cup. Christ's own Body and Blood were present under the appearances of bread and wine. Jesus' love and his sacrifice would forever be remembered in the celebration of the Eucharist. For Christians the Eucharist is the new Passover of God's people.

**The Final Hours** Jesus knew that one of his apostles would soon betray him. He knew that the next day would be one of suffering and of death. So he went to the Mount of Olives. His disciples went there, too. In these final hours before his suffering began, Jesus prayed to his Father in the olive grove called Gethsemane. And Jesus told his disciples that they should pray, too.

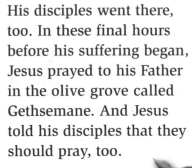

**Last Supper** the Passover meal that Jesus shared with his disciples on the night before he died

Leonardo da Vinci (1452–1519),
*The Last Supper*

As he prayed, Jesus asked to be relieved of the pain that he would suffer, and yet at the same time he wanted to do his Father's will. During his hours of prayer Jesus chose to be obedient and to trust his Father. Jesus freely chose to offer his life for us so that we might be freed from sin.

Jesus had given himself in the Eucharist and was now preparing to give his life for all of humanity.

## WE RESPOND

Illustrate the Passover of the Jewish people and the new Passover that has been given to us by Jesus Christ. What can you do to remember Jesus' Last Supper this week?

# Jesus gave his life for us.

## WE GATHER

✝ *Jesus, help us never to turn from you.*

What are the reasons that there might be unrest or revolt in some countries, cities, neighborhoods? What are some of the ways that governments deal with these problems? Are the ways always peaceful? always just?

## WE BELIEVE

While Jesus was praying in Gethsemane, Judas, one of his apostles, entered the garden. He came with Temple guards and a group of people who had been angered by Jesus' teachings. Judas had promised to hand over Jesus to these men for thirty pieces of silver. Judas had told them that the one he would kiss was the one they were looking for. So Judas went to Jesus, greeted him, and kissed him. Jesus said, "Friend, do what you have come for" (Matthew 26:50). Then the guards took hold of Jesus, and though Peter offered a struggle, they arrested Jesus.

First they took Jesus before Caiaphas, the high priest. Caiaphas insisted that Jesus was guilty of blasphemy, of referring to God in a disrespectful or irreverent way.

Then this group took him before Pontius Pilate, the Roman governor. When Judas learned what had happened to Jesus because of his betrayal, he regretted what he had done. He tried to return the thirty pieces of silver and said, "I have sinned in betraying innocent blood" (Matthew 27:4). But it was too late to stop what had begun!

Pilate found nothing for which to condemn Jesus. Yet some leaders of the people had said that Jesus must die because he called God his Father. Pilate feared that there would be unrest or even a revolt unless he took action. Pilate ordered that Jesus be whipped and crucified.

Jesus was crucified between two criminals. The dying Jesus was insulted by those who passed him as well as by the soldiers, chief priests, and scribes. They said that if he were the king of Israel he would be able to save himself as he had saved others. When Jesus took his last breath, the veil of the sanctuary in the Temple was torn in two. The soldier who stood in front of Jesus and watched him die said, "Truly this man was the Son of God!" (Mark 15:39).

View of Jerusalem including the Church of the Holy Sepulchre.

We further read in the Gospel of Mark that there were women watching from a distance. Mary Magdalene, Mary the mother of the younger James, and Salome had followed Jesus when he was in Galilee. Other women followers who had come with Jesus to Jerusalem were there, too.

After Jesus died, his body was taken down from the cross and placed in the tomb of Joseph of Arimathea, a follower of Jesus. A heavy stone was rolled across the entrance of the tomb. It was Friday, the day before the Jewish Sabbath. Christians call the day that marks Jesus' death Good Friday because it was on this day that Jesus died to save us. This is why we call Jesus our Redeemer. By his death and Resurrection Jesus gained our salvation and brought us the hope of new life.

## WE RESPOND

Let us make an imaginary pilgrimage now to the Holy Land. Let us walk where Jesus walked during the last days of his life.

Our first stop is the *Chapel of the Cenacle*. The word *cenacle* comes from a Latin word meaning "dining room." In the Upper Room on the second floor, Jesus celebrated the Last Supper with his apostles. They ate the Passover meal together, a meal that celebrated the passing over of the Jews from slavery to freedom. At this meal, Jesus gave us the gift of his Body and Blood, the Eucharist. This building is also the site honored as David's tomb. So in this one building we remember David, the king of Israel, and Jesus, a descendant of David and savior of the world.

The Garden of Gethsemane, Jerusalem

Our second stop is the *Garden of Gethsemane*. This garden was a special place for Jesus. This was where he went after the Last Supper to prepare for his eventual suffering on the cross. It was here that he endured the agony in the garden.

The Church of the Holy Sepulcher, Jerusalem.

Our last stop is the *Church of the Holy Sepulcher*. This is an impressive stone building with a shining dome. It combines two churches. The upper chapel of the church is said to be the site of Jesus' crucifixion. The site of Jesus' tomb is said to lie beneath the dome, but the actual tomb was destroyed.

If you were in these sacred places, what would you pray for? What would you say to Jesus, who died and rose here, and is with us now, today?

The Chapel of the Cenacle, Jerusalem.

# Jesus Christ rose from the dead.

## WE GATHER

✝ *Alleluia, we give praise to you, Jesus!*

Have you ever heard of or experienced an event that does not seem to have a natural explanation?

How did it make you feel? Why?

## WE BELIEVE

As it had been foretold in the Scriptures, Jesus was raised from the dead on the third day after his death. The mystery of Jesus' being raised from the dead is called the **Resurrection**.

📖 Mark 16:1–8

"When the sabbath was over, Mary Magdalene, Mary, the mother of James, and Salome bought spices so that they might go and anoint him. Very early when the sun had risen, on the first day of the week, they came to the tomb. They were saying to one another, 'Who will roll back the stone for us from the entrance to the tomb?' When they looked up, they saw that the stone had been rolled back; it was very large. On entering the tomb they saw a young man sitting on the right side, clothed in a white robe, and they were utterly amazed. He said to them, 'Do not be amazed! You seek Jesus of Nazareth, the crucified. He has been raised; he is not here. Behold, the place where they laid him. But go and tell his disciples and Peter, "He is going before you to Galilee; there you will see him, as he told you."' Then they went out and fled from the tomb, seized with trembling and bewilderment. They said nothing to anyone, for they were afraid."

*The Holy Women at the Sepulchre* by Laura James (Contemporary Artist)

Imagine that you are a news reporter in Jerusalem. You are interviewing Mary Magdalene and the other women on their return from Jesus' empty tomb. With a group role-play the interview.

Mark 16:9–11

**The Risen Jesus Appears to Mary** "When he had risen, early on the first day of the week, he appeared first to Mary Magdalene. . . . She went and told his companions who were mourning and weeping. When they heard that he was alive and had been seen by her, they did not believe."

We can read in the Gospel of Mark that the risen Christ appeared to other disciples, too. They also told the group what they had seen, but the group of disciples still did not believe. They finally believed once Christ appeared to them.

Through the gift of faith we believe in Jesus Christ and his Resurrection. By faith we not only believe in Jesus risen among us, but also live as his disciples each day.

### Key Word

**Resurrection** the mystery of Jesus' being raised from the dead

🎵 **Jesus Is Risen**

Refrain:

Alleluia! Alleluia! Alleluia!
Jesus is risen, alleluia!
That Easter morning at break of day,
friends of the Lord went to see where
   he lay.
The angel who sat at the tomb did say:
"He is not here, he is risen!" (Refrain)
All the apostles were filled with fear.
Then in the midst of them did he
   appear and say to them:
"Peace be upon you here.
See for yourselves, I am risen!" (Refrain)
Now it no longer could be denied,
seeing his feet and his hands and his side.
"Indeed you are Lord! You are God!"
   they cried.
"Conquering death, you have risen!"
(Refrain)

## As Catholics...

In the Gospel of Luke, we read that Mary Magdalene was one of the many people Jesus healed. She became one of his closest followers. She often traveled with Jesus and the apostles, and she was present at Jesus' death and burial. In the Gospel of John we read that the risen Jesus first appeared to Mary and sent her out to tell the other disciples the good news of his Resurrection. Mary Magdalene is a symbol of hope and the new life that comes from Christ. We honor Mary as a saint. Her feast day is July 22.

Think of a person that you consider a symbol of hope and new life. Why do you think this is so?

# Christ appeared to his disciples.

## WE GATHER

✝ *Jesus, help us to always believe in you.*

Think about the stories and events that you hear about or that people tell you about. Do you believe all of them? Why or why not?

## WE BELIEVE

The risen Jesus appeared to his disciples to strengthen them and to increase their faith in his Resurrection. He wanted his disciples to believe in all that he had told them and in what he had done for humanity.

Later on the day of Jesus' Resurrection, the apostles were gathered together behind locked doors. They feared that the people in authority might also arrest them. Jesus came and stood among them. He showed them his side and his hands and said, "Peace be with you. As the Father has sent me, so I send you" Then he breathed on them and said, "Receive the holy Spirit." (John 20:21, 22)

God breathed life into the first human beings. As God breathes life into every human being, Jesus breathed the gift of the Holy Spirit upon his disciples. This began the new life in which humanity now can share because of Jesus' Resurrection.

The Holy Spirit that Jesus breathed on his apostles is the same Holy Spirit who gives us life. The Holy Spirit guides us as we live each day. Jesus has not left us alone, but is with us always.

📖 John 20:24–29

Thomas, one of Jesus' apostles, was not with the others when Jesus appeared to them. He did not believe that they had seen Jesus. He said to the other apostles, "Unless I see the mark of the nails in his hands and put my finger into the nailmarks and put my hand into his side, I will not believe" (John 20:25).

Later in the week all of the disciples were together again, and Thomas was with them. They were inside and all the doors were locked. Jesus appeared right in the middle of them and told Thomas, "Put your finger here and see my hands, and bring your hand and put it into my side, and do not be unbelieving, but believe" (John 20:27). Thomas told Jesus he believed he was the Lord, his God. But Jesus reminded Thomas that he believed because he had now seen. Jesus said, "Blessed are those who have not seen and have believed" (John 20:29).

As disciples of Christ we are called to believe everything we have learned about Jesus from the gospels and the other writings of the New Testament. We are called to believe that Jesus Christ died and rose to new life. We are called to believe what the Church teaches us about Christ.

We believe that Jesus is the Son of God, our Savior. We believe that through the risen Jesus we have new life and the hope of sharing this life with him forever.

## WE RESPOND

Think about the appearances of Jesus after his Resurrection. Prepare a short advertisement using your favorite appearance to convince the public that Jesus is risen!

Review

**Complete the following.**

1. At the Last Supper when Jesus was celebrating the _____ meal with his disciples, he gave them the _____.

2. The mystery that Jesus _____ on the third day after his death is called the _____.

3. The risen Jesus appeared to his _____ to strengthen them and to increase their _____ in his Resurrection.

4. Christians call the day that marks Jesus' death _____ because on this day Jesus died to _____.

**Write True or False for the following sentences.**
**Then change the false sentences to make them true.**

5. _____ On the evening of the Resurrection the risen Jesus appeared to all his apostles.

_____

6. _____ On the night before he suffered and died, Jesus prayed to his Father.

_____

7. _____ Christians celebrate the Eucharist as the new Passover given to us by Christ.

_____

8. _____ By his death Jesus gains our salvation and brings us the hope of new life.

_____

**Write a paragraph to answer this question.**

9–10. What happened at the Last Supper?

ASSESSMENT

Design a mural or poster that illustrates Jesus as our Redeemer and Savior. Use the events in the chapter to help you. Include captions in your mural or poster to teach others about the saving work of Christ.

# We Respond in Faith

## Reflect & Pray

Jesus, you gave your life so that _____

_____

_____

Risen Jesus, come to us, too, and _____

_____

_____

**Key Words**

**Last Supper** (p. 260)
**Resurrection** (p. 265)

## Remember

- Jesus gave us a new covenant.
- Jesus gave his life for us.
- Jesus Christ rose from the dead.
- Christ appeared to his disciples.

## OUR CATHOLIC LIFE

### The Redemptorists

The Redemptorist Missionaries are priests, brothers, and lay missionaries who follow the example of Christ our Redeemer by preaching God's word to the poor and abandoned. This religious community, founded by Saint Alphonsus Liguori, serves all around the world to spread the good news and deepen the faith of youth, young adults, and adults. The Redemptorists work in parishes, preach at parish programs, run retreats and conference centers, work with those suffering from AIDS and other terminal illnesses, serve as missionaries throughout the world, and manage Liguori Publications, a Catholic publishing company.

# SHARING FAITH
## with My Family

## Sharing What I Learned

Discuss the following with your family:

- the Last Supper
- Jesus' final hours
- Jesus' death and Resurrection
- the appearances of the risen Jesus.

## A Family of Saints

**Saint Elizabeth of Portugal 1271–1336**

Saint Elizabeth of Portugal was born a Spanish princess. She is remembered for her charity and kindness toward the poor and as a peacemaker. We celebrate her feast day on July 4.

How can your family show charity and kindness to others?

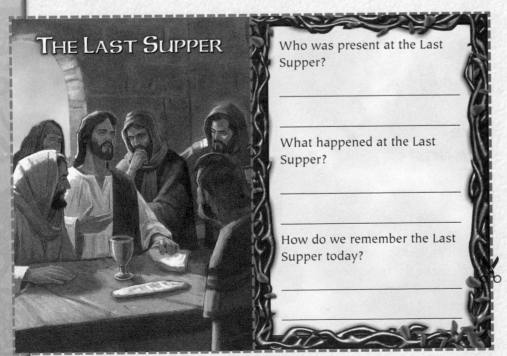

### THE LAST SUPPER

Who was present at the Last Supper?

_____

_____

What happened at the Last Supper?

_____

_____

How do we remember the Last Supper today?

_____

_____

## We Believe Trading Cards

Complete the facts on the back of the trading card. Then share with your family what you have learned about the Last Supper.

Visit Sadlier's
**www.WeBelieveweb.com**

**Connect to the Catechism**
For adult background and reflection, see paragraphs 1337, 609, 640, and 645.

# The Church Begins

## 24

## ✝ We Gather in Prayer

**Leader:** Come, Holy Spirit, fill the hearts of your faithful.

**All:** And kindle in them the fire of your love.

**Reader:** A reading from the Letter of Saint Paul to the Ephesians

"You are fellow citizens with the holy ones and members of the household of God, built upon the foundation of the apostles and prophets, with Christ Jesus himself as the capstone. Through him the whole structure is held together and grows into a temple sacred in the Lord; in him you also are being built together into a dwelling place of God in the Spirit . . . it has now been revealed to his holy apostles and prophets by the Spirit, that the Gentiles are coheirs, members of the same body, and copartners in the promise in Christ Jesus through the gospel." (Ephesians 2:19–22; 3:5–6)

The word of the Lord.

**All:** Thanks be to God.

**Leader:** The Holy Spirit moves us to become one in Christ's body, his Church. From the apostles to the martyrs to all the holy ones in the faith, we have learned that the Spirit knows our needs even before we ask the Father. Jesus teaches us to pray. The Spirit leads us to pray in freedom as sons and daughters of God. And so we pray.

**All:** Amen! Amen! Amen!

# With the coming of the Holy Spirit the Church began.

## WE GATHER

✝ *Holy Spirit, fill our hearts with your love.*

Have you ever been at a "Grand Opening" of a new store or business? What kind of things are happening? How are people acting and reacting to all the activities? Give some examples.

_____

_____

_____

_____

## WE BELIEVE

Jesus was about to change the disciples' lives again. He had to leave them as they knew him and return in all his glory to his Father in heaven. But he left them with the mission that he had begun. He had brought the good news of the Kingdom of God. He showed the people his Father's love and forgiveness. He spoke to them about the power of the Holy Spirit. He lived in the spirit of justice and peace. And Jesus passed his mission on to his disciples. He wanted them to continue to bring more people into the community of believers.

Jesus knew that the apostles and other disciples were fearful because of his arrest and crucifixion. He saw their hope now that he had risen and was with them. Yet he would soon leave them and he knew that they needed strength and courage to carry on his mission. He knew that the Holy Spirit was the power and force that would guide the community of believers. The Holy Spirit would help them to live out their faith and love in the one God.

Jesus told his disciples that they were his witnesses, the ones who would now spread the good news. Then he said, "And [behold]

I am sending the promise of my Father upon you; but stay in the city until you are clothed with power from on high" (Luke 24:49).

Jesus then went with his disciples "as far as Bethany, raised his hands, and blessed them. As he blessed them he parted from them and was taken up to heaven" (Luke 24:50–51). We call this the Ascension.

The disciples went back to Jerusalem as Jesus had instructed them. They were filled with joy and praised God, remembering all that had just taken place. Mary, the mother of Jesus, and other women and men who were disciples of Jesus prayed and stayed close to one another.

During this time after Jesus' Ascension, Peter told the others, "My brothers, the scripture had to be fulfilled which the holy Spirit spoke beforehand through the mouth of David, concerning Judas, who was the guide for those who arrested Jesus" (Acts of the Apostles 1:16).

Peter went on to say that Judas had died and that another person must be chosen to take Judas' place. This person must be a witness to everything the apostles had seen and heard. So they chose two men and then prayed, "You, Lord, who know the hearts of all, show which one of these two you have chosen to take the place in this apostolic ministry from which Judas turned away to go to his own place" (Acts of the Apostles 1:24–25).

These two men then chose lots. Matthias drew the one that showed that he had been chosen to take Judas' place as one of the apostles.

Acts of the Apostles 2:1–4, 7, 17, 41

**The Coming of the Holy Spirit** While the Jewish feast of Weeks, or Pentecost, was taking place the disciples were gathered together. "And suddenly there came from the sky a noise like a strong driving wind, and it filled the entire house in which they were. Then there appeared to them tongues as of fire, which parted and came to rest on each one of them. And they were all filled with the holy Spirit and began to speak in different tongues, as the Spirit enabled them to proclaim." (Acts of the Apostles 2:2–4) Everyone was astounded and Peter told them that the prophecy of Joel was now fulfilled.

"God says,
'that I will pour out a portion of my spirit
upon all flesh.'" (Acts of the Apostles 2:17)

How wonderful it was that each person understood what was being said in his or her own language! The fact that this happened helps us to know that Christ's message of love and peace is for all people.

We call the day the Holy Spirit came upon the first disciples **Pentecost**. It was on this day that Peter and the other apostles baptized about three thousand people. This was the beginning of the Church. After this day Peter and the other apostles continued to preach and baptize. Many believers became members of the Church. And the Church was made strong through the power of the Holy Spirit.

## WE RESPOND

What can you personally do to share Christ's message of love and peace? How can his message be shared throughout the entire world? Explain.

🎵 **Spirit of God, Come to Us**

Refrain:
Spirit of God, fill our hearts,
Spirit of God, fill our minds;
Help us to give, help us to live as
signs of your love.

We are your people, we are your own
faithful companions joined as one;
come to us now, Spirit of God,
enkindle within us the
fire of your love.
(Refrain)

Spirit of God, come to us;
Spirit of Jesus, live in us;
help us to be signs of your peace,
signs of compassion,
forgiveness and hope.
(Refrain)

**Key Word**

**Pentecost** the day on which the Holy Spirit came upon the first disciples

273

# The good news of Christ spread to many places.

## WE GATHER

✝ *Lord, help us to be faithful members of your Church.*

👤 Brainstorm a list of ways you spread important news so that everyone who needs to know about it gets the message.

## WE BELIEVE

From the beginning the apostles tried to help the members of the Church to live according to Jesus' teachings. In carrying out Jesus' command to love God, themselves, and others, the disciples shared everything. They contributed to a common fund to help needy members. We learn from Scripture that "they devoted themselves to the teaching of the apostles and to the communal life, to the breaking of the bread and to the prayers" (Acts of the Apostles 2:42).

Some disciples called themselves "followers of the Way," recalling that Jesus described himself as "the way, and the truth, and the life" (John 14:6). Others called themselves Nazarenes, indicating that they were followers of Jesus of Nazareth. It was not until about ten years after Jesus' death, in a large city called Antioch, that the followers of Jesus Christ were first called "Christians."

As the numbers of disciples increased and they spread throughout Judea and beyond, the Temple authorities in Jerusalem became uneasy. Peter and the other apostles were arrested. But they were released the next day because they had done nothing against the existing laws.

As Peter and the others continued to preach, fear about their influence and acceptance grew. It was not long before a persecution of Christ's disciples broke out.

📖 Acts of the Apostles 9:1–8, 17–18

One of the leaders of these persecutions was a young Pharisee and Roman citizen named Saul.

When Saul heard that Christians were active in Damascus, a busy commercial center in Syria, he asked the high priest for permission to arrest Christians there and bring them back to Jerusalem for trial. The high priest granted his request. As Saul approached Damascus, however, he had an experience that changed his whole life. A blinding light flashed around him. He fell to the ground and heard a voice saying to him "Saul, Saul, why are you persecuting me?" He said, "Who are you, sir?" The voice replied, "I am Jesus, whom you are persecuting" (Acts of the Apostles 9:4–5). With these words Jesus was telling Saul that in persecuting Christians, he was persecuting Jesus because Jesus and his followers were one body, the Church.

When Saul got up from the ground, he opened his eyes but could not see. The men he was traveling with brought him to Damascus. Three days later he recovered his sight in the presence of one of Jesus' disciples and Saul was baptized. This event is one of the most well-known examples of conversion in the Bible.

Within a short time Saul, better known by his Roman name, Paul, became one of the great leaders of the early Church. In three missionary journeys, Paul brought the good news of Jesus Christ to the major cities of the eastern Roman Empire.

- His first journey took him to the island of Cyprus and to Antioch and other cities of Syria and Asia Minor (modern Turkey).

- His second journey, which is the most extensive, included an eighteen-month stay in Corinth, Greece.

- Most of his third journey was spent establishing the Church community in Ephesus, a large and important city in Asia Minor.

During his travels Paul wrote letters to the new Christians in these places. Some of these letters can be found in the New Testament.

In caring for these members of the Church, Paul took all kinds of risks. He suffered insults, the hatred of his enemies, shipwreck, and even imprisonment. Yet Paul never wavered from his faith. He led many to believe in Jesus and to become members of the Church.

From the moment of his conversion, Paul's life was guided by his devotion to Jesus, who was the center of his preaching and teaching.

## WE RESPOND

Imagine that you, like Paul, have an experience that strengthens you to preach about Jesus Christ. What might that experience be?

Work in a group to make a map of the journeys that you would take to bring the good news of Jesus to those who need to hear it in today's world.

# Christians were persecuted for their faith.

## WE GATHER

✞ *Lord, help us to be your witnesses.*

Have you ever seen or experienced persecution? Why do you think so many people throughout the world are persecuted?

## WE BELIEVE

Paul's missionary trips were very important to the development of the Church. He preached the good news of Jesus Christ to people of different cultures and customs. Because of his work, Christianity spread beyond Judea and to people other than only those of the Jewish faith. It grew to include Greeks and Romans. Thus from its beginning, the Church has included people of different cultures who speak different languages, have unique customs, and live throughout the world.

As the Church grew, the Roman government became more threatened. Christians refused to honor and worship the false gods of the Roman Empire. More importantly, the Roman laws required people to acknowledge the emperor as a god, yet the Christians would not do this.

Christianity was not an accepted religion during the first three centuries, and this put the Christians at risk. Many had to keep their faith secret. They gathered for worship in the homes of fellow Christians, and tried to spread the good news without angering the Roman officials. The Romans believed that Christians put the authority and security of the empire at risk. These fears and misunderstandings led to the persecution of Christians. Some were imprisoned and forced to accept false gods. Others were ridiculed and treated as outcasts.

These conditions, however, did not stop Christians from believing in Christ. Many even became martyrs for their faith. A **martyr** is a person who dies rather than give up his or her belief in Jesus Christ. The word *martyr* actually comes from the Greek word for "witness." We do not have a record of all of the thousands of Christians who died for their faith. However, there are some martyrs whose stories have been passed down to us. Some of the information we have is folklore, but this adds to our desire to learn more about the great witness of the early days of the Church.

> **Key Word**
>
> **martyr** person who dies rather than give up his or her belief in Jesus Christ

**Saint Lawrence** Lawrence lived in Rome during the third century. He was one of the deacons of the Roman church. He had a great responsibility in caring for the goods of the church and making sure those in need were helped. In the year 257 Pope Sixtus was arrested and put to death. The following year Lawrence also became a martyr.

There are many legends and devotions surrounding Saint Lawrence. One of these is that when the pope was led away by the Roman soldiers, he told Lawrence that he would also die in three days. So Lawrence sold all the sacred vessels. He then gave all the church's money to the poor, the widows, and the orphans of Rome. When the chief Roman officer heard this, he ordered Lawrence to bring all the church's valuables to him.

Lawrence gathered all the Christians he could find and all the people who were neglected and abused by society. He then presented them to the chief Roman officer as "the Church's treasure." We celebrate Saint Lawrence's feast day on August 10.

**Saint Cecilia** Cecilia is another well-loved martyr and saint of the Church. She is believed to have lived in Rome during the 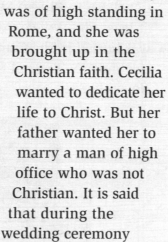 third century. Her family was of high standing in Rome, and she was brought up in the Christian faith. Cecilia wanted to dedicate her life to Christ. But her father wanted her to marry a man of high office who was not Christian. It is said that during the wedding ceremony Cecilia was silently singing to God and praying for his help. Cecilia convinced her husband that an angel of God protected her, and soon her husband and his brother became Christians. These two men were martyred, and Cecilia is said to have buried them. She, too, was then persecuted and martyred. We celebrate the feast day of Saint Cecilia, patroness of music, on November 22.

**Saint Agnes** Agnes lived during the third century in Rome. At age thirteen, she dedicated her life to Christ and vowed to remain pure of heart. It is said that she was a beautiful young woman whom many men wanted to marry. She refused to worship the false gods of many of the people of her time and was treated immodestly and ridiculed for her chaste ways. However, this abuse did not weaken her faith. She withstood the mistreatment and finally her life was taken because she refused to give up her Christian ways. Thus, she too died as a martyr. We celebrate Saint Agnes's feast day on January 21.

## As Catholics...

In recent years the Catholic Church has honored the Christian martyrs of the twentieth and twenty-first centuries. In May 2000, the Vatican welcomed Christians of different faith communities to participate in a prayer service to honor these martyrs. Among those remembered were Father Christian de Chergé and the monks of Our Lady of Atlas in Algeria (Catholic), Margherita Chou (Catholic), Pastor Paul Schneider (Lutheran), W.G.R. Jotcham (Baptist), and His Holiness Tichon, Patriarch of the Russian Orthodox Church. These women and men gave their lives as a witness to their faith in Christ. It is important to remember their lives and to work to stop religious persecution and violence.

Do some research and find out more about martyrs of recent centuries.

## WE RESPOND

List some ways people give witness to their faith today.

_____

_____

_____

_____

_____

_____

All Christians are called to be witnesses to Christ. How can you be a witness to Christ this week?

# Christianity became an accepted religion.

## WE GATHER

✞ *Father, lead us to be holy in you.*

In the United States we all are free to practice our religion. What are some ways this right is protected?

## WE BELIEVE

The fourth century was a dramatic one for the Church. In the year 313 the Roman emperors declared that Christianity was accepted in the Roman Empire. In the year 380 Christianity became the official religion of the Roman Empire. The years of persecution were finally ending. However, not all Romans accepted Christianity, and sometimes even members of the same family did not practice the same faith. The family of Saint Martin of Tours is one example of this.

**Saint Martin of Tours** Martin is one of the first saints that we remember not as a martyr but as a witness who was able to live out his Christian faith. Martin was born in a Roman province in the early years of the fourth century. He felt a strong calling to serve God. His parents continued to worship false gods, so Martin had to study Christianity secretly. At age fifteen he joined the Roman army. He did not want to serve in the military, but he was required to do so because his father had served in the military.

As a young soldier he showed great compassion for those in need. Once he passed a beggar and tore half of his cloak to cover the man and keep him warm. That night Jesus appeared to Martin and soon after Martin was baptized. A few years later he left the army and went to Tours, France. There he spoke out against those who were misinterpreting the faith. The people of Tours respected Martin greatly.

Eventually Martin became the bishop of Tours. He devoted his time to stopping false beliefs in France. He prayed, taught, and preached everywhere. Through his work many came to believe in Christ. Martin lived until he was at least eighty years old. At his request, he was buried in the Cemetery of the Poor. We celebrate the feast of this bishop and saint on November 11.

**Professing the Faith**   As we know, the apostles shared their faith with the early Church. Eventually it became necessary to summarize the faith into professions of faith, or creeds, for those being baptized. One of the earliest creeds, the Apostles' Creed is still prayed today. It can be found on page 325.

The Apostles' Creed is divided into three parts. The first part is about the first Person of the Blessed Trinity and the great work of creation. The second part is about the second Person of the Blessed Trinity and the redemption all of us have because of him. The final part is about the third Person of the Blessed Trinity from whom the Church and our holiness come.

During the fourth century, and later throughout the Church's history, some Church members questioned these teachings. It became necessary for the Church to come together to ensure that the teaching of Jesus and the apostles was passed on to future generations.

In the year 325 the bishops gathered together in Nicea for the first ecumenical council. An *ecumenical council* is a gathering of the pope and bishops to discuss and make decisions on issues of faith, Christian living, and the life of the Church. In Nicea they discussed Jesus, the Blessed Trinity, and the Church. They again gathered in Constantinople in 381 to make clear the Church's teachings on all these subjects. The result of these two councils is another creed which we still say today at Mass. It is the Nicene Creed. It can be found on page 327.

Both the Apostles' Creed and the Nicene Creed are part of Tradition. Tradition refers to the written and spoken beliefs and practices that have been passed down to us from the time of Christ and the apostles. Papal writings and council documents are other examples of Tradition, as is the Church's liturgy. The Catholic Church teaches us that Tradition is one of the two means by which God's Revelation comes to us. The Bible is the other. Together they make up the one source of Revelation. As the Church relies on the Bible as a book of faith, the Church looks to Tradition as a living witness of faith.

## WE RESPOND

Profess your faith by praying the Apostles' Creed or Nicene Creed together.

*The Third Council of Constantinople (680–681) from a fresco in the Vatican circa 1868.*

**Underline the correct answer.**

1. Christianity was (**accepted/not accepted**) as a religion during the first three centuries.

2. The Church began with the coming of (**the Holy Spirit/Matthias**).

3. (**Romans/Nazarenes**) were followers of Jesus Christ who were later called Christians.

4. The Apostles' Creed and the Nicene Creed are part of (**Tradition/Scripture**).

**Short Answers**

5. How does the Holy Spirit help Christ's disciples?

_____

6. What was the age of martyrs in the early Church?

_____

7. Why was the fourth century important for the Church?

_____

8. Why is Paul considered to be a great leader of the early Church?

_____

**Write a paragraph to answer this question.**

9–10. What are some ways Christians have given witness to Christ?

**ASSESSMENT** Imagine that you have been asked to give a presentation on the early Church. Prepare an outline including important dates, events, and people.

# We Respond in Faith

## Reflect & Pray

Come, Holy Spirit, fill our hearts. Help us _____

_____

Holy women and men who have gone before us, pray for us.

**Key Words**

Pentecost (p. 273)
martyr (p. 277)

## Remember

- With the coming of the Holy Spirit the Church began.

- The good news of Christ spread to many places.

- Christians were persecuted for their faith.

- Christianity became an accepted religion.

## OUR CATHOLIC LIFE

### Evangelization

We are called to give witness to our faith. We give witness when we speak and act based upon the good news. We tell others about the wonderful things that Christ has done. We show them what it means to be a disciple. Giving witness to our faith is an important part of the Church's mission of evangelization. Evangelization takes place in our everyday lives. We evangelize those who have not yet heard the message of Jesus Christ. We also evangelize those who have heard the message but need encouragement to live out the gift of faith that is theirs. You are an evangelizer! Live out the gospel and the people around you will see your faith in action.

# SHARING FAITH
## with My Family

## Sharing What I Learned

Discuss the following with your family:

- the coming of the Holy Spirit
- the story of Saint Paul
- the persecution of Christians
- the Apostles' Creed and the Nicene Creed.

## A Family of Saints

**Saint Catherine Laboure 1806–1876**

As a religious in the Daughters of Charity, Saint Catherine Laboure experienced visions of the Virgin Mary. In one of the visions, Mary instructed Catherine to have a medal made honoring the Immaculate Conception.

This medal is commonly known as the Miraculous Medal. We celebrate Saint Catherine Laboure's feast day on November 25.

How can your family honor Mary?

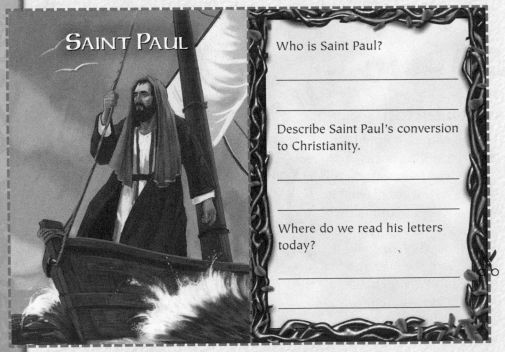

SAINT PAUL

Who is Saint Paul?

_____

_____

Describe Saint Paul's conversion to Christianity.

_____

_____

Where do we read his letters today?

_____

_____

## We Believe Trading Cards

Complete the facts on the back of the trading card. Then share with your family what you have learned about Saint Paul.

Visit Sadlier's
**www.WEBELIEVEweb.com**

**Connect to the Catechism**
For adult background and reflection, see paragraphs 732, 768, 2473, and 197.

# The Bible and the Church Today

## 25

## ✝ We Gather in Prayer

**Leader:** The prophets such as Amos, Micah, Jeremiah, Isaiah, and John the Baptist announced God's special love for those who are poor and in need. They called the people to live justly.

**Reader:** Jesus the Messiah, began his ministry by proclaiming these words of the prophet Isaiah in the synagogue in Nazareth,

"The Spirit of the Lord is upon me,
    because he has anointed me
        to bring glad tidings to the poor.

He has sent me to proclaim liberty to captives
    and recovery of sight to the blind,
        to let the oppressed go free,
    and to proclaim a year acceptable to the Lord" (Luke 4:18–19).

## 🎵 God Has Chosen Me

God has chosen me,
God has chosen me to bring good news to the poor.
God has chosen me,
God has chosen me to bring new sight to those searching for light:
God has chosen me, chosen me:

Refrain:
And to tell the world that God's kingdom is near,
To remove oppression and break down fear,
Yes, God's time is near,
God's time is near,
God's time is near, God's time is near.

God is calling me,
God is calling me in all whose cry is unheard.
God is calling me,
God is calling me to raise up the voice with no power or choice:
God is calling me, calling me: (Refrain)

# The New Testament is made up of different types of writings.

## WE GATHER

✝ *Jesus, you are Lord.*

Some families keep a scrapbook or memory box that is passed from generation to generation. What might be in such a book or box? Why? How does your family record and share memories?

## WE BELIEVE

The Bible is a book of faith. It is a record of the ways that God has remained faithful to his people. The Old Testament tells us who God is by telling us what God has done for the Jewish people and for us. It gives us a basic understanding of who God is and what our relationship to him should be.

Christians see the events and truths of faith in the Old Testament as leading us to Jesus and his teachings found in the New Testament. From the New Testament we learn about God's final Revelation in Jesus Christ and the salvation that comes from Christ. We learn about the first Christian communities and the beginning of the world-wide Church.

The New Testament is a collection of twenty-seven books. The writers of these books were inspired by the Holy Spirit to use their own abilities to record the truths of faith that are so important for living as Christians. Like the Old Testament, the New Testament includes different types of writings.

**The Gospels** The Gospels of Matthew, Mark, Luke, and John are in many ways historical writings. The writers of the gospels describe Jesus' mission and ministry, his call to discipleship, and his love. They help us to understand that Jesus Christ is Messiah and the Son of God. This is why Christians consider the gospels the most sacred books of the Bible.

Scholars believe that the Gospel of Mark was the first to be written around the years 65 to 70. The Gospels of Matthew and Luke are thought to have been written between the years 70 and 90, and the Gospel of John was completed between the years 90 and 100.

**The Letters to the Christian Communities**
The letters, or epistles, include twenty-one writings from leaders such as Paul, James, Peter, John, and Jude to different Christian communities. These letters have a variety of purposes. Some are written to discuss specific problems in the community, to instruct the people on how to live and worship, and to explain the role of the leaders of the community.

The letters include words of encouragement to new Christians who sometimes struggled in following Jesus' example of love and service. Many of these letters appear to have been written between the years 48–62. These were the years when Paul was in prison. A few letters were written much later, possibly during the early years of the second century.

**Other Writings**  The Acts of the Apostles and the Book of Revelation are the other books of the New Testament. The Acts of the Apostles records the coming of the Holy Spirit and the ministry of the Apostles. It describes the beginning and growth of the Church and the various missionary trips of the apostles and disciples. The Acts of the Apostles, which is actually a continuation of the Gospel of Luke, was probably written between the years 80 and 90.

The Book of Revelation is the final book in the New Testament. In many ways it is like parts of the Old Testament Books of Ezekiel, Zechariah, and Daniel. The Book of Revelation is based on visions and dreams and the interpretation of them. It is believed to have been written around the years 86 to 90.

As a Christian prophecy, the Book of Revelation deals with Christ's second coming at the end of time. The book uses symbols, poetry, and images. Sometimes its imagery is difficult to understand. However, the purpose of the Book of Revelation is not to foretell specific events, but to spread the message of God's Kingdom.

We treat both the Old and New Testaments as sacred, or holy. The Holy Spirit inspired the biblical writers, so God is the true author of Scripture. Our God is a living God, one who is present to us today and always. The Bible helps us to know that God loves us and is with us today. God is acting in our lives, calling us to learn from our ancestors in faith, calling us to respond to his love and to follow his Son.

## WE RESPOND

List some ways Scripture is a part of your life.

_____

_____

_____

_____

_____

_____

_____

# The Bible is an important source for Christian living and worship.

## WE GATHER

✝ *Help us to hear and live your word, Lord.*

Think about something new that you are learning to do, like rollerblade, play the piano, or use sign language. Who or what are your guides to learning these things?

## WE BELIEVE

The Bible is an important guide for Christian living. From the Bible we learn the Ten Commandments, the Beatitudes, the Great Commandment, and Christ's new commandment. These laws and teachings are the foundation of our moral life as Catholics. They help us to relate to God, ourselves, and one another.

Jesus built upon the teachings of the Old Testament writers. He used their words to teach his own disciples about following God's law. The Shema, the prayer prayed daily by Jews of Jesus' time and by Jewish people today, reminded the people to love God with all their hearts, souls, and strength. And the people had been instructed since the beginning of their covenant with God, "You shall love your neighbor as yourself" (Leviticus 19:18).

When Jesus was asked which commandment of God's law was the greatest he combined the two teachings into one. "You shall love the Lord, your God, with all your heart, with all your soul, and with all your mind. This is the greatest and the first commandment. The second is like it: You shall love your neighbor as yourself." (Matthew 22:37–39)

Jesus Christ is our model for just and right living. He obeyed God his Father and accepted the law as his guide. In fact, he told his disciples, "Do not think that I have come to abolish the law or the prophets. I have come not to abolish but to fulfill" (Matthew 5:17).

Jesus fulfilled the law by living it completely and totally. He showed us the way to love God and one another. His love changed the way people lived. He called each of us to follow his example when he gave us the *new commandment*. "I give you a new commandment: love one another. As I have loved you, so you also should love one another. This is how all will know that you are my disciples, if you have love for one another." (John 13:34–35)

**Prayer and Worship** Sacred Scripture is an essential part of the liturgy, the Church's official public worship. God's word is proclaimed at every celebration of the Mass. In fact, the first part of the Mass is called the Liturgy of the Word.

On Sundays and certain feast days of the Church, the Liturgy of the Word includes three readings and a responsorial psalm. The first reading is usually from the Old Testament. We hear of God's saving action in the lives of his people. We then sing or recite a responsorial psalm. The second reading is from one of the New Testament books other than the four gospels. This reading encourages us to follow Christ's teachings and to be faithful disciples. The third reading is always from one of the four gospels.

We show our reverence for the good news of Jesus Christ by standing for the proclamation of the gospel. The deacon or priest kisses the Book of Gospels, which was also honored in procession at the beginning of the Mass. And while the deacon or priest proclaims the gospel, altar servers often stand on either side of him holding candles. These are just some of the ways we show how important the gospels are to our lives as Christians.

The deacon or priest then gives a homily to help us understand what God's word means to us today. The homily helps us to reflect on the ways we are called to live as faithful followers of Christ.

Hearing the word of God is also a part of the other sacraments and liturgical celebrations of the Church. The Liturgy of the Hours is a beautiful combination of praying, singing, and listening to God's word.

We can use the Bible in study and personal prayer, too. By reflecting on God's word we can get to know God and ourselves better.

This reflection can help us to understand God's will for us.

## WE RESPOND

Discuss some ways that you can learn more about Scripture. This week choose one of these ways and then share what you have learned with your class.

## As Catholics...

Christ calls all of us to love one another as he has loved. When we read the gospels we find many examples of the way Jesus lived. He cared for the needs of others, especially those who were neglected, poor, or oppressed. Jesus identified himself with those he served, and he once told his disciples, "whatever you did for one of these least brothers of mine, you did for me" (Matthew 25:40).
The Corporal Works of Mercy come from this part of Matthew's Gospel. All the Works of Mercy are acts of love that help us to care for the needs of others. They can be found on page 329.

The Corporal Works of Mercy deal with the physical and material needs of others. The Spiritual Works of Mercy deal with the needs of people's hearts, minds, and souls.

Select one Work of Mercy and perform it this week.

# The Church continues Jesus' ministry through the seven sacraments.

## WE GATHER

✝ *Jesus, you are always near.*

Think of the people in your life who are special to you. Are there certain things that remind you of them even when they are not present? Discuss your answers.

## WE BELIEVE

The gospels record Jesus' ministry of welcoming, healing, forgiving, and feeding others. One special way the Church continues his ministry is through the sacraments. A sacrament is an effective sign given to us by Jesus through which we share in God's life. We call the life of God within us grace. The life of grace is God's gift to us. We can live each day knowing that God lives in us.

We believe that Christ instituted the sacraments so that his followers would always experience his presence. In the sacraments we find many parallels to the prayer and worship of the Israelites and the Jewish people today. For example, all of the celebration of the sacraments include readings from Scripture. They also include blessings and gestures that are based on Jewish rituals. In the Jewish faith the ritual gesture of anointing with oil was and is a sign of consecration for a God-given mission. Anointing with oil is an important part of the sacraments of Baptism, Confirmation, the Anointing of the Sick, and Holy Orders. The laying on of hands, which is also an essential part of the sacraments and is a sign of God's blessing and presence, comes from Jewish customs, too.

The sacraments are part of the liturgy of the Church, and they are our most important celebrations. The whole Body of Christ celebrates each sacrament. The priest and other members of the Church who participate in the sacraments represent the whole Church. The sacraments join Catholics all over the world with Jesus and with one another. They unite us as the Body of Christ.

**Sacraments of Christian Initiation**   Our initiation into the Church takes places through three sacraments: Baptism, Confirmation, and the Eucharist. Baptism begins our new life in Christ. Confirmation seals us with the Gift of the Holy Spirit and strengthens Christ's life in us. The Eucharist nourishes us with the Body and Blood of Christ so that we, too, can become more Christ-like.

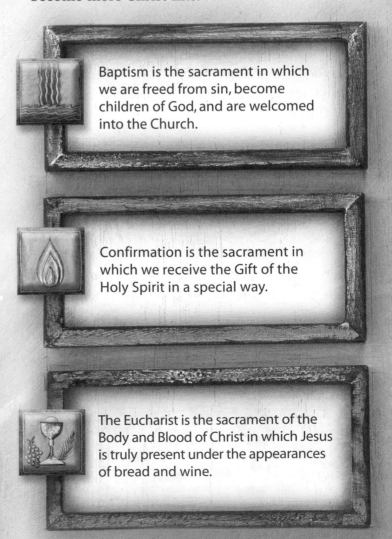

Baptism is the sacrament in which we are freed from sin, become children of God, and are welcomed into the Church.

Confirmation is the sacrament in which we receive the Gift of the Holy Spirit in a special way.

The Eucharist is the sacrament of the Body and Blood of Christ in which Jesus is truly present under the appearances of bread and wine.

**Sacraments of Healing**  The sacraments of Reconciliation and the Anointing of the Sick are known as sacraments of healing. Through these sacraments we experience God's forgiveness, peace, and healing touch.

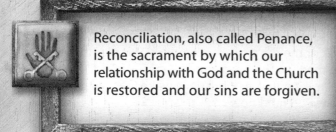

Reconciliation, also called Penance, is the sacrament by which our relationship with God and the Church is restored and our sins are forgiven.

The Anointing of the Sick is the sacrament by which God's grace and comfort are given to those who are suffering because of their old age or because they are seriously ill.

**Sacraments at the Service of Communion**
Church members who receive these sacraments are strengthened to serve God and the Church through one of two particular vocations. This sacrament helps them to be faithful and true to their vows.

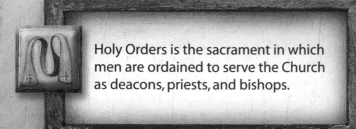

Holy Orders is the sacrament in which men are ordained to serve the Church as deacons, priests, and bishops.

Matrimony is the sacrament in which a man and a woman become husband and wife and promise to be faithful to each other for the rest of their lives.

## WE RESPOND

Write your answer to each of these questions.

What sacraments have you received?

_____

_____

How have you participated in the celebration of these sacraments?

_____

_____

How did your family and parish take part?

_____

_____

What are some signs of these sacraments?

_____

_____

Why are these sacraments important to your parish? to you?

_____

_____

Share your experiences with the class. Brainstorm ways you can encourage people your age to participate in the sacraments.

# The Church continues Jesus' ministry through its work for social justice.

## WE GATHER

✝ *Holy Spirit, fill me with love for God and others.*

👤 Make a list of words and actions that would describe people who try to do the things God asks them to do.

## WE BELIEVE

Through the prophets of the Old Testament, God spoke to his people. He told them to be faithful to the covenant and true to him, the one true God. The prophets encouraged the people to have hope and to trust in God. They called the people to work for social justice, and told them that love of God could not be separated from love of neighbor.

John the Baptist proclaimed the same message of the prophets who had gone before him. He prepared people for the Messiah who would bring a reign of true justice.

This is exactly what Jesus Christ, the Son of God and Messiah, did. Jesus worked for justice. He tried to make sure that people had what they needed. He healed the sick and fed the hungry. He listened to people when they told him about their needs. Jesus stood up for those who were neglected or ignored by society. And he spoke out against leaders who did not take care of people.

**Catholic social teaching** calls us to work for justice and peace as Jesus did. Jesus' life and teaching are the foundation of Catholic social teaching. There are seven themes of Catholic social teaching.

👤 Read the chart and discuss the questions listed at the end of each theme.

## Themes of Catholic Social Teaching

### Life and Dignity of the Human Person
Human life is sacred because it is a gift from God. Because we are all God's children, we all share the same human dignity. Our dignity—our worth and value—does not come from the way we look or the things we accomplish. Our dignity comes from being made in the image and likeness of God. This dignity makes us equal. As Christians we respect all people, even those we do not know.

### Call to Family, Community, and Participation
We are all social. We need to be with others to grow. The family is the basic community in society. In the family we grow and learn values. We learn what it means to be part of a group. Families are groups of people that contribute to society in many ways. As Christians we are involved in our family life and community.

### Rights and Responsibilities of the Human Person
Every person has a fundamental right to life. This includes the things we need to have a decent life: faith and family, work and education, health care and housing. We also have a responsibility to others and to society. We work to make sure the rights of all people are being protected.

### Option for the Poor and Vulnerable
We have a special obligation to help those who are poor and in need. This includes those who cannot protect themselves because of their age or their health. At different times in our lives we are all poor in some way and in need of assistance.

### The Dignity of Work and the Rights of Workers
Our work is a sign of our participation in God's work. People have the right to decent work, just wages, safe working conditions, and to participate in decisions about their work. There is value in all work. Our work in school and at home is a way to participate in God's work of creation. It is way to use our talents and abilities to thank God for his gifts.

### Solidarity of the Human Family
Solidarity is a feeling of unity. It binds members of a group together. Each of us is a member of the one human family, equal by our common human dignity. The human family includes people of all racial, cultural, and religious backgrounds. We all suffer when one part of the human family suffers whether they live near us or far away from us.

### Care for God's Creation
God created us to be stewards, or caretakers, of his creation. We must care for and respect the environment. We have to protect it for future generations. When we care for creation, we show respect for God the Creator.

## Questions

What are some ways the dignity of students or teachers is not respected during class? Why do you think this happens?

What are some conflicts in your school that have been resolved in a way that recognizes the dignity of those involved?

What are some virtues that individuals practice? that families practice? that neighbors practice?

How does the practice of these virtues influence society as a whole?

What is the difference between needing and wanting something?

What are some ways people might be poor?

What are some ways people are vulnerable?

How might different kinds of work make people feel?

How can we make people feel respected and valued for whatever work they do?

What are some problems or challenges that we face in our country?

How are they similar to those of other countries? How are they different?

What are some examples of society not protecting the environment?

How can these situations be changed?

**Key Word**

**Catholic social teaching**
the teaching of the Church that calls all members to work for justice and peace as Jesus did

The whole Church is called to live by this social teaching. Together we can work to change the things in society that allow unjust behaviors and conditions to exist.

### WE RESPOND

In groups select one theme of Catholic social teaching. Dramatize some examples of people following the teaching and of people not following it. What are the effects of each of these examples on our society?

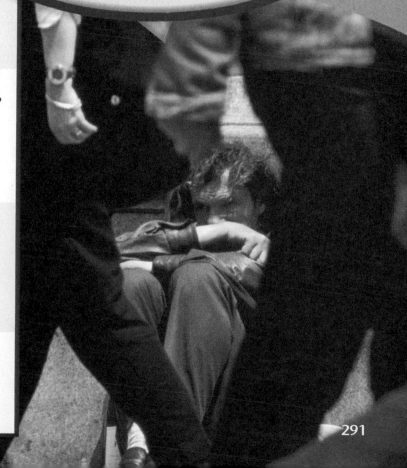

# Review

**Write True or False for the following sentences.
Then change the false sentences to make them true.**

1. _____ Catholic social teaching calls us to work for justice and peace as Jesus did.

   _____

2. _____ The writers of the New Testament were inspired and guided by Paul to record the truths of faith God wanted revealed to us.

   _____

3. _____ The sacraments join Catholics all over the world with Jesus and one another, and unite the Church as the Body of Christ.

   _____

4. _____ The dignity of work is an important source for Christian living and worship.

   _____

**Short Answers**

5. What kinds of books are in the New Testament?

   _____

6. How can we live out Jesus' new commandment?

   _____

7. What is a sacrament?

   _____

8. There are seven themes of Catholic social teaching. List three.

   _____

**Write a paragraph to answer this question.**

**9–10.** How does the Church use Scripture?

**ASSESSMENT** You have been asked to teach some younger children about the Bible. Use the lessons in the chapter to help you gather information. Be creative. Make charts, graphics, posters, and so on. Share your presentation with your class.

# We Respond in Faith

**Catholic social teaching** (p. 291)

## Reflect & Pray

God, in your word _____

_____

For your sacraments, Lord, we _____

_____

## Remember

- The New Testament is made up of different types of writings.

- The Bible is an important source for Christian living and worship.

- The Church continues Jesus' ministry through the seven sacraments.

- The Church continues Jesus' ministry through its work for social justice.

## OUR CATHOLIC LIFE

### Catholic Campaign for Human Development

The Catholic Campaign for Human Development (CCHD) is a national program of the U.S. Catholic bishops. CCHD focuses on the causes of poverty in the United States and works to eliminate poverty and its effects. CCHD provides money and support to thousands of local programs across the U.S. In the past CCHD has sponsored a Multi-Media Youth Arts Contest for youth. The contest is a way to increase awareness of Catholic social teaching and to learn ways communities are working to end injustice. By using visual arts, literature, or audio-visual displays, youths show the importance of living the gospel message.

IF YOU WANT PEACE WORK FOR JUSTICE
PAUL 6

# SHARING FAITH
## with My Family

### Sharing What I Learned

Discuss the following with your family:

- the New Testament
- Jesus' new commandment
- the seven sacraments
- Catholic social teaching.

### A Family of Saints

**Saint Thomas Aquinas 1226–1274**

Saint Thomas Aquinas is known as one of the greatest theologians in the history of the Church. He was a Dominican priest and a brilliant student. He is the patron saint of all universities and of students.

We celebrate his feast day on January 28.

How can your family learn more about the Church?

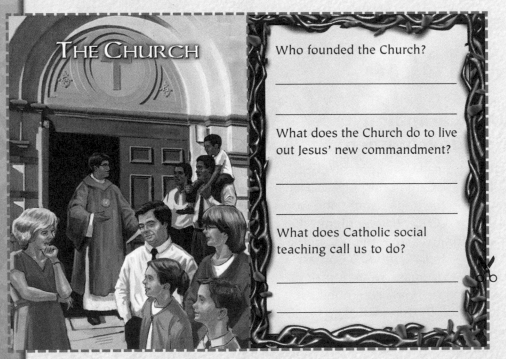

**THE CHURCH**

Who founded the Church?

_____

_____

What does the Church do to live out Jesus' new commandment?

_____

_____

What does Catholic social teaching call us to do?

_____

_____

### We Believe Trading Cards

Complete the facts on the back of the trading card. Then share with your family what you have learned about the Church.

**Connect to the Catechism**
For adult background and reflection, see paragraphs 126, 133, 1210, and 2420.

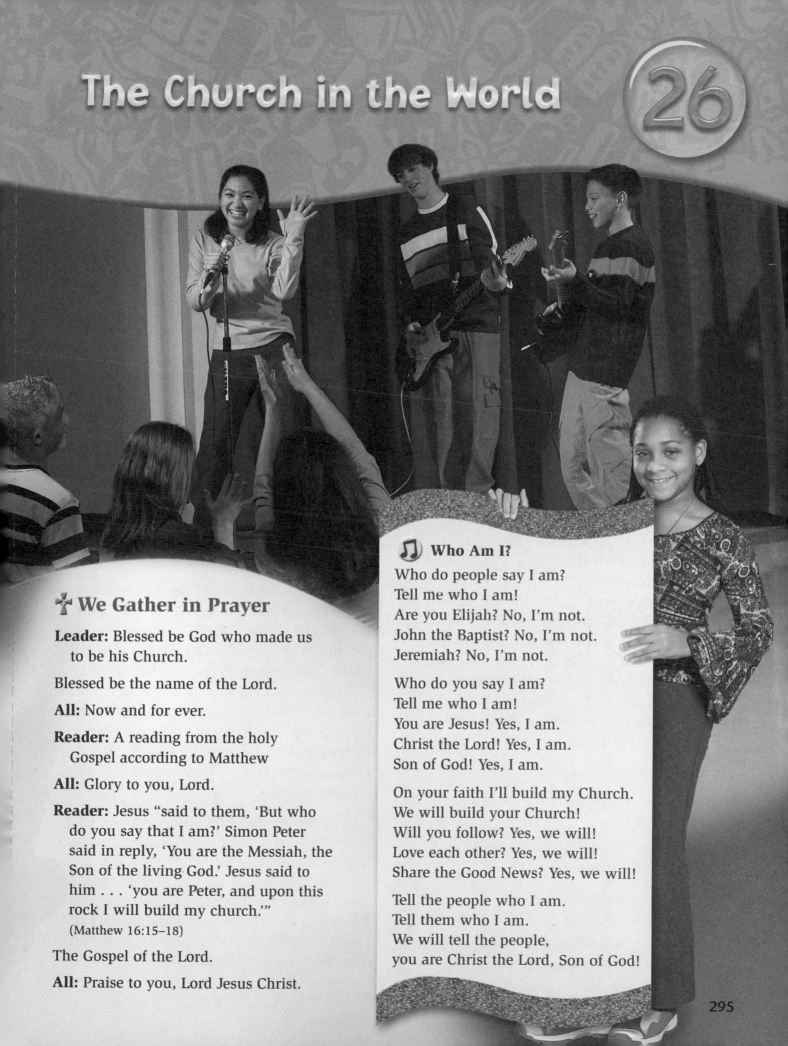

# The Church in the World

26

## ✝ We Gather in Prayer

**Leader:** Blessed be God who made us to be his Church.

Blessed be the name of the Lord.

**All:** Now and for ever.

**Reader:** A reading from the holy Gospel according to Matthew

**All:** Glory to you, Lord.

**Reader:** Jesus "said to them, 'But who do you say that I am?' Simon Peter said in reply, 'You are the Messiah, the Son of the living God.' Jesus said to him . . . 'you are Peter, and upon this rock I will build my church.'"
(Matthew 16:15–18)

The Gospel of the Lord.

**All:** Praise to you, Lord Jesus Christ.

## 🎵 Who Am I?

Who do people say I am?
Tell me who I am!
Are you Elijah? No, I'm not.
John the Baptist? No, I'm not.
Jeremiah? No, I'm not.

Who do you say I am?
Tell me who I am!
You are Jesus! Yes, I am.
Christ the Lord! Yes, I am.
Son of God! Yes, I am.

On your faith I'll build my Church.
We will build your Church!
Will you follow? Yes, we will!
Love each other? Yes, we will!
Share the Good News? Yes, we will!

Tell the people who I am.
Tell them who I am.
We will tell the people,
you are Christ the Lord, Son of God!

295

# We live as one people.

## WE GATHER

✝ *Holy Spirit, increase our faith.*

Sometimes we may say to others that we believe in peace, justice, and family. What do you believe in? How do you show others what you believe in?

## WE BELIEVE

Each time we gather for Mass, we profess our faith as a community. We do this by praying the Apostles' Creed or the Nicene Creed. We declare our belief in the Blessed Trinity, Christ, and the Church. In the Nicene Creed we state, "We believe in one holy catholic and apostolic church." One, holy, catholic, and apostolic are the four essential features, or identifying marks, of the Church. They are also called the **marks of the Church**.

The members of the Church believe in and follow the one Lord, Jesus Christ. The Church is one because its members are joined to Christ, who "is the head of the body, the church" (Colossians 1:18). Saint Paul wrote, "As a body is one though it has many parts, and all the parts of the body, though many, are one body, so also Christ. For in one Spirit we were all baptized into one body, whether Jews or Greeks, slaves or free persons" (1 Corinthians 12:12–13).

The Church is one because:

- Jesus Christ unites us by his death and Resurrection
- the one Holy Spirit draws us together and guides us as a community
- the pope and bishops are called to lead us and continue the work of the apostles
- the seven sacraments unite us and enable us to share in God's grace.

Members of the Church share the same Baptism in the name of the Father, and the Son, and the Holy Spirit. Because of our common Baptism, we participate in the Eucharist, another very important sign of our unity. In the Eucharist, we are nourished by the word of God and receive the Body and Blood of Christ. We are joined more closely to Christ and one another to form the Body of Christ, the Church. And we show that we are filled with the life of Christ by the way that we live.

**The Church and Other Christian Communities**

The Catholic Church teaches that it is the Church founded by Christ himself. It is the one, holy, catholic, and apostolic Church. However, the Catholic Church respects all other Christians, recognizes the good in other Christian traditions, and has an especially close connection to the members of the Orthodox Churches. Other followers of Christ include: Episcopalians, Lutherans, Methodists, Presbyterians, Baptists, and Pentecostals.

Catholics have many things in common with other Christians. Most Christians are baptized and believe that Jesus is both divine and human. They believe that he died and rose to save us from sin. Christians also share the belief that the Bible was inspired by the Holy Spirit. For Christians throughout the world the Bible is the most important book.

But Jesus wanted his followers to be united. At the Last Supper Jesus prayed, "I pray not only for them, but also for those who will believe in me through their word, so that they may all be one" (John 17:20–21). So the Catholic Church works with other Christian communities to bring about the unity of the Church. This work to promote the unity among all Christians is called **ecumenism**.

The task of ecumenism involves all of us. We are called to know and understand our faith and the teachings of the Church. We are called to participate in our parish and grow as disciples of Christ. We are called to pray that all Christians may be one. A special time to pray for this is during the Week of Prayer for Christian Unity that takes place each January.

## WE RESPOND

Make a poster illustrating some possible ways to bring about ecumenism.

How can you show that you believe in ecumenism?

### Key Words

**marks of the Church** the four essential features of the Church: one, holy, catholic, and apostolic

**ecumenism** the work to promote unity among all Christians

Ecumenical Prayer Service, Toronto, Canada

# We live as a holy people.

## WE GATHER

✝ *Father, holy is your name.*

The word *holy* is an adjective. What are some of the nouns you would use it to describe? What in your life do you consider holy?

## WE BELIEVE

We learn from the Old Testament stories of creation that the one true God is good and holy. We know that he shared his goodness with all of his creation, most especially with humans. When God's people struggled to remain good and faithful, God continued to be with them. His prophets called the people to be holy through worship and just living. God so loved his people and wanted to share his life with them that he sent his only Son to be their Messiah.

Christ offered his goodness and holiness to all of us through his life, death, Resurrection, and Ascension. Christ shares his holiness with us today through the Church. **Holiness** is sharing in God's goodness and responding to his love by the way we live. This holiness comes from the gift of God's life that he shares with us through the sacraments and from living as faithful Christians every day. The gifts of the Holy Spirit help us to respond to the love God offers us, and to follow Christ's example of loving service.

The apostles taught the early Christians that by Baptism they shared in the very life of Christ. They knew that this union with Christ meant that they shared in his holiness, too. All the baptized were considered "holy ones." Saint Paul wrote to the new community at Corinth, "Do you not know that you are the temple of God, and that the Spirit of God dwells in you? . . . the temple of God, which you are, is holy" (1 Corinthians 3:16, 17).

To Paul, *holy* was another way of saying "belonging to God." He told the Corinthians, "you have been sanctified in Christ Jesus, called to be holy, with all those everywhere who call upon the name of the Lord Jesus Christ" (1 Corinthians 1:2).

Paul, Peter, and the other apostles encouraged Christ's disciples to live lives of holiness. We, too, share this call to holiness. We look to Jesus as our model for holy living. We live this life of grace as Jesus' disciples. He lived his life in perfect love of God the Father and in service to others, and he wants us to lead holy lives, too. Our holiness grows as we respond to God's love in our lives and live as Christ asks us to live.

👤 List some signs of holiness in the world today. Who are some people who you think live holy lives?

**Models of Holiness** From the beginning of the Church, some of God's holy ones have been remembered in a special way. The martyrs were the first to be honored for heroic virtue and faithfulness to God. "Heroic virtue" is a term used to describe people who are brave, committed to the faith, and Christ-like in distinctive ways. Heroic virtue motivates people to do things that are very difficult.

**Key Word**

**holiness** sharing in God's goodness and responding to his love by the way we live; our holiness comes through grace

Saints have stood up for their faith in many ways. Some saints preached the good news of Christ in times when the Church was misunderstood by society. Others put Jesus' words into action in the midst of discrimination or injustice. Many others dedicated their lives to prayer and penance. These women and men are friends and servants of God. Their lives are models for us.

The Church officially declares a disciple of Christ a saint by a process called canonization. We remember and celebrate each canonized saint on a special day during the Church year. For many saints, this day is the day of their death, which we see as the beginning of their new life with God in heaven.

The lives of the saints teach us about true discipleship. Because the saints are closely united to Christ, they pray for us constantly. They help the Church to grow in holiness. Their love for the Church is great.

It is important to remember that we are all God's holy ones and that his Church is holy. But we are human, and the Church is a human community. We are tempted and at times we do not live as God calls us to live. However, through the grace of the sacrament of Reconciliation, we are again freed from sin and made holy. The sacrament of the Eucharist also strengthens us to follow Christ's example of holiness. Praying, respecting all people, living fairly, and working for justice and peace help us to respond to God's grace in our lives and to help the Church to grow in holiness.

## WE RESPOND

How can you grow in holiness this week?

In groups identify some ways you and your families can show others that you "belong to God."

_____

_____

_____

As a class plan to present some of these ways to a class of younger students. Design the presentation to include role-plays that involve the younger students.

## As Catholics...

On All Saints' Day, November 1, we remember and honor all of Christ's faithful followers who lived holy lives on earth and now live in happiness with God forever. We not only celebrate the lives of canonized saints but also all people who are saints with God. This is a good time to celebrate the lives of our patron saints—the saints whose names we share, the saints for whom our schools and parishes are named, and the saints that our families honor.

On All Souls' Day, November 2, we remember all people who have died, particularly those in our own families and parishes. We pray that they may know God's love and mercy and share in eternal life.

Who are some of the people you remember on these special days?

Blessed Pierre Toussaint

Saint Elizabeth of Portugal

Saint Cecilia

Saint Martin of Tours

Saint Paul

Saint Mary Magdalene

# We live as a welcoming people.

## WE GATHER

✝ *God our Father, help us to love all your children.*

There are specific conditions to being a member of certain clubs or groups. Discuss what conditions you think are necessary to being in the choir, on a sports team, in the chess club, or in the art club.

## WE BELIEVE

The word *catholic* means "universal." The Church is open to all people everywhere. We welcome all who seek God's love and mercy. This has been true since the beginning of the Church.

Jesus commissioned the apostles and sent them to make disciples of all nations. Some of them traveled to Rome, Antioch, and other parts of the world to preach the gospel message. They baptized believers and established local Church communities. This was the beginning of the universal Church.

Catholics belong to a great variety of cultures, and they live their faith in different ways. Their different customs and traditions are a true gift to the Church. We are blessed that all are part of the life of the Church. All of us together are still one in Christ.

No matter what the racial or cultural heritage of our parish communities, we are a community of faith. We may be from different countries. We may speak different languages and have different customs. But we are united by our love for Christ and our common call to holiness. Together we make the Church catholic, and we participate in the sacraments, learn about our faith, and grow as members of the Church. We are united and strengthened to love as Jesus loved and to continue his work for justice and peace.

🧍 Illustrate ways your parish is one community made up of many different people.

**The Mission of the Church**   The Church is missionary because it is catholic. All people are invited to believe in Jesus and to be baptized in the faith of the Church. Extending this invitation to faith is an important part of the Church's mission. The mission of the Church is to share the good news of Christ and to spread the Kingdom of God.

We are the Church, and each of us is called to take part in the mission of the Church. We are called to share the good news of Christ and to live lives of holiness. We can do this by our prayers, good works, and everyday living.

Some members of the Church share in its mission as missionaries. Single and married people, priests, and religious sisters and brothers can be missionaries. Students of many ages, adults, and entire families can serve as missionaries.

Missionaries share their faith with those they serve. They also may build homes, schools, and hospitals with the people that they serve. They may teach people to farm and to provide for their needs in other ways, too. These works of service put the good news of Christ into action.

**Respect for All Faiths** There are many other religions beside Christianity. As Catholics we respect the rights of others to practice and live their faith. As you have learned, Christianity has its roots in Judaism. The Jewish people are our ancestors in faith, and many of our beliefs, prayer practices, and traditions are based in Judaism. For example, we share the belief in the one true God and follow the Ten Commandments.

Today Jewish people everywhere continue to live their faith in the one true God. God's covenant with the Jewish people is a wonderful sign of God's great love for the people he first made his own. Jewish people continue to live by that covenant today.

Islam is another religion with which Christians and Jews share belief in the one true God. People who practice the religion of Islam are called Muslims. Muslims, Jews, and Christians have the important connection of worshiping God and consider Abraham a common ancestor. Muslims follow the teachings of the prophet Muhammad, who lived in the sixth and seventh centuries.

People of other religions and faiths include Buddhists, Hindus, and members of many native tribes. There are many other people of faith. They, too, follow a set of beliefs and show their faith in different ways. In communities around the world, there are people of different religions living and working together. The Church respects the rights of all people to practice their faith, and we join with them and with people of no religious belief in trying to make the world a better place for all people.

## WE RESPOND

What might your class do to show respect for people whose beliefs are not the same as yours? List three ideas here and then decide on ways to make them a part of your daily life.

_____

_____

_____

_____

_____

# We live as a faithful people.

## WE GATHER

✝ *Holy Spirit, guide all those who spread the good news of Christ.*

✗ Write some sentences in which the word *foundation* is used in different ways. Share your sentences with the class.

## WE BELIEVE

The Church is apostolic because it is built on the faith of the apostles. ". . . you are fellow citizens with the holy ones and members of the household of God, built upon the foundation of the apostles and prophets, with Christ Jesus himself as the capstone" (Ephesians 2:19–20).

Jesus chose the apostles to care for and lead the community of believers. The faith we profess and practice is based on the faith that the apostles shared and spread. For instance, the Apostles' Creed tells us about Jesus, his teachings, and the teachings of the apostles. The Apostles' Creed has an important place in the Church. From the early years of the Church in Rome, this was the creed that those being baptized professed.

The life and leadership of the Church is based on that of the apostles. When the apostles established local communities of believers, the apostles appointed local leaders to represent them in the community. The apostles passed on to these leaders what Christ had given them: the Gift of the Holy Spirit and the authority to carry out the mission of Jesus Christ. These leaders preached the good news and shared the teachings of the apostles. They continued the apostles' ministry and acted under their leadership. They were the successors of the apostles and eventually became known as bishops.

As the Church continued to grow, the bishops, the successors of the apostles, commissioned others to continue the ministry of the apostles. In this way, the leadership of the Church throughout history can be traced back to the apostles.

The bishops of today are called to continue the ministry of the apostles. As the bishop of Rome, the pope is the successor of the apostle Peter, who was the first leader of the Church of Rome. The pope continues Peter's ministry and has a special responsibility to care for the Church. The bishops, with the pope as their head, are called to lead and guide the whole Church.

The whole Church shares in the mission that Christ first gave to his apostles. But as a body has different parts with different functions, so the members of the Church have different roles in sharing in this mission.

**The Laity** The laity are the baptized members of the Church who share in the Church's mission to bring the good news of Christ to the world. The laity are also known as laypeople or the Christian faithful. Right now you are a layperson. All Catholics begin their lives as members of the Christian faithful. Most remain laypeople their entire lives, and serve God and share in the mission of the Church as single people or married people.

You are a layperson, and every day you are growing as Jesus' disciple. You do not have to wait to be an adult to be an active member of the Church. You can live and share your faith right now. As a layperson you are called to share the good news at home, in school, and in your neighborhood. You can take part in your parish celebrations and activities. Every day you can live as Jesus taught. You can be an example of Christian living for others.

Laypeople are called to bring the good news of Christ to their work places and local communities. Women and men in the laity are called to be involved in city, state, and national governments. In these situations they often take on leadership positions and make many decisions. They have a responsibility to act and make decisions based on the teachings of Jesus and on their faith.

Laypeople are called to participate in the celebration of the sacraments and to support their parishes. They may serve on the parish pastoral council or in the various parish ministries. In their dioceses they may lead or work in areas such as catechesis, education, worship, youth ministry, and peace and justice ministries.

It is truly a blessing that all in the Church can work to bring about God's reign. We are one people who can show by our love of others that we are living as Christ's disciples in the world.

## WE RESPOND

What are the different ways that the Church serves the world?

What are the different ways that people your age participate in the mission of the Church?

**Complete the following.**

1. The Church is one because _____

   _____

2. The Church is holy because _____

   _____

3. The Church is catholic because _____

   _____

4. The Church is apostolic because _____

   _____

**Circle the letter of the correct answer.**

5. _____ is sharing in God's goodness and responding to his love by the way we live.

   **a.** Ecumenism   **b.** Catholic   **c.** Holiness

6. The _____ are all the baptized members of the Church who share in the Church's mission to bring the good news of Christ to the world.

   **a.** bishops      **b.** laity      **c.** disciples

7. The Catholic Church believes it is the Church founded by _____.

   **a.** Jesus Christ  **b.** Peter    **c.** Paul

8. The work to promote unity among all Christians is called _____.

   **a.** ecumenism  **b.** holiness  **c.** marks of the Church

**Write a paragraph to answer this question.**

9–10. What can young people do to help the Church to grow?

ASSESSMENT

Your class has been asked to make a Catholic Church "quilt" to be displayed during Christian Unity Week. Think about the words *one*, *holy*, *catholic*, and *apostolic*. How can you represent the meaning of each of these words on a quilt square? Be creative. Cut words or images from magazines, download images from a computer, write a poem or song, and so on. Attach your ideas on four fabric squares or sheets of paper. Present your "quilt" to your class or family.

#  We Respond in Faith

## Reflect & Pray

Christ, you call us to holiness. I can respond to your call by

_____

_____

Christ, you call us to be one. Send your Spirit to us that we may be united.

 **Key Words**

**marks of the Church** (p. 297)
**ecumenism** (p. 297)
**holiness** (p. 298)

## Remember

- We live as one people.
- We live as a holy people.
- We live as a welcoming people.
- We live as a faithful people.

## OUR CATHOLIC LIFE

Tell your story here.

Place your photo here.

# SHARING FAITH
## with My Family

## Sharing What I Learned

Discuss the following with your family:

- the marks of the Church
- ecumenism
- holiness
- the mission of the Church.

MAKE THE WORLD BETTER PLACE

## A Family of Saints

**Saint Maximilian Kolbe 1894–1941**

Saint Maximilian Kolbe was a Franciscan priest. During World War II, he was imprisoned in a Nazi concentration camp. There he offered his life in place of another man, a husband and father, who had been chosen to die. Saint Maximilian is an example of unselfish love for all people. We celebrate his feast day on August 14.

How can your family show love in your parish and community?

## OUR FAMILY

What mark of the Church would best describe your family? Why?

_____

_____

How does your family show respect to people of other faiths?

_____

_____

Name one way your family can grow in holiness this year.

_____

_____

## We Believe Trading Cards

Complete the facts on the back of the trading card. Then share with your family ways you can live out your faith.

Visit Sadlier's

www.WeBelieveweb.com

**Connect to the Catechism**
For adult background and reflection, see paragraphs 820, 826, 835, and 863.

# Easter

## 27

"The love of God has been poured into our hearts by his Spirit living in us, alleluia."

Introductory Rites, Pentecost Vigil Mass

# During the Easter season, we celebrate our new life in Christ and the coming of the Holy Spirit.

## WE GATHER

✝ *Lord Jesus, may we rise with you to new life in the Holy Spirit!*

Think of a time when a person was welcomed into your family. How did you celebrate?

## WE BELIEVE

The Easter season is a special time to rejoice in the new life we have in Christ. It is a time for bringing new members into the Church—for celebrating the sacraments of Baptism and Confirmation, both of which lead to the table of the Eucharist. And during the Easter season the whole Church grows in their experience of the risen Christ, and through liturgical celebrations, reflects with joy on Christ's Paschal Mystery. We welcome the new members of the Church and pray with them each week.

The Easter season lasts for fifty days. During this time we celebrate the Resurrection and Ascension of Jesus Christ and the coming of the Holy Spirit on Pentecost. We hear stories of the risen Jesus' appearances to his disciples. We learn about the beginning of the Church from the Acts of the Apostles.

**Easter Monday in Nigeria**   The day after Easter Sunday is an important day of worship in Nigeria. In many towns and villages Catholics and other Christians gather in a common place which they name "Galilee" for the day. They believe that, like the apostles and first disciples, they are to be in "Galilee" to meet the risen Lord. Christians of all faiths gather together to celebrate Christ's Resurrection with preaching, singing and dancing, sharing a meal, and participating in all types of sports and games. This "Galilee" gathering is possible because Easter Monday is traditionally a public holiday in Nigeria.

**Ascension** During the season of Easter we recall the last event of Jesus' public life, his Ascension. Jesus ascended or returned to his father in heaven forty days after he rose from the dead. Thus the Church celebrates the feast of the Ascension around forty days after Easter. In many dioceses of the United States this feast is a holy day of obligation. We read about Jesus' Ascension in the Acts of the Apostles.

Acts of the Apostles 1:3–12

Forty days after his Resurrection, the risen Jesus had gathered with his apostles outside of Jerusalem. He told them, "'You will receive power when the holy Spirit comes upon you, and you will be my witnesses in Jerusalem, throughout Judea and Samaria, and to the ends of the earth.' When he had said this, as they were looking on, he was lifted up, and a cloud took him from their sight." (Acts of the Apostles 1:8–9).

The apostles went back to the upper room and waited in prayer.

Christ the Redeemer,
Rio de Janiero

## Pentecost

**Pentecost** Fifty days after Easter we celebrate the feast of Pentecost. The word *Pentecost* comes from the Greek word *penta*, meaning fifty. Pentecost is celebrated on the last Sunday and final day of the Easter season. On Pentecost Sunday we celebrate the coming of the Holy Spirit to the first disciples. We also celebrate the beginning of the Church, and we rejoice because the Holy Spirit fills our hearts today.

The Jewish feast of Pentecost was celebrated fifty days after Passover, as a thanksgiving for the harvest. The "first fruits" of field and orchard were blessed and shared. So it is fitting that on this feast God the Father and God the Son, chose to share the "first fruits" of Jesus' Resurrection—the Holy Spirit, the power sent from on high. This Gift of the Holy Spirit was a great gift of God's love. The apostles now shared in the fellowship of the Holy Spirit.

What a difference the Holy Spirit made in the lives of the apostles! During Jesus' trial and death, the apostles were afraid. After his Resurrection, they remained hidden. When the Holy Spirit came, the apostles began to remember the words of Jesus and to act on them. They began preaching and teaching. They were no longer alone. Neither are we alone because the Holy Spirit will be with us always.

The apostles and Mary spent the time between the Ascension and Pentecost in prayer. The Church keeps the days between Ascension and Pentecost as days of waiting and prayer for the Holy Spirit. During this time the liturgy is full of prayerful longing for the coming of the Holy Spirit.

## WE RESPOND

Pray this prayer together.

"Father,
let your Spirit come upon us with power
   to fill us with his gifts.
May he make our hearts pleasing to you,
   and ready to do your will."

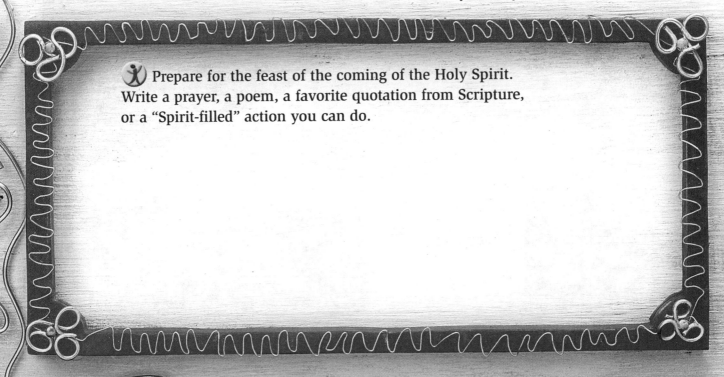

Prepare for the feast of the coming of the Holy Spirit.
Write a prayer, a poem, a favorite quotation from Scripture,
or a "Spirit-filled" action you can do.

# ✝ We Respond in Prayer

**Leader:** Lord, send out your Spirit.

**All:** And renew the face of the earth.

**Reader:** A reading from the first Letter of Saint Paul to the Corinthians

"There are different kinds of spiritual gifts but the same Spirit; there are different forms of service but the same Lord. . . As a body is one though it has many parts, and all the parts of the body, though many, are one body, so also Christ. For in one Spirit we were all baptized into one body, whether Jews or Greeks, slaves or free persons, and we were all given to drink of one Spirit." (1 Corinthians 12:4–5, 12–13)

The word of the Lord.

**All:** Thanks be to God.

## 🎵 Envía Tu Espíritu

Refrain

Envía tu Espíritu, envía tu Espíritu,
envía tu Espíritu,
sea renovada la faz de la tierra.
Sea renovada la faz de la tierra.

Spirit of the living God,
burn in our hearts,
and make us a people of hope
and compassion. (Refrain)

Wind of promise, wind of change,
friend of the poor,
empower your people to make
peace and justice. (Refrain)

# SHARING FAITH
## with My Family

## Sharing What I Learned

Discuss the following with your family:

- the Easter season
- the Ascension
- Pentecost.

## Around the Table

As a family, decide to do some of the spirit-filled actions from the list below. You may want to make your choice a summer-long activity.

- Help out at a soup kitchen or collect canned goods.

- Volunteer for neighborhood, parish, or school clean-up.

- Run a yard sale or lemonade stand and give the proceeds to a favorite cause.

- Donate toys in good condition to a thrift shop or to a children's society.

- Mow lawns or do grocery shopping for elderly or housebound neighbors.

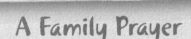

## A Family Prayer

Pray this prayer during the days between the Ascension and Pentecost.

**Leader:** Come, Holy Spirit, fill the hearts of your faithful.
**All:** And kindle in them the fire of your love.
**Leader:** Send forth your Spirit and they shall be created.
**All:** And you will renew the face of the earth.
**Leader:** Lord,
by the light of the Holy Spirit
you have taught the hearts
of your faithful.
In the same Spirit
help us to relish what is right
and always rejoice in your
consolation.
We ask this through Christ our Lord.
**All:** Amen.

Visit Sadlier's

**www.WeBelieveweb.com**

**Connect to the Catechism**
For adult background and reflection, see paragraph 690.

## The Teapot

Lisa knew what was coming when she saw Gram setting the teapot on the table. Lisa knew this meant listening to another story about it.

The story was interesting the first few times Lisa heard it. As a young woman Lisa's grandmother had come from China. She was poor and had very few possessions when she arrived in the United States. The teapot was one of them. It had been carefully wrapped and carried from place to place as Gram settled into her new home. The teapot represented an important part of Gram's childhood and heritage.

A few days later Lisa's friend Rachel came over. As they passed through the kitchen, Rachel spotted the teapot sitting on the table.

"Oh, look," she cried. "Isn't that beautiful? Where did you get it?"

Lisa told Rachel the story of the teapot and about her grandmother's journey from China to the United States. Rachel listened carefully. "You are so lucky," she said. Lisa looked at the teapot and smiled. "I guess I am," she replied.

• Why is it important to share our family stories?

"Make known to me your ways, LORD;
  teach me your paths.
Guide me in your truth and teach me,
  for you are God my savior."

Psalm 25: 4–5

## Because *We Believe*

The Bible is the written record of God's Revelation. It has a divine author, God, and many human authors. As they worked, the human authors were guided by God the Holy Spirit. The special guidance that the Holy Spirit gave to these human authors of the Bible is called divine inspiration. This inspiration of God the Holy Spirit means that the human authors wrote without any error, God's saving truth. God is the true author of the whole Bible. Thus, the Bible is the word of God.

The Bible, helps us to know the good news of Jesus Christ as lived out in the Church, past and present. As such it includes teachings and practices from the time of Jesus and the apostles. It includes the creeds, the teachings of the Church, documents issued by Church councils, the Church's worship, and other things. Tradition helps us to understand the meaning of God's Revelation in our lives today.

How do we show that we believe this?

We can come to know something about God by paying attention to the people in our lives.

## With Your Class

Research the history of your parish. You may want to interview someone that has worked in the parish for a number of years. Here are some questions to consider.

- How did the parish begin? Who helped to establish the parish?

- How did the parish get its name?

- Is this its original location? Why was this spot picked to build a parish?

- What special or significant events have taken place in the parish?

Write a story about your parish and illustrate it with photos or your own pictures. Then share it with another class.

## With Your Family

Read page 313 together. Talk about the way the Bible was inspired and written.

Have a family storytelling session. Ask each member to tell a story that he or she has heard about the family's history. Or recall a memory to start a new story.

How does your family pass memories on? List the ways.

_____

_____

_____

_____

_____

_____

"In Sacred Scripture, the Church constantly finds her nourishment and her strength, for she welcomes it not as a human word, 'but as what it really is, the word of God.'"

*(Catechism of the Catholic Church, 104)*

## Pray Together

**Write a prayer for your family.**

_____

_____

_____

_____

_____

## Lost and Found

Nancy was annoyed. Nancy's mother told her that she had to take care of her brother, Andrew. Nancy had planned to meet her friends at the baseball game. If she really wanted to go, she would have to take Andrew with her.

At the ball field, Nancy told Andrew to be quiet and not to embarrass her in front of her friends. Nancy and her friends met as the game was getting underway. Nancy was having a good time until she realized that Andrew was nowhere in sight. Nancy walked all around the bleachers, but she couldn't find Andrew.

As she broadened her search to the entire park, Nancy began to feel more annoyed. It was a pain having to take care of her brother. Nancy kept walking and walking. There was no sign of Andrew. Nancy began to worry. What if she lost her little brother?

Near the food stands, Nancy spotted Andrew sitting on a bench. His head was down, and it looked like he had been crying. "Where have you been?" Nancy demanded. Andrew started to cry again. Nancy gave her brother a hug and said, "Stop crying, Andrew. I am here. Everything is fine."

- Why is it sometimes hard to be faithful to one another in our families?

> "You shall be my people, and I will be your God."
>
> Jeremiah 30:22

## Because *We Believe*

God made a sacred promise, a *covenant*, with the patriarchs and their families. He promised to be their God and to watch over them. Through faith, these people learned what it meant to be a part of God's family. They lived their lives trying to follow God's commands. Sometimes it was difficult to be faithful to the covenant. However, God remained faithful.

Sometimes the people went through difficult situations and tried to make the best decisions. God sent prophets to guide the people and to challenge them to live according to his ways.

Faith is a gift from God that enables us to believe in him and accept all that he has revealed. Through the gift of faith we can see our lives and the world around us as God sees them. We start to live the way God wants us to live.

We all have ways in which we are challenged each day to be faithful and loving to each other, and to trust in God's constant concern for us. Caring for each other, forgiving each other, and being faithful to one another are ways in which God's covenant continues to be lived out today in the lives of those who believe.

How do we show that we believe this?

The Old Testament often contains stories of people and their families. Many of these people are good examples for us of how to be faithful and to trust in God.

## With Your Class

Talk about people in your community or parish who are living examples of being faithful to God and one another. What qualities do these people share?

Select one of these people you would especially like to remember. Write a profile of faith describing how this person remains faithful in his or her life. If possible, ask this person to join in a discussion on faithfulness with your class.

### Profile of Faith

_____
_____
_____
_____
_____
_____
_____

**"To live, grow, and persevere in the faith until the end we must nourish it with the word of God."**

*(Catechism of the Catholic Church, 162)*

## With Your Family

Read pages 315 and 316 together. Talk about what it means to be faithful to God and to one another.

Imagine you were writing an advice column for families. How would you answer the following questions?

What makes a family strong?

- How can families stay close to one another?
- What can families do to help others who are in need?
- How can families remain faithful to God?

## Pray Together

**I trust in your faithfulness.**
  **Grant my heart joy in your help,**
**That I may sing of the Lord,**
  **"How good our God has been to me!"**

Psalm 13:6

NOW WHAT?
Bring this page back to school ☐   Keep this page at home ☐

# SHARING FAITH
## in Class and at Home

## Small Steps

Ethan was still trying to wake up as his father drove him to school. The car felt warm and cozy, especially when he watched the rain pound against the windshield. It startled him when his father stopped the car and rolled down the window. He handed something to a woman standing on the corner. "Thank you and God bless you," Ethan heard the woman say.

"Who was that?" he asked.

"Didn't you see her sign?" his father responded. "It said, 'Need help with the rent.' Imagine being thrown out of your home on a day like this. I gave her some money."

Ethan looked back. Other cars were driving by the woman. She stood alone, holding her sign and shivering in the driving rain.

Later that week, Ethan's class had a discussion about social justice. There were so many problems in the world—poverty, war, racism, violence, pollution, and unemployment. The class wanted to support a project in order to make a difference. Then, Ethan thought of the woman and her sign on the street corner. Ethan raised his hand. "I would like to help," he said.

- What do you think Ethan is going to say to the class?

"I say to you, whatever you did for one of these least brothers of mine, you did for me."

Matthew 25:40

## Because *We Believe*

The Old Testament helps us understand who God is and how he has acted in the lives of his people. From the Old Testament we learn what our relationship with God should be. The gospels of the New Testament tell us the good news of Jesus Christ. Jesus worked for justice and peace. He stood up for those who were neglected or ignored by society. He spoke out against leaders who did not take care of people.

Catholic social teaching calls us to work for justice and peace as Jesus did. As individuals we will probably never solve the massive problems that exist in our world. But together as disciples of Jesus Christ, we can make a difference. It starts and continues with small steps that, together, lead to great things.

How do we show that we believe this?

Catholic social teaching calls us to work for justice and peace as Jesus did.

## With Your Class

The Church responds in two ways to follow Catholic social teaching. These ways are sometimes called the "two feet" of social ministry.

**1. Charity:** helping people to survive their present crisis by doing such things as providing food, housing, and clothing.

**2. Justice:** helping to remove the causes of social problems through doing such things as working to change laws and institutions.

Pick an area of social concern, such as poverty, homelessness, and so on. Trace two footprints on a sheet of construction paper. On one, list the responses that could be made for the social concern out of *charity*. On the other, list the responses that could be made out of *justice*.

Share your responses with the rest of the class. Perhaps your group can make one of these responses happen.

**"There are no just structures without people who want to be just."**

*(Catechism of the Catholic Church, 2832)*

## With Your Family

Read page 317 together. Talk about social justice and what it means to follow Jesus' teachings.

What has inspired your family to respond to someone in need? Talk about any specific things you have done to reach out to others.

Using the chart, make a list of things your family has done or can do as a way to carry out Catholic social teaching. For example:

**What Our Family Has Done**

_____

_____

_____

_____

_____

**What Our Family Can Do**

_____

_____

_____

_____

_____

## Pray Together

**"Whatever you do, in word or deed,
do everything in the name
of the Lord Jesus, giving thanks
to God the Father through him."**

Colossians 3:17

**NOW WHAT?**
Bring this page back to school ☐    Keep this page at home ☐

**Fill in the circle beside the correct answer.**

1. The Church teaches us that _____ is one of the two means by which God's Revelation comes to us. The Bible is the other.

   ○ Tradition          ○ liturgy          ○ the council of Nicea

2. In the first part of the Sermon on the Mount Jesus gave guidelines that describe the way to live as his disciples. These are the _____.

   ○ gospels          ○ Beatitudes          ○ Lord's Prayer

3. _____ did not believe that the other apostles had seen Jesus.

   ○ The apostle          ○ Mary Magdalene          ○ Joseph of Arimethea
      Thomas

4. On his way to _____ to persecute Christians, Saul had an experience that changed his life.

   ○ Antioch          ○ Damascus          ○ Ephesus

5. One, holy, catholic, and apostolic are the four _____.

   ○ themes of Catholic      ○ marks of the Church    ○ models of holiness
      social teaching

6. The apostle _____ was chosen to take Judas's place.

   ○ Matthias          ○ Paul          ○ Jerome

7. As a Christian prophecy, the Book of Revelation deals with _____.

   ○ the ministry of      ○ the life and        ○ Christ's second coming
      the apostles           work of Jesus

8. The work to promote the unity of all Christians is called _____.

   ○ ecumenism          ○ social justice          ○ holiness

**Write True or False for the following sentences. Then change the false sentences to make them true.**

9. \_\_\_\_\_ We call the power of God's love coming into the world and into our lives the gospel.

10. \_\_\_\_\_ For Christians the Eucharist is the new Passover of God's people.

11. \_\_\_\_\_ The gospels are effective signs given to us by Jesus through which we share in God's life, which we call grace.

12. \_\_\_\_\_ It was at Antioch, about ten years after Jesus' death, that his followers were first called Nazarenes.

13. \_\_\_\_\_ The Lord's Prayer is one of the most important prayers in the gospels and of the Church.

14. \_\_\_\_\_ Christians call the day Christ died Good Friday because it was on this day that Jesus died to save us.

15. \_\_\_\_\_ Catholic social teaching calls us to work for justice and peace as Jesus did.

16. \_\_\_\_\_ The apostles are all the baptized members of the Church who share in the Church's mission to bring the good news of Christ to the world.

**Answer the questions.**

17–18. To be a Christian in Rome meant to be at risk of being persecuted. Many kept their faith a secret. If you were a Christian then and were arrested, what would you tell the Roman authorities?

19–20. The mission of the Church is to share the good news of Christ and to spread the Kingdom of God. As members of the Church, each of us is called to take part in this mission. How can you, as a sixth grader, do this?

**Explain the importance to Christians of each of these passages from Scripture. Then illustrate each passage.**

1. "Now this is eternal life, that they should know you, the only true God, and the one whom you sent, Jesus Christ." (John 17:3)

2. "God created man in his image; in the divine image he created him; male and female he created them." (Genesis 1:27)

3. "Have dominion over the fish of the sea, the birds of the air, and all the living things that move on the earth." (Genesis 1:28)

4. "This is the sign of the covenant I have established between me and all mortal creatures that are on earth." (Genesis 9:17)

5. "Do not do the least thing to him. I know now how devoted you are to God, since you did not withhold from me your own beloved son." (Genesis 22:12)

## Across

1. Moses' brother, who helped him explain God's message to the Israelites.

3. The sweet, bread-like food God provided to the Israelites in the wilderness.

5. Poetic prayers intended to be chanted or sung in public worship.

8. David's son, who succeeded him as king of Israel.

11. The first king of Israel, chosen by God and anointed by Samuel.

12. David's father, who summoned his son from the fields at Samuel's command.

13. The center of worship of the one true God that Solomon built in Jerusalem.

14. A Moabite woman whose story shows us that sadness can be turned into joy when we follow God's plan for us.

## Down

1. The _____ of the covenant, the box in which the tablets of the Ten Commandments were kept.

2. The land God promised to the Israelites.

4. The night on which God spared the Israelites as he struck down the firstborn of the Egyptians.

5. Delilah, who betrayed Samson, was a _____ woman.

6. The man to whom God spoke from a burning bush, calling him to lead his people from slavery.

7. The son of Hannah whom God called to be a prophet.

9. Through God's actions and her firm faith in him, _____ helped free Israel from its enemies.

10. A poem or song expressing sorrow, mourning, or regret.

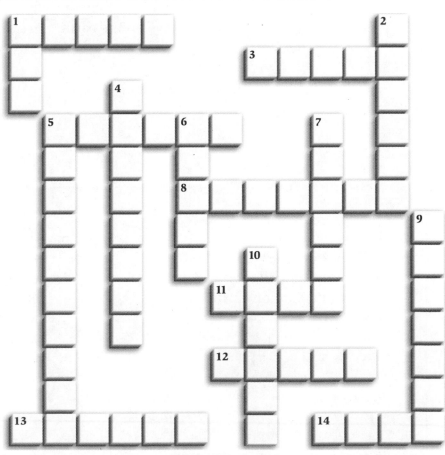

| Amos | Elijah | Elisha | Ezekiel | John |
|------|--------|--------|---------|------|
| Habakkuk | Isaiah | Jeremiah | Malachi | Micah |

## Write the name of the prophet that fits the description below.

**1.** This man was the first prophet sent by God to the northern kingdom of Israel to preach that the one true God is the only God; his name means "Yahweh is my God."

**2.** God summoned this shepherd from the southern kingdom of Judah to call the people of the northern kingdom back to God.

**3.** When God's people were in exile in Babylon, God told them that Babylon was an instrument for purifying Judea of its sins.

**4.** The prophet Elijah anointed this man and threw his cloak over him as a sign that he was called to the mission of a prophet.

_____    _____    _____    _____

**5.** This prophet was accused of blasphemy, attacked, and imprisoned by God's people, but he continued to speak out against the sins he saw around him.

**6.** This prophet mentioned a messenger who would prepare the way for repentance and true worship.

**7.** This prophet and priest warned God's people against all forms of social injustice, idolatry, and superstition.

_____    _____    _____

**8.** This great prophet foretold that salvation would come only through the suffering of a servant of the Lord. This servant would be without sin.

**9.** This prophet foretold that a new David would restore the chosen people.

**10.** This son of Elizabeth and Zechariah preached and prophesied throughout Judea to prepare the way for the coming of the Messiah.

_____    _____    _____

**As a member of the Church, you are called to continue Jesus' ministry. Choose four from the following and write a summary:**

• the Lord's Prayer

• the Beatitudes

• Spiritual Works of Mercy

• Corporal Works of Mercy

• the seven sacraments

• the seven themes of Catholic social teaching

• the Bible.

_____

_____

_____

_____

_____

_____

_____

_____

_____

_____

_____

_____

_____

_____

_____

**Then describe ways that each of the four you have summarized above can be used to spread the good news of Jesus Christ. Present your ideas in the form of a demonstration, a poster, or a song.**

# Prayers and Practices

## Glory to the Father

Glory to the Father, and to the Son,
and to the Holy Spirit:
as it was in the beginning,
is now, and will be for ever. Amen.

## Our Father

Our Father, who art in heaven,
hallowed be thy name;
thy kingdom come;
thy will be done on earth
as it is in heaven.
Give us this day our daily bread;
and forgive us our trespasses
as we forgive those
who trespass against us;
and lead us not into temptation,
but deliver us from evil. Amen.

## Hail Mary

Hail Mary, full of grace,
the Lord is with you;
blessed are you among women,
and blessed is the fruit
of your womb, Jesus.
Holy Mary, Mother of God,
pray for us sinners,
now, and at the hour of our death.
Amen.

## Morning Offering

O Jesus, I offer you all my prayers,
works, and sufferings of this day
for all the intentions of your most
Sacred Heart. Amen.

## Evening Prayer

Dear God, before I sleep
I want to thank you for this day,
so full of your kindness and your joy.
I close my eyes to rest
safe in your loving care.

## Apostles' Creed

I believe in God, the Father Almighty,
creator of heaven and earth.
I believe in Jesus Christ,
his only Son, our Lord.
He was conceived by the power
of the Holy Spirit
and born of the Virgin Mary.
He suffered under Pontius Pilate,
was crucified, died, and was buried.
He descended to the dead.
On the third day he rose again.
He ascended into heaven,
and is seated at the right hand
of the father.
He will come again to judge
the living and the dead.

I believe in the Holy Spirit,
the holy catholic Church,
the communion of saints,
the forgiveness of sins,
the resurrection of the body,
and the life everlasting. Amen.

Note:
The Ten Commandments are found on page 110.
The gifts of the Holy Spirit are found on page 147.
The Beatitudes are found on page 251.
The seven sacraments are found on pages 288–289.
The seven themes of Catholic social teaching are found on pages 290–291.
The Prayer to the Holy Spirit is found on page 312.

# The Angelus

The angel spoke God's message to Mary,
and she conceived of the Holy Spirit.
Hail Mary....

"I am the lowly servant of the Lord:
let it be done to me according to your word."
Hail Mary....

And the Word became flesh
and lived among us.
Hail Mary....

Pray for us, holy Mother of God,
that we may become worthy of the promises
of Christ.

Let us pray.
Lord,
fill our hearts with your grace:
once, through the message of an angel
you revealed to us the Incarnation of your Son;
now, through his suffering and death
lead us to the glory of his resurrection.
We ask this through Christ our Lord.
Amen.

# Hail, Holy Queen

Hail, holy Queen, mother of mercy,
hail, our life, our sweetness, and our hope.
To you we cry, the children of Eve;
to you we send up our sighs,
mourning and weeping in this land of exile.
Turn, then, most gracious advocate,
your eyes of mercy toward us;
lead us home at last
and show us the blessed fruit of your womb, Jesus:
O clement, O loving, O sweet Virgin Mary.

# The Canticle of Mary, the Magnificat

"My soul proclaims the greatness of the Lord;
 my spirit rejoices in God my savior.
For he has looked upon his handmaid's lowliness;
 behold, from now on will all ages call me
  blessed.
The Mighty One has done great things for me,
 and holy is his name.
His mercy is from age to age
 to those who fear him.
He has shown might with his arm,
 dispersed the arrogant of mind and heart.
He has thrown down the rulers from their thrones
 but lifted up the lowly.
The hungry he has filled with good things;
 the rich he has sent away empty.
He has helped Israel his servant,
 remembering his mercy,
according to his promise to our fathers,
 to Abraham and to his descendants forever."

(Luke 1:46—55)

# Memorare

Remember, most loving Virgin Mary,
never was it heard
that anyone who turned to you for help
was left unaided.

Inspired by this confidence,
though burdened by my sins,
I run to your protection
for you are my mother.
Mother of the Word of God,
do not despise my words of pleading
but be merciful and hear my prayer.
Amen.

# Nicene Creed

We believe in one God,
the Father, the Almighty,
maker of heaven and earth,
of all that is seen and unseen.

We believe in one Lord, Jesus Christ
the only Son of God,
eternally begotten of the Father,
God from God, Light from Light,
true God from true God,
begotten, not made, one in Being
with the Father.
Through him all things were made.
For us men and for our salvation
he came down from heaven:
by the power of the Holy Spirit
he was born of the Virgin Mary,
and became man.

For our sake he was crucified
under Pontius Pilate;
he suffered, died, and was buried.
On the third day he rose again
in fulfillment of the Scriptures;
he ascended into heaven
and is seated at the right hand
of the Father.
He will come again in glory to judge
the living and the dead,
and his kingdom will have no end.

We believe in the Holy Spirit, the Lord,
the giver of life,
who proceeds from the Father and the Son.
With the Father and the Son he is
worshiped and glorified.
He has spoken through the Prophets.

We believe in one holy catholic
and apostolic Church.
We acknowledge one baptism for the
forgiveness of sins.
We look for the resurrection of the dead,
and the life of the world to come.
Amen.

# The Rosary

A rosary is made up of groups of beads arranged in a circle. It begins with a cross followed by one large bead and three small ones. The next large bead (just before the medal) begins the first "decade." Each decade consists of one large bead followed by ten smaller beads.

Begin the rosary with the Sign of the Cross. Recite the Apostles' Creed. Then pray one Our Father, three Hail Marys, and one Glory to the Father.

To pray each decade, say an Our Father on the large bead and a Hail Mary on each of the ten smaller beads. Close each decade by praying the Glory to the Father. Pray the Hail, Holy Queen as the last prayer of the rosary.

The mysteries of the rosary are special events in the lives of Jesus and Mary. As you pray each decade, think of the appropriate Joyful Mystery, Sorrowful Mystery, Glorious Mystery, or Mystery of Light.

The Five Joyful Mysteries
1. The Annunciation
2. The Visitation
3. The Birth of Jesus
4. The Presentation of Jesus in the Temple
5. The Finding of Jesus in the Temple

The Five Sorrowful Mysteries
1. The Agony in the Garden
2. The Scourging at the Pillar
3. The Crowning with Thorns
4. The Carrying of the Cross
5. The Crucifixion and Death of Jesus

The Five Glorious Mysteries
1. The Resurrection
2. The Ascension
3. The Descent of the Holy Spirit upon the Apostles
4. The Assumption of Mary into Heaven
5. The Coronation of Mary as Queen of Heaven

The Five Mysteries of Light
1. Jesus' Baptism in the Jordan
2. The Miracle at the Wedding at Cana
3. Jesus Announces the Kingdom of God
4. The Transfiguration
5. The Institution of the Eucharist

# Stations of the Cross

From the earliest days of the Church, Christians remembered Jesus' life and death by visiting and praying at the places where Jesus lived, suffered, died, and rose from the dead.

As the Church spread to other countries, not everyone could travel to the Holy Land. So local churches began inviting people to "follow in the footsteps of Jesus" without leaving home. "Stations," or places to stop and pray, were made so that stay-at-home pilgrims could "walk the way of the cross" in their own parish churches. We do the same today, especially during Lent.

There are fourteen "stations," or stops. At each one, we pause and think about what is happening at the station.

1. Jesus is condemned to die.
2. Jesus takes up his cross.
3. Jesus falls the first time.
4. Jesus meets his mother.
5. Simon helps Jesus carry his cross.
6. Veronica wipes the face of Jesus.
7. Jesus falls the second time.
8. Jesus meets the women of Jerusalem.
9. Jesus falls the third time.
10. Jesus is stripped of his garments.
11. Jesus is nailed to the cross.
12. Jesus dies on the cross.
13. Jesus is taken down from the cross.
14. Jesus is laid in the tomb.

# The Canticle of Zechariah

"Blessed be the Lord, the God of Israel,
for he has visited and brought redemption
    to his people.
He has raised up a horn for our salvation
within the house of David his servant,
even as he promised through the mouth of his
    holy prophets from of old:
        salvation from our enemies and from the
        hand of all who hate us,
            to show mercy to our fathers
        and to be mindful of his holy covenant
and of the oath he swore to Abraham our father,
and to grant us that, rescued from the hand
    of enemies,
without fear we might worship him in holiness
    and righteousness
        before him all our days.
And you, child, will be called prophet of the Most High,
for you will go before the Lord to prepare his ways,
to give his people knowledge of salvation
    through the forgiveness of their sins,
because of the tender mercy of our God
    by which the daybreak from on high will visit us
to shine on those who sit in darkness and
    death's shadow,
        to guide our feet into the path of peace."

(Luke 1:68–79)

# Act of Contrition

My God,
I am sorry for my sins with all my heart.
In choosing to do wrong
and failing to do good,
I have sinned against you
whom I should love above all things.
I firmly intend, with your help,
to do penance,
to sin no more,
and to avoid whatever leads me to sin.
Our Savior Jesus Christ
suffered and died for us.
In his name, my God, have mercy.

# Prayer for My Vocation

Dear God,
You have a great and loving plan
for our world and for me.
I wish to share in that plan fully,
faithfully, and joyfully.

Help me to understand what it is
you wish me to do with my life.
Help me to be attentive to the signs
that you give me about preparing for the future.

Help me to learn to be a sign
of the kingdom, or reign, of
God whether I'm called to the
priesthood or religious life,
the single or married life.

And once I have heard and understood
your call, give me the strength
and the grace to follow it
with generosity and love. Amen

# The Precepts of the Church

1. Celebrate Christ's Resurrection every Sunday (or Saturday evening) and on holy days of obligation by taking part in Mass and avoiding unnecessary work.

2. Lead a sacramental life. Receive Holy Communion frequently and the sacrament of Reconciliation regularly. We must receive Holy Communion at least once a year between the first Sunday of Lent and Trinity Sunday. We must celebrate Reconciliation once a year if we have committed mortal, or serious, sin.

3. Study Catholic teaching throughout life, especially in preparing for the sacraments, and continue to grow in faith.

4. Observe the marriage laws of the Church and give religious instruction and formation to one's children.

5. Contribute to the support of the Church: one's own parish community, priests, the whole Church, and the pope.

6. Do penance, including not eating meat and fasting from food on certain days.

7. Join in the missionary work of the Church.

# Corporal Works of Mercy

Feed the hungry.
Give drink to the thirsty.
Clothe the naked.
Visit the imprisoned.
Shelter the homeless.
Visit the sick.
Bury the dead.

# Spiritual Works of Mercy

Admonish the sinner.
   (Give correction to those who need it.)

Instruct the ignorant.
   (Share our knowledge with others.)

Counsel the doubtful.
   (Give advice to those who need it.)

Comfort the sorrowful.
   (Comfort those who suffer.)

Bear wrongs patiently.
   (Be patient with others.)

Forgive all injuries.
   (Forgive those who hurt us.)

Pray for the living and the dead.

# The Holy Days of Obligation

(as celebrated by the Church in the United States.)

Solemnity of Mary, Mother of God (January 1)

Ascension (when celebrated on Thursday during the Easter Season)

Assumption of Mary (August 15)

All Saints Day (November 1)

Immaculate Conception (December 8)

Christmas (December 25)

# Glossary

**ark of the covenant** (p. 113)
a wooden box in which the tablets of the Ten Commandments were kept

**Beatitudes** (p. 250)
teachings of Jesus that describe the way to live as his disciples

**Bible** (p. 25)
the written record of God's Revelation and his relationship with his people

**blasphemy** (p. 191)
a thought, word, or act that refers to God without respect or reverence

**Blessed Trinity** (p. 23)
the three Persons in one God: God the Father, God the Son, and God the Holy Spirit

**Book of Genesis** (p. 33)
the first book in the Bible

**Canaan** (p. 69)
an area in western Palestine that included most of present-day Israel

**Catholic social teaching** (p. 291)
the teaching of the Church that calls all members to work for justice and peace as Jesus did

**conscience** (p. 39)
the ability to know the difference between good and evil, right and wrong

**covenant** (p. 33)
an agreement between God and his people

**divine inspiration** (p. 25)
the special guidance that the Holy Spirit gave to the human authors of the Bible

**Divine Revelation** (p. 23)
God's making himself known to us

**ecumenism** (p. 297)
the work to promote unity among all Christians

**exodus** (p. 98)
the biblical word describing the Israelites' departure from slavery to freedom

**faith** (p. 69)
a gift from God that enables us to believe in him and accept all that he has revealed

**free will** (p. 39)
the freedom and ability to choose

**gospel** (p. 57)
the good news about God at work in Jesus Christ

**holiness** (p. 298)
sharing in God's goodness and responding to his love by the way we live; our holiness comes through grace

**hope** (p. 199)
a gift from God that enables us to trust in God's promise to be with us always; it enables us to be confident in God's love and care for us

**human dignity** (p. 39)
the value and worth that comes from being made in God's image and likeness

**idolatry** (p. 173)
giving worship to a creature or thing instead of to God

**Incarnation** (p. 225)
the truth that the Son of God, the second Person of the Blessed Trinity, became man

**Kingdom of God** (p. 248)
the power of God's love coming into the world and into our lives

**lamentation** (p. 196)
a sorrow that is expressed in the form of a poem

**Last Supper** (p. 260)
the Passover meal that Jesus shared with his disciples on the night before he died

**manna** (p. 109)
a sweet bread-like food that God provided for the Israelites in the desert

**marks of the Church** (p. 297)
the four essential features of the Church: one, holy, catholic, and apostolic

**martyr** (p. 277)
person who dies rather than give up his or her belief in Jesus Christ

**miracle** (p. 109)
an extraordinary event that is beyond human power and brought about by God

**monarchy** (p. 134)
kingdom or empire ruled by one person, either a king or queen

**Mount Sinai** (p. 109)
a mountain peak in the rocky southern part of the Sinai peninsula

**Nazirite** (p. 125)
a person consecrated to God who promised not to drink wine or strong drink, touch anyone or anything that had died, or cut or shave his or her hair

**original sin** (p. 50)
the first sin that weakened human nature and brought ignorance, suffering, and death into the world; we all suffer from its effects

**parable** (p. 211)
short story that has a message

**Passover** (p. 103)
the event in which God passed over the whole of Egypt, taking the lives of every firstborn Egyptian and sparing the Israelites

**patriarch** (p. 69)
a father, or founder, of a clan, a group of related families

**Pentecost** (p. 273)
the day on which the Holy Spirit came upon the first disciples

**pharaoh** (p. 75)
the king of Egypt

**prophet** (p. 132)
someone who speaks on behalf of God, defends the truth, and works for justice

**proverb** (p. 200)
a brief saying that gives wise advice

**providence** (p. 75)
God's plan for and protection of all creation

**psalm** (p. 150)
a poetic prayer designed to be sung or chanted to some kind of musical accompaniment

**Resurrection** (p. 265)
the mystery of Jesus' being raised from the dead

**sin** (p. 150)
a thought, word, deed, or omission against God's law

**soul** (p. 45)
the invisible spiritual reality that makes each of us human and that will never die

**steward** (p. 47)
a person who is given both the authority over what he or she cares for and the responsibility for seeing that it lives and grows

**superstition** (p. 196)
the false belief that living creatures or things possess powers that in fact they do not have

**Ten Commandments** (p. 111)
the laws of God's covenant given to Moses on Mount Sinai

**torah** (p. 203)
the Hebrew name for the first five books of the Old Testament

**Tradition** (p. 25)
the Revelation of the good news of Jesus Christ as lived out in the Church, past and present

**vocation** (p. 191)
God's call to serve him in a special way

**wisdom** (p. 147)
the knowledge and ability to recognize and follow God's will in our lives

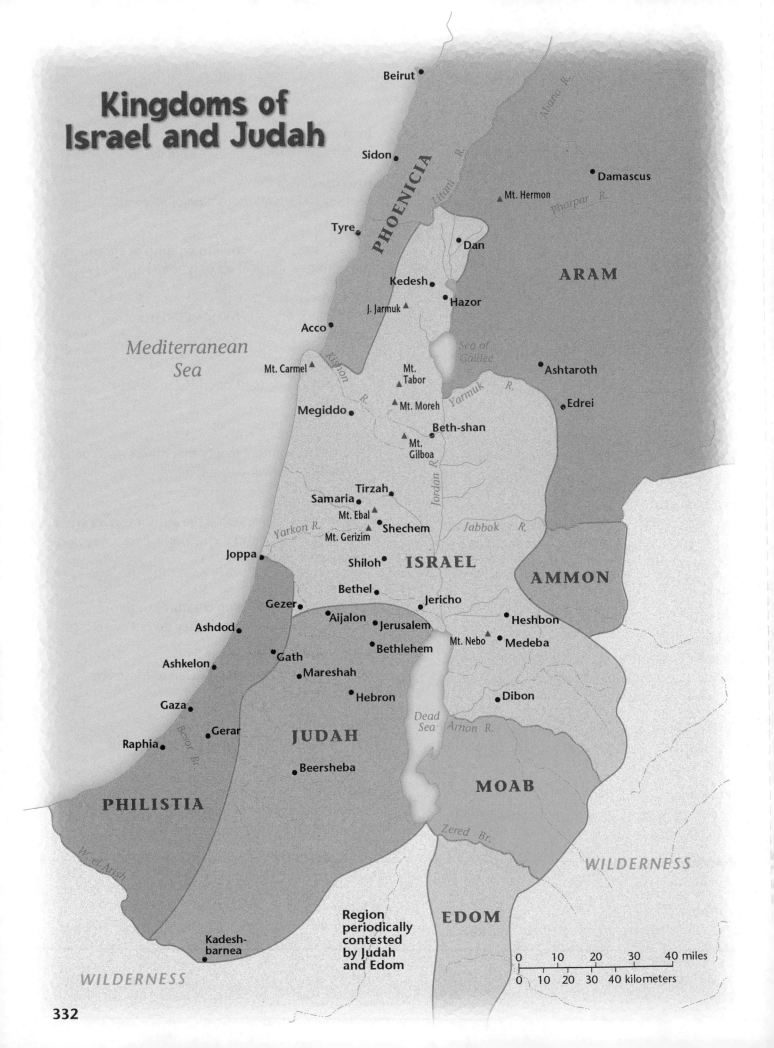

# Kingdoms of Israel and Judah

Beirut

Sidon

**PHOENICIA**

Tyre

*Abana R.*

*Litani R.*

Damascus

Mt. Hermon

*Pharpar R.*

Dan

**ARAM**

Kedesh

Hazor

J. Jarmuk

Acco

Sea of Galilee

*Mediterranean Sea*

Mt. Carmel

*Kishon R.*

Mt. Tabor

Ashtaroth

Mt. Moreh

*Yarmuk R.*

Megiddo

Beth-shan

Edrei

Mt. Gilboa

*Jordan R.*

Tirzah

Samaria

Mt. Ebal

*Yarkon R.*

Shechem

Mt. Gerizim

*Jabbok R.*

Shiloh

**ISRAEL**

**AMMON**

Bethel

Jericho

Joppa

Heshbon

Gezer

Aijalon

Jerusalem

Mt. Nebo

Medeba

Ashdod

Bethlehem

Gath

Mareshah

Ashkelon

Hebron

Dibon

Gaza

*Dead Sea*

Gerar

*Besor Br.*

Raphia

**JUDAH**

*Arnon R.*

Beersheba

**MOAB**

**PHILISTIA**

*Zered Br.*

*W. el-Arish*

**WILDERNESS**

Region periodically contested by Judah and Edom

**EDOM**

| 0 | 10 | 20 | 30 | 40 miles |

| 0 | 10 | 20 | 30 | 40 kilometers |

Kadesh-barnea

**WILDERNESS**

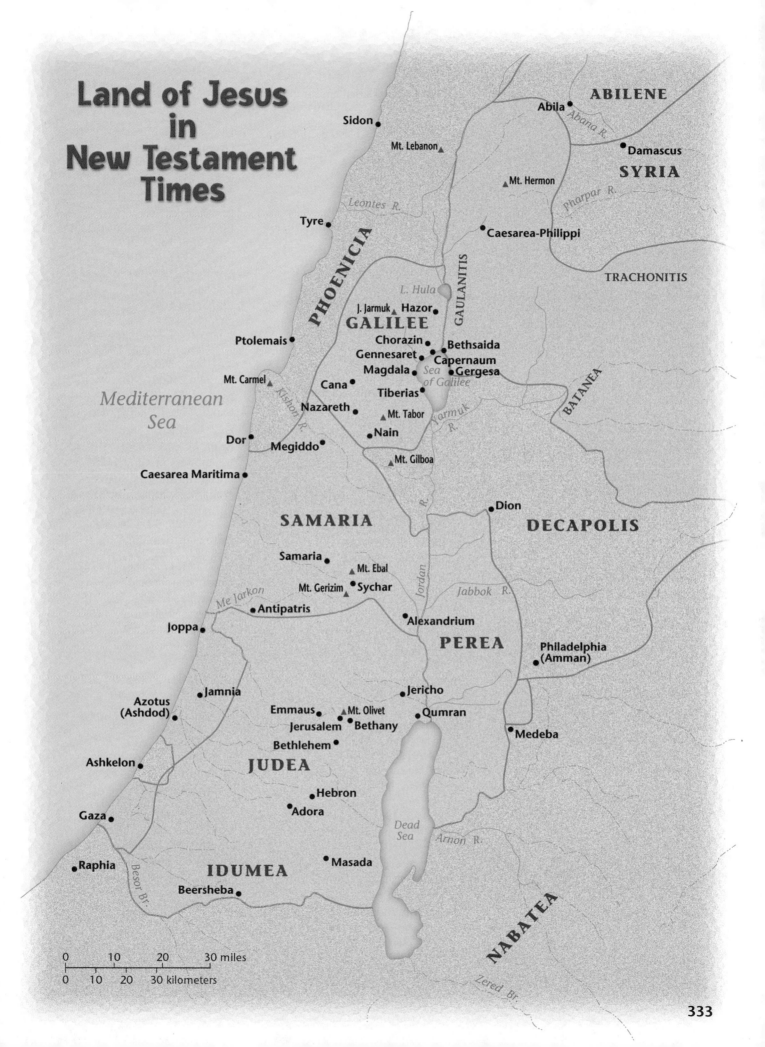

# Land of Jesus in New Testament Times

**ABILENE**

Abila • · *Abana R.*

Sidon •

Mt. Lebanon ▲

· **Damascus**

**SYRIA**

▲ Mt. Hermon · *Pharpar R.*

*Leontes R.*

**PHOENICIA**

Tyre •

· Caesarea-Philippi

**GAULANITIS**

*L. Hula*

J. Jarmuk ▲ · Hazor •

**GALILEE**

Ptolemais •

Chorazin • · Bethsaida
Gennesaret • · Capernaum
Magdala • *Sea of Galilee* · Gergesa

**TRACHONITIS**

Mt. Carmel ▲

Cana • Tiberias •

Nazareth • *Sea of Galilee*

*Kishon R.*

▲ Mt. Tabor

*Yarmuk R.*

**BATANEA**

Dor • Nain •

Megiddo • ▲ Mt. Gilboa

*Mediterranean Sea*

Caesarea Maritima •

*R.*

· Dion

**DECAPOLIS**

**SAMARIA**

Samaria •

▲ Mt. Ebal

*Jordan*

Mt. Gerizim ▲ • Sychar

*Jabbok R.*

*Me Jarkon*

Antipatris •

· Alexandrium

**PEREA**

Joppa •

· Philadelphia (Amman)

Jamnia •

Azotus (Ashdod) •

· Jericho

Emmaus • ▲ Mt. Olivet

Jerusalem • • Bethany

· Qumran

Bethlehem •

· Medeba

Ashkelon •

**JUDEA**

· Hebron

*Dead Sea*

Gaza • • Adora

*Arnon R.*

Raphia • **IDUMEA**

• Masada

*Besor Br.*

Beersheba •

**NABATEA**

| 0 | 10 | 20 | 30 miles |
| 0 | 10 | 20 | 30 kilometers |

*Zered Br.*

333

# Index

The following is a list of topics that appear in the pupil's text.
**Boldface** indicates an entire chapter or section.